Uncle John's
NEW & IMPROVED
FUNNIEST EVER

Bathroom Readers'
Institute

Portable Press
San Diego, California

Portable Press
An imprint of Printers Row Publishing Group
10350 Barnes Canyon Road, Suite 100, San Diego, CA 92121
www.portablepress.com • mail@portablepress.com

Printers Row Publishing Group is a division of Readerlink Distribution Services,
LLC. Portable Press, Bathroom Readers' Institute, and Uncle John's Bathroom
Reader are registered trademarks of Readerlink Distribution Services, LLC.

All notations of errors or omissions should be addressed to Portable Press,
Editorial Department, at the above address.

Publisher: Peter Norton • Associate Publisher: Ana Parker
Publishing/Editorial Team: Vicki Jaeger, Lauren Taniguchi, Stephanie Romero
Editorial Team: JoAnn Padgett, Melinda Allman, Dan Mansfield
Production Team: Jonathan Lopes, Rusty von Dyl

Cover design by Rusty von Dyl

ISBN: 978-1-68412-390-2

Uncle John's New & Improved Funniest Ever
Library of Congress Cataloging in Publication Control Number:
    2018015338 (print)

Printed in the United States of America

23 22 21 20 19   3 4 5 6 7

Articles in this edition have been included from the following books:

Uncle John's Giant 10th Anniversary BR © 1997
Uncle John's Absolutely Absorbing BR © 1999
Uncle John's All-Purpose Extra-Strength BR © 2000
Uncle John's Supremely Satisfying BR © 2001
Uncle John's Ahh-Inspiring BR © 2002
Uncle John's Electrifying BR for Kids Only! © 2003
Uncle John's Presents Book of the Dumb © 2003
Uncle John's Unstoppable BR © 2003
Uncle John's Book of Fun BR For Kids Only! © 2004
Uncle John's Slightly Irregular BR © 2004
Uncle John's BR Colossal Collection of Quotable Quotes © 2004
Uncle John's BR Tees Off on Golf © 2005
Uncle John's Fast-Acting Long-Lasting BR © 2005
Uncle John's BR Christmas Collection © 2005
Uncle John's BR Book of Love © 2006
Uncle John's Curiously Compelling BR © 2006
Uncle John's BR Wonderful World of Odd © 2006
Uncle John's BR Quintessential Collection of Notable Quotables © 2006
Uncle John's Triumphant 20th Anniversary BR © 2007
Uncle John's BR Takes a Swing at Baseball © 2008
Uncle John's Unsinkable BR © 2008
Uncle John's Certified Organic BR © 2009
Uncle John's Endlessly Engrossing BR © 2009
Uncle John's Heavy Duty BR © 2010
Uncle John's BR The World's Gone Crazy © 2010
Uncle John's BR Plunges Into New York © 2011
Uncle John's BR Tunes Into TV © 2011
Uncle John's BR Vroom! © 2011
Uncle John's 24-Karat Gold BR © 2011
Uncle John's The Enchanted Toilet BR For Kids Only! © 2012
Uncle John's Kid-Topia BR For Kids Only! © 2012
Uncle John's BR Nature Calls © 2012
Uncle John's BR Plunges Into California © 2012
Uncle John's Fully Loaded 25th Anniversary BR © 2012
Uncle John's Perpetually Pleasing Bathroom Reader © 2013
Uncle John's Canoramic Bathroom Reader © 2014
Uncle John's Factastic Bathroom Reader © 2015

CONTENTS

Because the BRI understands your reading needs, we've
divided the contents by length as well as subject.
Short—a quick read
Medium—2 to 3 pages, but still brief

"FOR SALE BUY OWNER"
Short

Medium

IT'S SCIENCE!
Short

Medium

JOKESJOKESJOKESJOKES
Short

Medium

TALK WORDY TO ME
Short

EW, THIS TASTES FUNNY
Short

Medium

TWO THUMBS UP YOURS
Short

Medium

THE WILD SIDE
Short

Medium

LIFE & DEATH
Short

Medium

NICE WORK IF YOU CAN AVOID IT
Short

Medium

PRANK YOU VERY MUCH
Short

Medium

GET LIT
Short

Medium

TAKE ME TO YOUR LEADER
Short

Medium

SONG & DUNCE
Short

Medium

*   *   *

"Any time Detroit scores more than 100 points and holds the
other team below 100 points, they almost always win."

—Doug Collins, basketball analyst

INTRO-DUCK-TION

Whenever I tell people that I make *Uncle John's Bathroom Readers* for a living, they either say, "Uncle Whooey's *What?*" and then give me a strange look. Or, if they know the series (whew!), they often say, "Oh, your books are so *funny!*"

…Which I find a bit odd. I mean, sure, we can be found in the humor section, but we never actually set out to make a "funny" book. Rather, we try to pack our books full of entertaining articles that are fun to read. Many of them happen to be funny. And because a lot of our articles are on the serious side, we offset them with sillier stuff. That's where this book comes in.

For the *New & Improved Funniest Ever*, we pored through the entire *Bathroom Reader* series—that's more than 120 books spanning 30 years—to find the most hilarious reading that has ever graced our pages. We really pulled out all the stops by mixing and matching and massaging our best stuff to take it to a whole new level of humor. Inside these pages you'll find the original "tickle your funny bone" hits and soon-to-be-favorites as well.

Result: This is *the* funniest book in the history of Western civilization—now even newer and more improved! You think I'm kidding? In what other single book will you find cheesy action movie one-liners, stories of real-world irony (take that, Alanis Morissette), glorious government goofs, and a story about a cow with such awful flatulence that she became a "four-legged flame-thrower"? Whatever your preferred brand of humor—light or dark, crass or clever, or just plain weird—you'll find it splattered all over these pages.

Before you dive in, we'd like to take this opportunity to thank YOU, our loyal readers. Without you, we're just cracking ourselves up—and it's much funnier when someone laughs along. So happy reading! And as always…

Go with the Flow!

—**Uncle John and the BRI staff**

A SHAGGY DOG STORY

Wanna hear a joke?

A "shaggy dog story" is a classic style of joke—one that goes on for a long time and escalates in detail and scope before ultimately ending in a short, ironic punch line or pun. It gets its name from a joke that dates to the 1940s—and it was actually about a shaggy dog. By increasing the level of detail, the storyteller can easily stretch it out 5 or 10 minutes (or longer), but be prepared: Your audience may think you're the funniest person on Earth…or they may want to hurt you. Today, comedians still tell long, meandering "shaggy dog stories" about a number of topics.

One famous example was the basis for the 2005 movie *The Aristocrats*. We can't print that one (it's X-rated), but here's a brief version of the original shaggy dog story.

A wealthy man lost his beloved, valuable pet dog, an incredibly shaggy dog, maybe the shaggiest in the world. The man took out a newspaper advertisement that read, "Lost: World's Shaggiest Dog. Large Cash Reward." A young boy saw the ad and wanted the reward, so he decided he'd find the world's shaggiest dog and return it. The boy combed his town, and the next town over, and the one after that, looking for shaggy dogs. He found some in pet stores and dog pounds, and they were shaggy…but not shaggy enough.

Finally, at the 30th dog pound he visited, the boy found an incredibly shaggy dog. The dog was so shaggy that he tripped over his own fur, because it covered both his paws and his eyes. When it barked, you couldn't even hear the sound because it got lost in the dog's layers of fur. It was the shaggiest dog the boy had ever seen in his life, and there was no way a dog could ever be shaggier.

So, the boy bought the dog and carried it all the way to the home of the wealthy man who'd placed the ad for the lost shaggy dog. (He had to carry it because the dog was so shaggy it couldn't see or walk properly.) The boy went to the rich man's home and rang the doorbell. The man answered the door, glanced at the dog, and then said to the boy, "Not that shaggy."

George Washington liked to tell dirty jokes.

"BIDET TO YOU, SIR!"

*We'd be flushed with embarrassment if we didn't drop
in at least a few bathroom quotes from TV land.*

"Welcome. I am honored to accept your waste."

—**Japanese toilet, *The Simpsons***

Charles: "You serve our food *and* build latrines?"

Igor: "Don't worry, sir, I washed my hands before I built the latrine."

—***M*A*S*H***

Elizabeth: "That's it, Mark. I'm not staying here anymore. Every faucet leaks. Your toilet actually *rocks*."

Mark: "I kind of like that."

—***ER***

"This toilet comes with a lifetime guarantee! So we'll never have to worry about buying another one. And when I die, Kyle will inherit the throne. It'll be just like Shakespeare!"

—**Jim, *According to Jim***

"How many of you kids want to wake up in a public bathroom lying in a pool of what you hope is your own filth?"

—**Jerri, *Strangers with Candy***

Janitor: "You've been stealing pudding cups and toilet paper?"

J.D.: "No! I hate pudding and I don't use toilet paper. I have one of those French things that shoots water up your butt."

Janitor: "Bidet?"

J.D.: "Bidet to you, sir!"

—***Scrubs***

"The toilets of today aren't worthy of the name. They come in designer colors and they're too low. When you flush them, they make this weak, almost apologetic sound. Not the Ferguson! When you flush, *BAWOOSH!* A Ferguson says, 'I'm a toilet! Sit down and give me your best shot!'"

—**Al Bundy, *Married...
with Children***

"Listen, you, I'll use these facilities when I'm damn well ready! Until then you shall continue to sanitize my crevice and be damn grateful for the opportunity! Starting right...hmmp...hmmp, well then, not now, but soon!"

—**Baby Stewie, *Family Guy***

To get a hippo to open its mouth, try tickling its nose.

POLI-TALKS

Why are we so annoyed by politicians? It might have something to do with utterances like these.

"The top half of the students are well-educated, the bottom half receive extra help, but the middle half we're leaving out."

—Marcia Neal (R), candidate for the Colorado State Board of Education (she won)

"My fear is that the whole island will become so overly populated that it will tip over and capsize."

—Rep. Hank Johnson (D-GA), on why U.S. troops shouldn't be sent to Guam

"Yes, I have some friends who are NASCAR team owners."

—Mitt Romney, when asked whether he follows NASCAR

"What do you want me to tell Romney? I can't tell him to do *that* to himself. You're crazy. You're absolutely crazy. You're getting as bad as Biden."

—Clint Eastwood, talking to an empty "Obama" chair at the 2012 GOP convention

"I've known eight presidents, three of them intimately."

—V.P. Joe Biden

"Fool me once, shame on you. Fool me twice, shame on you."

—Rep. Virginia Foxx (R-NC)

"It's going to take an individual that has testicular fortitude."

—Paul Gibson, Sheet Metal Workers' Union president, on why Hillary Clinton should be president

"When they ask me who's the president of Ubeki-beki-beki-beki-stan-stan, I'm going to say, you know, 'I don't know. Do you know?'"

—Herman Cain (R), presidential candidate, explaining his foreign policy credentials

"There's a lot of—I don't know what the term is in Austrian—'wheeling and dealing.'"

—Barack Obama, unaware that there's no Austrian language (they speak German)

"And you can always follow me on Tweeter."

—Gov. Rick Perry (R-TX), accepting an award for his work in "new media activism"

PEZ flavor flops: yogurt, eucalyptus, and chlorophyll.

CAN'T MAKE THIS STUFF UP

We're still scratching our heads over these.

MUSTACHE QUOTES FROM JOHN OATES

*John Oates is one-half of the popular rock duo, Hall & Oates.
From 1976–1990, they scored 16 top-ten hits. Almost as
famous as the music: Oates' mustache.*

"A good mustache makes a man for many reasons."

"Having a mustache and never smiling became a permanent component of
my persona through the quaintly self-important decade of the '70s."

"I couldn't wait to grow a mustache. I stopped shaving my upper lip the day
I graduated from high school."

"My mustache has become this weird iconic representation of a certain era."

"The mustache represented the old John. I didn't want to be that guy
anymore, so I shaved it off. It was ritualistic in a way."

* * *

NAME CHANGERS

• Sheila Ranea Crabtree hated her first name; she thought it was ugly. She
went by her middle name as a teenager, but didn't think that one fit her
personality, either. So, with the blessing of her husband and children, the
Ohio woman had her name legally changed to Sexy Crabtree.

• A man in New Zealand lost a bet and had to legally change his name.
Good news: His new name is one letter shy of the government's 100-letter
maximum. Bad news: His name is now Full Metal Havok More Sexy
N Intelligent Than Spock And All The Superheroes Combined With
Frostnova.

Olive Oyl's shoe size: 14AAAAAA.

LOUD NOISES!!!

The world's so damn loud, we can't even hear ourselves complain!

GOING CUCKOO

Residents of a Phoenix, Arizona, neighborhood complained to city officials about the bells of Cathedral of Christ the King Church. They chimed on the hour, every hour, every day, every week. "It makes us feel like captives in our own homes," said one citizen. Officials finally put an end to the siege: They took the church's bishop, Rick Painter, to court, where he was sentenced to probation. From now on, if the church bells ring on any day but Sunday, the bishop will go to jail.

REVENGE OF THE NOISEMAKERS

In the middle of the night in May 2009, Marsha Coleman of Salem, Oregon, couldn't sleep because of the loud party going on next door. So she went over and asked the neighbors to *please* keep it down. Bad move: After she got back home, some of the drunken revelers showed up on her porch and banged repeatedly on her door. Frightened, she called 911. A deputy rushed to Coleman's house and was in the middle of taking her statement when they heard another series of loud knocks on the door. Then they heard a slurring voice yell, "This is the Marion County Sheriff!" The deputy opened the door and found one of the partiers, 32-year-old David Bueno, whose party ended right there, as he was arrested for impersonating an officer and disturbing the peace.

THOSE DAMN KIDS!

An 82-year-old German man was fed up by an annoying song coming in through his window. It happened in the morning, the afternoon, and the middle of the night. He kept yelling out his window for the neighborhood kids to shut up, but the song would start playing again. It was so annoying that he finally called the police—who instantly solved the case. How? An officer found a greeting card on the man's windowsill. It was the kind that has a tiny speaker inside and plays a song every time the card shakes… which happened every time a breeze came in through the window. The man was "happy, relieved, and a little embarrassed."

In Glasgow, Scotland, it is a crime for a man to hug a store mannequin.

EVERYONE'S A COMEDIAN

But few are as funny at it as these folks.

"If I had to describe myself in one word, it would be 'bad at following directions.'"
—**Matt Roller**

"'Employee of the Month' is a good example of how somebody can be both a winner and a loser at the same time."
—**Demetri Martin**

"A lot of people think kids say the darnedest things, but so would you if you had no education."
—**Eugene Mirman**

"I bought a book on hair loss, but the pages kept falling out."
—**Jay London**

"While driving I had an accident with a magician. He came out of nowhere!"
—**Auggie Cook**

"I'm paranoid. On my stationary bike I have a rearview mirror."
—**Richard Lewis**

"I stop my microwave at 0:01 to feel like I'm a bomb defuser."
—**Jerry Seinfeld**

"One new plastic surgery technique is called lipgrafting, wherein fat cells are removed from one part of your body that is too large, such as your buttocks, and injected into your lips; people will then be literally kissing your ass."
—**Dave Barry**

"Doesn't Prince Charles look like somebody kissed a frog, and it hasn't changed all the way?"
—**Wendy Liebman**

"I must be going bald. It's taking longer and longer to wash my face."
—**Harry Hill**

"I have a lot of growing up to do. I realized that the other day while sitting in my fort."
—**Zach Galifianakis**

"I met a beautiful girl at a barbecue, which was exciting. Blonde, I think—I don't know. Her hair was on fire. And all she talked about was herself. You know those kind of girls. It was just me, me, me. Help *me*. Put *me* out."
—**Garry Shandling**

To increase milk production, Oregon farmer Arie Jongeneel makes his cows sleep on water beds.

"I didn't know what Facebook was, and now that I do know, I have to say, it sounds like a huge waste of time. I would never say the people on it are losers, but that's only because I'm polite."

—**Betty White**

"When I was a kid, I couldn't wait for the first snowfall. I would run to the door and yell, 'Let me in! Let me in!'"

—**Emo Philips**

"My brothers would never let me play with them, so to get back at them I put Vaseline on the Twister mat. Left arm, BROKEN!"

—**Brian Regan**

"I buy books on suicide at bookstores. You can't get them at the library, because people don't return them."

—**Kevin Nealon**

"There's a metal train that's a mile long, and a lightning bolt strikes the back. How long until it reaches and kills the driver, provided he's a good conductor?"

—**Bo Burnham**

"An escalator can never break; it can only become stairs."

—**Mitch Hedberg**

"I got kicked out of ballet class because I pulled a groin muscle. It wasn't mine."

—**Rita Rudner**

"I went to a bookstore and asked the woman, 'Where's the self-help section?' She said if she told me, it would defeat the purpose."

—**George Carlin**

"I've got a great doctor. If you can't afford the operation, he touches up your X-rays."

—**Henny Youngman**

"You offer a sincere compliment on a great mustache and suddenly she's not your friend."

—**Marty Feldman**

"Sometimes, when I'm feeling down, I like to take a home pregnancy test. Then I can say, 'Hey, at least I'm not pregnant.'"

—**Daniel Tosh**

"I saw a guy hitchhiking with a sign that said 'Heaven.' So I hit him."

—**Steven Wright**

"The guy who invented the hokey-pokey just died. It was a weird funeral. First, they put his left leg in…"

—**Irv Gilman**

An average of two people per year die from flatulence.

HOW TO DRIVE PEOPLE NUTS

Bored? Here's a thought: Why not drive the people around you absolutely insane? Here's how.

• Call an addiction hotline and explain that you're hooked on phonics.

• Go to the airport wearing a suit of armor and try walking through the metal detector.

• Wash out a gas can, punch a hole in it, then fill it with water and carry it down a busy lunch-hour sidewalk while smoking the biggest cigar you can find.

• Call the Q-Tips 800 number and say that one of the cotton swab parts just came off in your ear. When they reply, keep shouting, "What? What did you say?"

• Go to the polar bear enclosure at the zoo and shout, "C'mon Larry, enough's enough! Take off that costume and come back to the office!"

• Fill an inflate-a-date with helium and release it at rush hour on a windy day. Chase it down the street, yelling, "Come back here, you tramp!"

• Call National Acme Co. Ask if they have any products you could use to kill a roadrunner.

• Rush yourself to the ER and explain to the night nurse that you were resting on your leg for a long time and now it feels like pins and needles. Ask if they'll have to amputate.

• In the middle of the night, noisily bury a fully dressed mannequin in your backyard. Arrange lawn furniture on the fresh mound and sit down in it quickly when the police arrive.

• Get a video camera and micro-phone and chase a local TV news crew around. Interrupt on-the-scene shots by shouting questions like "Where have all the cowboys gone?"

• Ask strangers if they have change for a nickel.

• In the bathroom at work, utter loud, pain-wracked screams, then emerge holding a large hen's egg.

Boo goo: When frightened, ladybugs squirt a smelly liquid from their knees.

A BORING PAGE

Does everything have to be exciting?

YAWN
The "Boring 2010" conference took place in London. About 200 people attended. Among the activities: milk tasting, a PowerPoint presentation of a man's changing tastes in necktie colors, and a speech called "My Relationship with Bus Routes."

WHATEVER

In 1964 artist Andy Warhol released what is possibly the most boring movie ever made. Called *Empire*, the grainy, black-and-white silent film is just one continuous shot of New York City's Empire State Building on a night when nothing happened. Warhol filmed the building for six hours, but to make the movie even less interesting, he recorded it at a slower speed so it lasts eight hours.

YUP

To many, the phrase "boring museum" is redundant, but some museums are more boring than others. Examples: the Cement Museum in Spain, the Wallpaper Museum in France, and the Occupational Health and Safety Museum in Germany.

MEH

What's the world's most boring city? It could be Brussels, Belgium. According to a poll of 2,400 travelers conducted by the website TripAdvisor.com, aside from the famous waffles, there's not much of interest there.

ARE WE DONE YET?

In 2010 British researcher William Tunstall-Pedoe designed a computer program that scanned all the news from every single day in the century to determine the most boring day of the 20th century. The "winner": April 11, 1954. On that day, no one famous was born, no one famous died, and there were no big news events. Even the weather was boring.

"The Sequoia School District now has a minority population of 57%." —*San Francisco Chronicle*

TECH SUPPORT

Real confused calls from real confused computer users.

Caller: I'm having a problem with my mouse. It's squeaking.

Tech: I'm sorry, did you say squeaking?

Caller: That's right. The faster I move it across the screen, the louder it squeaks.

Tech: Are you pressing your mouse up against the screen?

Caller: Well, sure! The message says, "Click here to continue."

Caller: My computer locked up, and no matter how many times I type "11," it won't unfreeze.

Tech: What do you mean, "type 11?"

Caller: The message on my screen says, "Error Type 11."

Tech: Click on "cancel."

Caller: Capital?

Tech: "Cancel."

Caller: Sorry, it only says "OK" and "cancel."

Caller: I was printing something.

Tech: From before you called?

Caller: No, from Microsoft Word.

Tech: Okay ma'am, do you see the button on the right-hand side of your mouse?

Caller: No, there's a printer and a phone on the right-hand side of my mouse.

Tech: I need you to right-click on the desktop. Did you get a pop-up menu?

Caller: No.

Tech: Okay. Right-click again. Do you see a pop-up menu?

Caller: No.

Tech: Sir, can you tell me what you have done up until this point?

Caller: Sure. You told me to write "click" and I wrote "click."

Tech: What is the prompt on the screen?

Caller: It's asking for "Enter Your Last Name."

Tech: Okay, so type in your last name.

Caller: How do you spell that?

Tech: Tell me, is the cursor still there?

Caller: No, I'm alone right now.

Dolly Parton once lost a Dolly Parton look-alike contest.

THE HENLEY-ON-TODD

It's just like any other boat race, minus one important thing: water.

IN THE MIDDLE OF NOWHERE

Located nearly 1,000 miles from the nearest ocean, the small Australian town of Alice Springs, New South Wales, is about as landlocked as it gets: it's in the desert. Even the Todd River, which cuts through the center of town, is bone-dry. Yet, amazingly, every year 20,000 tourists flock to Alice Springs for a boat race.

The idea for the race was hatched in 1962 when a local meteorologist named Reg Smith and his friends were brainstorming ideas for charity events that would draw visitors to the small desert town. Mocking stuffy English rowing races like the Henley-on-Thames (between Cambridge and Oxford Universities), Smith suggested they hold a boat race on the dry river. "What about the boats?" asked one of Smith's friends. "Do we tow them or push them?"

"Neither," replied Smith, "we cut the bottoms out and carry them." The race, dubbed the Henley-on-Todd Regatta, has taken place in the third week of August ever since (except in 1993, when, ironically, the races were canceled because of heavy rains that flooded the dry river).

AND THEY'RE OFF!

The main event is called Bring Your Own Boat, and it's just as Smith described: teams bring a bottomless boat and then hold it up from the inside as they race "Fred Flintstone style" around the sandy riverbed. In 2014 a family calling themselves the "Fab Four" brought the first ever "submarine" to the event. (It was yellow.) Other events include the Bathtub Derby, in which contestants are carried around the course in bathtubs, and Sand-Skiing, which is exactly what it sounds like.

The final event is called Battle of the Boats. A pirate ship, Viking ship, and navy ship (built over the frames of four-wheel-drive trucks) race each other through the sandy riverbed. As the name implies, this is more of a battle than a race. Pirates, Vikings, and sailors bombard each other with flour cannons, confetti, and water balloons…and usually end up drenching the spectators.

What do the winners receive (other than a good night's sleep)? Not a whole lot. There are prizes supplied by sponsors, as well as a "cash prize lucky draw" for $500. But the main reason that thousands of people flock to the Henley-on-Todd Regatta every year is to have fun in the sun and not take life too seriously.

Better not to think about it? *Lasagna* comes from the Latin word for "chamber pot."

BOB ROCK ROCKS!

The term aptronym was coined by humorist Franklin P. Adams to describe the amusing situation when a person's name is "apt" for his or her profession— like toilet manufacturer Thomas Crapper. Here are some more.

• **Vince Offer.** TV infomercial pitchman (ShamWow)

• **Usain Bolt.** Olympic gold medalist and one of the fastest runners in the world

• **Neil Moore.** Catholic priest from Portland, Oregon

• **Margaret Court.** Legendary tennis player

• **Marilyn vos Savant.** *Parade* columnist who reportedly has an extremely high IQ of 228

• **Bob Rock.** Music producer

• **Cecil Fielder.** Baseball star (1985–98)

• **Chuck Long.** NFL quarterback (1986–91)

• **Lord Igor Judge.** Chief justice of England's highest court

• **Margaret Spellings.** Secretary of Education (2005–09)

• **David Dollar.** Economist at the World Bank

• **Larry Speakes.** White House spokesman (1981–87)

• **Greg Weiner.** *Playgirl Magazine* photographer

• **Jules Angst.** German research psychiatrist specializing in anxiety

• **Chandler Robbins.** Ornithologist and author of *Birds of North America*

• **Richard Smalley.** University professor who researched nano-technology

• **Emily Hornett.** Prominent entomologist (the science of insects)

• **Alto Reed.** Saxophonist with Bob Seger and the Silver Bullet Band

• **Tommy Tune.** Broadway dancer and choreographer

• **Dr. William Dement.** A professor of behavioral sciences

• **Jeffrey M. Advokat.** Lawyer in New Jersey

• **Laura Knott-Twine.** Founder of Connecticut's Windham Textile & History Museum

• **Vania Stambolova.** Bulgarian Olympic hurdler who, in the 2012 Olympics, stumbled over a hurdle and didn't finish the race

SMELLY BEEF WATER

*Perfume is a huge industry, from famous brands like Chanel No. 5
and White Diamonds to some truly bizarre concoctions.
But who wouldn't want to smell like a burger?*

WHAT'S THAT SMELL? Flame

BACKGROUND: During the 2008 Christmas season, Burger King sold a novelty cologne for men called Flame—designed to mimic the smell of flame-broiled beef patties. Flame was available only in limited quantities through Burger King's website and at a single cosmetics boutique in New York called Ricky's. Despite its scarcity and poor reviews (one critic likened the scent to "a Burger King when it's burning down in a horrible grease fire"), within a week the entire stock had sold out. It originally cost $3.99, but bottles of the smelly beef water were soon selling for $70 on eBay. Demand was so high that Burger King relaunched the cologne in the summer of 2009 with a series of print ads featuring *America's Got Talent* judge Piers Morgan, photographed nearly naked, next to the tagline "The scent of seduction with a hint of flame-grilled meat."

WHAT'S THAT SMELL? *Star Trek* cologne and perfume

BACKGROUND: Three separate scents were marketed in 2009 as tie-ins with the reboot of the *Star Trek* movie series.

• **Tiberius.** Named after the captain of the Starship *Enterprise*, James Tiberius Kirk, and the (over)actor who played him, William Shatner. So does it smell like ham? No, it smells like vanilla and sandalwood. According to the manufacturer, the scent is for men who, like Kirk, are "casual, yet commanding."

• **Red Shirt.** This one pays homage to an in-joke among Trekkies. In many 1960s *Star Trek* episodes, the main crew explores a mysterious planet and one anonymous crew member—known as a "red shirt"—gets killed by hostile alien natives. Red Shirt, the cologne, is a "daring scent for those brave enough to place no trust in tomorrow."

• **Pon Farr.** A fragrance for women, this one is named after (and could theoretically trigger) the Vulcan mating ritual.

In 2006 Dong Changsheng of China pulled a 3,300-lb. car 32 feet using his lower eyelids.

WHAT'S THAT SMELL? Politics

BACKGROUND: During the hoopla surrounding the 2008 U.S. presidential election, a company called Nature's Garden created three different scents designed to allow consumers to display their political affiliation via their personal odor. Republican smells like "love of country and a strong family unit" (and apples), Democrat exudes "a love for mankind" (and clover), and Independent evokes "the desire to preserve the quality of our environment" (it smells like daffodils).

WHAT'S THAT SMELL? Virtue

BACKGROUND: According to California perfumers IBI, if you wear Virtue, you can actually smell like Jesus. Using the Bible as a guide to what kind of plants were used as perfumes in the Holy Land when Jesus walked the Earth, IBI scientists claim that Virtue is a close approximation of what Christ and his followers would have smelled like. It's a sweet blend consisting mostly of apricot, with a dash of frankincense and myrrh, which were given to Jesus at birth by the three wise men.

WHAT'S THAT SMELL? Play-Doh

BACKGROUND: One of the most memorable parts of playing with Play-Doh was the musky, almost candylike odor of the clay when it's soft and fresh out of the can. Turns out that the scent comes largely from wheat flour, so it's pretty easy to reproduce. In 2006 Demeter Fragrance did just that, creating a Play-Doh perfume in honor of the toy's 50th anniversary. It smells exactly like Play-Doh. (Demeter makes many other perfumes that evoke nostalgia for childhood, including Crayon and Tootsie Roll.)

*   *   *

POSITIVELY NEGATIVE

During a lecture, a linguistics professor said to his students, "In English, a double negative forms a positive. For example, 'He doesn't have no apples' actually means he does have apples. In some languages, such as Russian, a double negative is actually still a negative. However, there is no language in which a double positive can form a negative."

Just then, one of the students huffed and said, "Yeah, right."

The gold chains worn by Mr. T on *The A-Team* weighed between 35 and 40 pounds.

A DARK AND STORMY WRITE

Created in the early 1980s by literary professor Scott Rice, the Bulwer-Lytton Fiction Contest dares writers to compose the worst opening sentence to the worst of all possible novels. Here are some really good really bad ones.

BUT FIRST...
The sentence that started it all, from the 1830 novel *Paul Clifford* by English author Edward George Bulwer-Lytton: "It was a dark and stormy night; the rain fell in torrents—except at occasional intervals, when it was checked by a violent gust of wind which swept up the streets (for it is in London that our scene lies), rattling along the housetops, and fiercely agitating the scanty flame of the lamps that struggled against the darkness." Now settle in for some modern-day longwindedness...

• **It was a dark** and stormy night—actually not all that dark, but more dusky or maybe cloudy, and to say "stormy" may be overstating things a bit, although the sidewalks were still wettish and smelled of ozone, and, truth be told, characterizing the time as night is a stretch as it was more in the late, late afternoon because I think Oprah was still on.
  – Gregory Snider, MD, Lexington, KY, 2004 runner-up

• **Jack planted the magic beans** and in one night a giant beanstalk grew all the way from the earth up to the clouds—which sounds like a lie, but it can be done with genetic engineering, and although a few people are against eating gene-engineered foods like those beans it's a high-paying career to think about for when you grow up.
  —Frances Grimble, San Francisco, CA, 2004 Children's Lit winner

• **On reflection,** Angela perceived that her relationship with Tom had always been rocky, not quite a roller-coaster ride but more like when the toilet-paper roll gets a little squashed so it hangs crooked and every time you pull some off you can hear the rest going bumpity-bumpity in its

---

When you laugh, you expel air at speeds up to 70 mph.

holder until you go nuts and push it back into shape, a degree of annoyance that Angela had now almost attained.

—**Rephah Berg, Oakland, CA, 2002 winner**

AND A FEW BY THE GOOD BAD WRITERS AT THE BRI

• **He couldn't sleep** so he did what he always did when he couldn't sleep—he thought about riding a unicorn, like the one he'd dreamt about as a child, the dream which he wasn't totally convinced was a dream, but in actuality was a reality—then he awoke and realized he wasn't really sleeping, but was dreaming about wanting to sleep; he thought it all terribly ironic, until, he noticed, there at the foot of his bed, was the ghost of John Quincy Adams.

—**Brian Boone**

• **The weary foot soldier** peered out from his squalid foxhole and saw them: a plethora of attacking aliens advancing toward him—or maybe it was a myriad of aliens, he thought, pondering the quantitative value of plethoras versus myriads, to and fro, until, sadly, he was instantly vaporized by what his fellow soldiers (who'd barely escaped themselves) would later describe as "a sh*tload of aliens."

—**Jay Newman**

• **Though it sickened her** to think that, once again, the old men would ogle her generous hips under the voluminous corduroy skirt, and desire her supple skin, aromatic with Yardley oatmeal soap that you could only find at a Rexall pharmacy, she steeled herself, tightening her moist lips like two tiles in a badly built shower, and pushed through the door of the stamp-collectors' shop.

—**Amy Miller**

• **Staring intently across the office** through the bleak October twilight, Matt eyed the empty orange-juice container that he'd "decorated" with a Sharpie to look like a jack-o-lantern face, silently hating the fact that his lame co-workers had actually entered it in the demeaning office pumpkin-decorating contest, but also secretly pissed off that he hadn't won and hadn't even gotten an honorable mention for "Most Economical."

—**Gordon Javna**

Google's original name was BackRub.

CLASSIC MUPPETS

Jim Henson and Frank Oz—along with a team of talented writers and performers—brought life to a bunch of fabric, fake hair, and plastic eyes.

Statler: "I like this show so far."
Waldorf: "It hasn't started yet."
Statler: "That's what I like about it!"

"Only time can heal your broken heart, just as only time can heal his broken arms and legs."

—**Miss Piggy**

Loretta Swit: "You can't just pick Miss Piggy up and throw her out in the snow!"
Kermit: "Not without a forklift, I can't!"

"Kermit, cancel my bread impersonation act! They didn't deliver my poppy seeds. You wouldn't want me to walk out there *naked*, would you?"

—**Gonzo**

Dr. Bob: "How could you love him? You're a nurse."
Nurse Piggy: "That may be true, but I am a woman first."
Dr. Bob: "No, you're not. You're a pig first. Nurse second. I don't think 'woman' made the top 10."

Kermit: "A tap-dancing chicken act? Gonzo, I've never heard of anything as ridiculous as a dancing chicken!"
Gonzo: "How about a talking frog?"

Dr. Teeth: "Hey, hey, what's this bummer called again?"
Floyd: "Minuet in G Major."
Dr. Teeth: "Uh, we'll send it back to the minors."

Waldorf: "That number scared the pants off of me!"
Statler: "Are you sure you didn't just forget to put them on?"

Dancer: "I hear you come from a broken home."
Animal: "Yeah, I broke it myself!"

"Who's Jim Henson, for God sakes? I'm up here working my tail off! I hear his name bandied about a lot. He seems to have his hand in a lot of things around here, but I don't particularly know what that means."

—**Kermit**

Results of a two-year FBI study: The lyrics to the song "Louie Louie" are unintelligible.

CLAPPERS, SNAPPERS...

...and other weird achievements that rhyme with "-apper."

CLAPPER. Kent French has beaten his own hand-clapping speed record several times. It's currently 721 claps in one minute—about 12 per second. Navneet Singh of India set the record for clapping with *one* hand in 2007. Number of singlehanded claps: 284 in one minute.

SNAPPER. Scott Woodson, a teenager from Mountville, Pennsylvania, developed a way to manipulate his joints so that every finger snap becomes three snaps. Woodson holds the record for finger-snapping, with 162 snaps in 10 seconds.

SLAPPER. At a 2009 event for the World Record Appreciation Society (an organization whose members set mundane records), a man named Lawson Clarke took a record 46 slaps to the face, from 46 different people, in one minute.

RED SNAPPER. In 1996 Doc Kennedy was fishing in Port Fourchon, Louisiana, when he caught a 50 lb., 4 oz., 41-inch red snapper—the largest one on record.

GIFT WRAPPER. Ann Erickson of Utah won the 2009 "Scotch Brand Most Gifted Wrapper" contest for her speed and accuracy in wrapping a toy helicopter, jigsaw puzzle, bicycle, and sailboat.

RAPPER. Twista, who had a #1 hit in 2004 with the rapid-fire rap song "Slow Jamz," made *Guinness World Records* in 1992 for fastest rapper, able to enunciate 11.2 syllables per second.

CRAPPER. Avant-garde artist Michelle Hines decided in 1995 that she wanted to produce the largest poop possible. Working with nutritionists at the University of Michigan, Hines ate a fiber-rich diet and took fiber supplements for a week before finally producing—on a bowling alley that donated its floor for the event—a turd measuring 26 feet long, the entire length of Hines's digestive tract. (To prevent any premature evacuations, Hines wore a "plug.")

OOPS!

Everyone loves tales of outrageous blunders.
Here are the most "LOL" goofs from our archives.

VOICE FROM BEYOND

A French ventriloquist named Jacques de Putron was attending his friend's funeral and decided to have a little fun. When the deceased's wife, Claudia Sassi, 57, approached the closed casket, de Putron threw his voice and said, "Let me out! Let me out!" The shock of hearing her dead husband call to her was too much for Sassi; she collapsed and later died of shock. De Putron, who was not charged with a crime, explained to police that it was "just a joke."

MAJOR-LEAGUE DUSTUP

Not long after the 2001 anthrax attacks, when U.S. citizens were still on high alert, witnesses observed a small plane fly over Seattle's Safeco Field during a Mariners game. A small bag fell from the plane, hit the roof, and burst into a big puff of dust. The authorities evacuated the ballpark and tracked down the plane's owner, who confessed to dropping the bag. But it wasn't anthrax, he said. It was the ashes of his dead friend, whose last wish was to be scattered over the field. But Safeco's retractable roof was closed that day, so the pilot just dropped his buddy onto the roof and flew away.

BOUND AND STUPID

An artist named Trevor Corneliusien, 26, decided to paint a portrait of his ankles bound in chains. Afterward, however, he couldn't find the key to the lock—which wouldn't have been that big of a deal had he been at home. But the artist was camping in a remote area north of Baker, California. It took him 12 hours to hop through the desert and reach a gas station for help.

UNHOLY WATER

"It's a miracle!" shouted the townspeople in Wadowice, Poland, when water began flowing from the base of a statue of Pope John Paul II, who was born there. Soon believers from all over Europe were flocking to Wadowice to bottle some of the "holy water" for themselves. But their revelry came to an end when the town's mayor admitted that the water was coming from an ordinary pipe that had been installed to make the statue look "pretty."

THE STRAIGHT STORY

In June 2008, at the U.S. Olympic Trials in Eugene, Oregon, sprinter Tyson Gay won the 100-meter race. OneNewsNow.com—a news service run by the conservative American Family Association—reported the story, but because they use computerized word-replacement filters that substitute "family-friendly" words for ones they find objectionable, readers were told that the 100-meter race was won by "Tyson Homosexual."

SMART CAR...DUMB TRUCK

Truck driver Klaus Buergermeister was cruising at about 60 mph on the autobahn in Germany when he was pulled over by a police officer. Why? There was a little Smart Car wedged to the front of his truck—with a terrified driver inside. Buergermeister, 53, had pushed the car for two miles without even knowing it. "I thought I felt a bump," he told police, but figured he'd drove over a pothole "or something." Buergermeister wasn't charged with a crime, and the Smart Car driver, Andreas Bolga, 48, was uninjured. "I tried to drive away but couldn't," explained Bolga. "I looked up through my sunroof and could see the driver, but he didn't notice me."

MAN VS. DRYER

In 2009, 42-year-old Dave Chapman was doing a load of laundry at a friend's house in Waipopo, New Zealand. That evening, thinking his friend had put his clothes in the dryer, Chapman went to the laundry room to change. "By then, I'd had a fair bit to drink," he later said. He removed everything but his T-shirt, and then looked inside the front-loading dryer for a clean pair of underwear. Not finding any, he stuck his head inside. Still no underwear. So he climbed in even farther, past his shoulders...and got stuck. And the dryer was still hot. Chapman started thrashing about but couldn't get out. But he did manage to dislodge the dryer from on top of the washer, and both dryer and drunken man crashed down onto the floor. His friends rushed in but were unable to free him (or stop laughing), so they called for help. It took four firefighters—two holding the dryer, and two holding his legs—to free the half-naked man, whom they described as "agitated."

Phone booths in Chicken Port, Brazil, are shaped like chickens.

DO NOT USE TOILET BRUSH ORALLY

And other actual warning labels on the things you buy.

On a Duraflame fireplace log: "Caution—Risk of Fire."

On a compact disc player: "Do not use the Ultradisc 2000 as a projectile in a catapult."

On a propane blowtorch: "Never use while sleeping."

On a box of rat poison: "Warning: Has been found to cause cancer in laboratory mice."

On an air conditioner: "Avoid dropping air conditioners out of windows."

On a vacuum cleaner: "Do not use to pick up anything that is currently burning."

On a Batman costume: "Warning: Cape does not enable user to fly."

On a bottle of hair coloring: "Do not use as an ice cream topping."

On a curling iron: "Warning: This product can burn eyes."

On a cardboard sunshield for a car: "Do not drive with sunshield in place."

On a toner cartridge: "Do not eat toner."

On a toilet bowl cleaning brush: "Do not use orally."

On a pair of shin guards: "Shin pads cannot protect any part of the body they do not cover."

On a portable stroller: "Caution: Remove infant before folding for storage."

On a plastic, 13-inch wheelbarrow wheel: "Not intended for highway use."

On a laser pointer: "Do not look into laser with remaining eye."

In a microwave oven manual: "Do not use for drying pets."

In the instructions for a digital thermometer: "Do not use orally after using rectally."

"Genies won't let you wish for more wishes. Solution: Wish for more genies." —Aaron Karo

REALITY BITES

We offer these dumb and bizarre quotes from reality TV shows to save you the trouble of having to watch them yourself. You're welcome.

"I've got eyes and ears in the back of my head."
—**Jo, *The Apprentice 2* (U.K.)**

"The monkfish wasn't technically raw because only a little part of it was raw."
—**Matt, *Hell's Kitchen***

"Simon gave me advice—he always refers to a fortune cookie and says the moth who finds the melon…finds the cornflake always finds the melon, and one of you didn't pick the right fortune."
—**Paula Abdul, *American Idol***

"Is there chicken in chickpeas?"
—**Helen, *Celebrity Big Brother 2* (U.K.)**

"I'm just trying to take in everything you've done, and then pepper it with a little Stevie B."
—**Stephen Baldwin, *Celebrity Apprentice***

"I'm not willing to alienate Giselle, because she's the only one with a straightening iron."
—**Elyse, *America's Next Top Model***

"Shut up! I really mean that, from the bottom of my heart."
—**Chef Ramsay, *Hell's Kitchen***

"I'm so angry, I'm fuming! I'm fumigating!"
—**Nadia, *Celebrity Big Brother***

"I backstabbed and lied a lot, but I feel like I've accomplished so much, and I'm so proud."
—**Todd, winner of *Survivor: China***

Studies show: Married men change their underwear twice as often as single men.

THE CABBAGE PATCH CONSPIRACY

The next time you want to buy a cute doll for a kid,
make sure to test it first with your Geiger counter.

CONSPIRACY THEORY: Cabbage Patch Kids weren't innocent dolls—they were designed to prepare Americans for what post-apocalyptic humans will look like.

DETAILS: In the early 1980s, President Ronald Reagan feared that a nuclear war with the Soviet Union was inevitable. Survivors, if any, would likely be horribly physically deformed; the offspring of nuclear victims would be even more gruesome. So Reagan assigned government scientists to determine what post-apocalyptic humans would look like...and to come up with a way to accustom Americans to their appearance. The scientists exposed human test subjects to high levels of radiation, then took samples of their altered DNA, and bred babies. Result: infants with tiny, beady eyes, chubby limbs with undifferentiated fingers and toes, and mashed-in faces. The government then hired Coleco Toys to make dolls based on the infants. Coleco gave the dolls an innocuous name, explained their odd appearance with a fairy tale about the children growing in the ground, and released them to toy stores. The toys were a huge success. Mission accomplished.

THE TRUTH: Cabbage Patch Kids first appeared in the 1901 novel *Mrs. Wiggs of the Cabbage Patch*, about a widowed woman with five children in Cabbage Patch, Louisiana. Georgia doll maker Xavier Roberts began handmaking dolls based on the characters in the novel in 1978—three years before Reagan took office. Coleco bought the rights to mass-produce the dolls in 1983.

Richard Joltes, a college student who worked at a West Virginia Sears in the early 1980s, claims to be the source of the "mutant" theory. Why? He hated the dolls, and whenever he sold one he'd tell the customer, "I heard these things were designed to get people used to what mutants might look like after a nuclear war." Soon, other cashiers started doing it, too. Then Joltes told the tale in political science classes during discussions about President Reagan's far-reaching nuclear policy. The legend spread...and mutated.

The coaching staff for a synchronized swimming team includes a makeup artist.

FOUND ON ROAD DEAD

No matter how much you love your car, when it breaks down, you hate it.
Fortunately for bathroom readers, some people have channeled their
hatred for their cars into these awesome automotive acronyms.

DODGE
Drips **O**il & **D**rops
Grease **E**verywhere
Dead **O**n **D**ay **G**uarantee
Expires
Dear **O**ld **D**ad's **G**arage
Experiment

PINTO
Put **I**n **N**ickel **T**o **O**perate

HONDA
Had **O**ne, **N**ever **D**id **A**gain
Hang **O**n, **N**ot **D**one
Accelerating
Hallmark **O**f **N**on-**D**escript
Automobiles

SAAB
Swedish **A**bstract **A**rt **B**ackfire
Something **A**lmost
Automobilish, **B**roken
Shape **A**ppears **A**ss-**B**ackwards
Still **A**in't **A** **B**eemer

AUDI
Accelerates **U**nder **D**emonic
Influence
Another **U**gly **D**eutsche
Invention

VOLVO
Very **O**dd-**L**ooking **V**ehicular
Object

FORD
Fix **O**r **R**epair **D**aily
Fast **O**nly **R**olling **D**ownhill
First **O**n **R**oad to **D**ump
Found **O**n **R**oad **D**ead
Fix **O**r **R**ecycle **D**ilemma
Follow **O**ur **R**usty **D**ogsled
Forlorn, **O**ld, **R**otten **D**ustbin
Frequent **O**verhaul, **R**apid
Deterioration
Fraternal **O**rder of **R**estored
DeSotos

BUICK
Butt-**U**gly **I**mitation **C**hrome **K**ing

FIAT
Feeble **I**talian **A**ttempt at
Transportation
Fix **I**t **A**gain, **T**ony!

JEEP
Junk **E**ngineering **E**xecuted
Poorly
Just **E**mpty **E**very **P**ocket

Q: What's the definition of a surprise? A: A fart with a lump in it.

BRITISH BUFFOONERY

"You don't frighten us, English pig dogs! Go and boil your bottoms, you sons of a silly person!" —*John Cleese*, Monty Python and the Holy Grail

WE ARE NOT AMUSED
England's Queen Victoria loved Lewis Carroll's book *Alice's Adventures in Wonderland* so much that she requested a copy of his next book. Carroll, a math professor at Oxford, was happy to oblige, so he sent the queen his next book *Syllabus of Plane Algebraical Geometry—Systematically Arranged with Formal Definitions, Postulates, and Axioms.*

PERSISTENCE SQUARED
A 22-year-old Briton, Graham Parker, bought a Rubik's Cube in 1983. He started trying to solve it, and kept trying...for 26 years. Finally, in 2009, at age 48, Parker solved it. "I've missed many important events," he said, "and I've had wrist and back problems from spending hours on it, but when I clicked that last bit into place, I wept."

SYMPHONIES OF SUCK
• The maker of Great Britain's most successful snoring remedy, Helps Stop Snoring, made a public call for recordings of heavy snorers in 2009. They then assembled the snore recordings into a snore-version of the Christmas song "Silent Night," and put it up on their website. They called it the world's first "snorechestra." (Everyone who sent in their snores was given a year's supply of anti-snoring products.)

• Founded by English college students in 1970, the Portsmouth Symphonia was unique in that fully two-thirds of its members did not know how to play a musical instrument. Result: Their music (if you could call it that) was appallingly bad...but also "refreshingly original," as one reviewer wrote. "Unhampered by preordained melody, the orchestra tackled the great compositions, agreeing only on when they should start and finish. The cacophony which resulted was naturally an immense hit." Conductor Leonard Bernstein credited the Symphonia with "changing his attitude to *The William Tell Overture*...forever."

In high school, Hillary Clinton was president of teen idol Fabian's fan club.

I APOLOGIZE IN YOUR GENERAL DIRECTION

In an exhibit called "The Roman Experience," the Deva Museum in Chester, England, invited visitors to stroll through streets constructed to look as they did during Roman times. Hoping to provide an authentic experience, the staff wanted to add an authentic odor to the Roman latrines. They found one called "Flatulence" from Dale Air, a company that designs aromas for museums. Unfortunately, Flatulence proved a bit too authentic, causing several schoolchildren to vomit. Museum supervisor Christine Turner apologized: "It really was disgusting." Dale Air director Frank Knight added, "We feel sorry for the kids, but it is nice to see that the smell is so realistic!"

SCROOGED

In December 2002, Reverend Lee Rayfield of Maidenhead, England, held a special Christmas service just for children. A horrified shock went through the room when Rayfield delivered an unexpected message: Santa Claus, he told the kids, is *dead*. In order to deliver presents to all the children in the world, he explained, the reindeer would have to travel 3,000 times the speed of sound—which would make them all burn up in less than a second. The audience included "a lot of young children who still believe in Santa Claus," said one angry parent, "or did until last night."

END OF THE ROAD

Residents in a neighborhood in Conisbrough, Doncaster, were tired of tourists stopping to take pictures of one of their street signs. "We've even had people flashing their bottoms for photographs," said Paul Allot. On top of that, residents weren't getting their mail because delivery drivers didn't believe it was a real road. The council agreed and changed the street to Archers Way. However, an Internet petition has since sprung up to change it back to its original name, which comes from an Old English term for a rain barrel—"water butt." So what was the name of the street? Butt Hole Road.

BARRED BARD

Officials at England's Norwich Prison were fed up with prisoners' profane language, so they hired college Shakespeare professor Jane Wirgman to teach them better English. Thanks to Wirgman, prisoners at Norwich now insult each other with lines from Shakespeare plays, saying things like "thou odiferous stench" and "thou crusty botch of nature."

THOU ART A FLESH-MONGER!

The Bard's best barbs.

"Go, prick thy face, and over-red thy fear, Thou lilyliver'd boy."
—**Macbeth**

"Thou art like a toad; ugly and venomous."
—**As You Like It**

"He's a disease that must be cut away."
—**Coriolanus**

"Thou art a flesh-monger, a fool and a coward."
—**Measure for Measure**

"Thy tongue outvenoms all the worms of Nile."
—**Cymbeline**

"You scullion! You rampallian! You fustilarian! I'll tickle your catastrophe!"
—**Henry IV, Part 2**

"Methink'st thou art a general offence and every man should beat thee."
—**All's Well That Ends Well**

"Thou clay-brained guts, thou knotty-pated fool, thou whoreson obscene greasy tallow-catch!"
—**Henry IV, Part 1**

"You are as a candle, the better burnt out."
—**Henry IV, Part 2**

"I scorn you, scurvy companion. What, you poor, base, rascally, cheating, lack-linen mate! Away, you mouldy rogue!"
—**Henry IV, Part 2**

"Thou art unfit for any place but hell."
—**Richard III**

"Thine face is not worth sunburning."
—**Henry V**

"It is certain that when he makes water, his urine is congealed ice."
—**Measure for Measure**

"I do wish thou wert a dog, That I might love thee something."
—**Timon of Athens**

Celebrity fact: Scooby-Doo is his nickname. His real name is Scoobert.

CHINDOGU

Chindogu \chin-doh-goo\ n. 1) an almost useless object; 2) an invention that actually exists, but that consumers would be too embarrassed to use; 3) an object that is not for sale, and that nobody would buy anyway.

BACKGROUND
Since the 1990s, writer Kenji Kawakami has been collecting unusual inventions that he calls *chindogu* (Japanese for "weird tool"). These objects offer clever (and strange) solutions to everyday problems. But what makes them unusual isn't their brilliance or simplicity. In fact, chindogu inventions are complicated, inconvenient, wildly impractical, embarrassing when used in public and, ultimately, completely useless.

The "rules of chindogu": The invention cannot be patented ("If the idea's worth stealing, it's not chindogu"), it cannot be for sale, it must actually exist, and it must "challenge the suffocating dominance of utility." To join the society, a prospective member has to invent a new chindogu. But watch out—many truly useless ones have already been invented. Here are some classics:

• **COMMUTER'S HELMET.** This red hard hat straps to your head, then sticks to the wall of a train with a toilet plunger, preventing you from toppling over if you fall asleep. A handy card attached to your forehead lists your destination, so someone can wake you when it's time to disembark.

• **PORTABLE CROSSWALK.** Finding a safe place to cross the street can be a challenge. But now there's the Portable Crosswalk, a roll-up mat that's printed with white stripes. Simply choose a spot, unroll the crosswalk into the street, and walk out into traffic.

• **HAY FEVER HAT.** Do you sneeze a lot? This headgear consists of a roll of toilet paper that sits on top of your head, secured by a halo-shaped frame and chinstrap. At the first sign of a sneeze, just reach up and pull.

• **SWEETHEART'S TRAINING ARM.** Teach your loved one to hold hands properly with this artificial limb. Designed to dangle by your side as you walk down the street, the Training Arm lets your significant other perfect their hand-holding techniques—pressure, duration, finger position, etc.—without subjecting you to embarrassing sweaty palms.

Mosquitoes prefer blondes to brunettes.

• **AUTOMATED NOODLE COOLER.** Who hasn't put a forkful of noodles in their mouth, only to find out that they're scalding hot? The Noodle Cooler solves all that. A small battery-operated fan attaches to your fork, spoon, or chopsticks, blowing a cooling breeze across the noodles as you bring them to your mouth. (Also works for soups and stews.)

• **CAT TONGUE SOOTHER.** Designed for anyone who feeds their cat hot "people food," this invention does for cats what the Noodle Cooler does for humans. This little fan attaches to the rim of the cat's food bowl, cooling the meal to a safe temperature.

• **AUTOMATIC CHEW COUNTER.** Experts agree: Most people don't chew their food enough. For a strong jaw and good digestion, adults should chew at least 2,000 times per meal. But who keeps count? Enter the Chew Counter, a strap that runs under your jaw and records each chew on a digital readout. Also recommended for dieters to practice "vigorous air-chewing."

• **PERSONAL RAIN SAVER.** With fresh water becoming such a valuable resource, it's a shame that so much of it is washed into gutters on rainy days. Now you can capture your own rainwater with this device, an inside-out umbrella that you hold over your head. A drain in the handle siphons rainwater into your own shoulder-harnessed reservoir tank. As the description says, "Every drop that falls is yours to keep."

• **WIDE-AWAKE OPENER.** Students, workaholics, and narcoleptics can finally keep their eyes open with this simple device. Attach the gentle alligator clips to your eyelids, then set the padded ring—attached to the clips with short tethers—on top of your head. Keeps your eyes open no matter how late it is or how boring the lecture.

• **EARRING SAFETY NETS.** These are just what they sound like: little nets, similar to the kind you catch goldfish with, attached to clamps that sit on the shoulders of your jacket or blouse. Large enough to catch any falling or flying earring, these ensure you never lose another one.

• **DADDY NURSER.** For millions of years, mothers have enjoyed bonding with their babies through the experience of nursing. Now Dad can finally feel the joy of breast-feeding, too. Twin breast-shaped bottles attach to a harness that the father wears like a brassiere. Fill them with formula or breast milk, and let the bonding begin.

House pets? Plants grow better when you pet them.

"I'LL HAVE THE HUSBAND AND WIFE LUNG SLICE"

In China, menus in restaurants frequented by Western tourists are carefully translated into English and easy to understand. But if you eat where the locals eat, you may experience a phenomenon known as "Chinglish"— translations that are incomprehensible and often hilarious.

BONE APPÉTIT

Translating Chinese into English is made difficult because 1) many Chinese symbols are pictographs, or graphic depictions of the words they denote, and 2) pictographs are combined to create symbols for new words. The word "calf," for example, combines the symbols for "cow" and "boy." That's how "cowboy leg" finds its way onto some menus where leg of veal is served.

Chinese symbols can also mean more than one thing. The character for "dry" (one of the two symbols used in the name for the "dry pot" style of cooking) can also mean "do." In English, "do" can be a slang term for…well, this book is PG-rated, so we can't really spell it out. But that's why, when a dish called "dry-pot rabbit" is on the menu, the English translation sometimes describes the rabbit performing an intimate act on the cooking pot that, had it involved another bunny instead of the cooking pot, would have increased the population of rabbits in the vicinity.

GOOD EATIN'

How would you translate buffalo wings into Mandarin? How about corn dogs, ladyfingers, tater tots, toad-in-the-hole, or spotted dick (two English pub favorites)? It's easy to see where misunderstandings can arise. The Chinese, it turns out, also love colorful idiomatic names. According to legend, a popular tofu dish called Bean Curd Made by a Pockmarked Woman really was created by such a woman. And because a Sichuan dish of minced pork on beanthread noodles looks like ants climbing a tree, that's what it's called. So sometimes even when a dish is correctly translated, it can seem pretty odd to the uninitiated.

"Whoever wrote this doesn't understand comedy." —Kim Basinger, on a screenplay by Neil Simon

Here are some real examples of items found on menus in China:

Salty Egg King Steams the Vegetable Sponge

Beauty Vegetables

Blow up a Flatfish with No Result

Bacteria Dictyophore Wu Chicken

Ginger Burping Milk (hot)

Sydney and White Tree Fungus Braise Pig Heart

Elder Brother the Ground Is Second

The Palace Quick-Fries Dices Chicken Powered

Hand Pills to Fight Pork (handmade pork balls)

Wood Mustache Meat

Steamed Red Crap with Ginger

Pot Zhai Double Dong Belly

Government Abuse Chicken

Fishing Fans to Burn Dry Sausages

Plaster w/Coconut Juice

Strange Flavor Noodles

Spiced Salt Blows Up Pig Hand

The Black Fryings the Breeze Ball

Health Demolition Tofu Recipe

Husband and Wife Lung Slice

West the Flower Fries the Rib a Meat

Open Space Pfiddlehead Stewed Meat

Chicken Rude and Unreasonable

Dishes with Human Pickles

Decayed Thick Gravy Fillet

Peasant Family Stir-Fries Flesh for a Short Time

Carbon Burns Fresh Particularly Most

Good to Eat Mountain

Strange Flavor of Inside Freasuse

A Previous Small

Fragrant Bone in Garlic in Strange Flavor

The Incense Burns Screw

The Farmer Is Small to Fry King

Man Fruit Braise the North Almond

Slippery Meat in King's Vegetables in Pillar

Big Bowl Four Treasure Frog

A West Bean Pays the Fish a Soup

Eating spicy foods is a common cause of stinky feet.

THE HITCHHIKER'S GUIDE TO DOUGLAS ADAMS

Combining a droll British sense of humor with science fiction, author Douglas Adams (1952–2001) garnered a huge cult following, thanks to witty—and bizarre—observations like these.

"In the beginning, the Universe was created. This has made a lot of people very angry and has been widely regarded as a bad move."

"Nothing travels faster than the speed of light with the possible exception of bad news, which obeys its own special laws."

"The major difference between a thing that might go wrong and a thing that cannot possibly go wrong is that when a thing that cannot possibly go wrong goes wrong it usually turns out to be impossible to get at or repair."

"It is no coincidence that in no known language does the phrase 'As pretty as an airport' appear."

"If it looks like a duck, and quacks like a duck, we have at least to consider the possibility that we have a small aquatic bird of the family *Anatidae* on our hands."

"If you try and take a cat apart to see how it works, the first thing you have in your hands is a non-working cat."

"I think fish is nice, but then I think that rain is wet, so who am I to judge?"

"I'm spending a year dead for tax reasons."

"One always overcompensates for disabilities. I'm thinking of having my entire body surgically removed."

"The knack of flying is learning how to throw yourself at the ground and miss."

"You live and learn. At any rate, you live."

"I may not have gone where I intended to go, but I think I have ended up where I needed to be."

Studies show that men prefer classical Muzak while on hold; women prefer light jazz.

JOKE ORIGINS

Classic jokes are essentially oral traditions that get passed from person to person for decades until someone decides to write them down. We asked our resident jokestorian, Bozo Newman, to find the origins of a few classics. Honk honk!

KNOCK-KNOCK!

During Prohibition in the 1930s, if you wanted to get into a speakeasy, you would knock on the door, someone would ask, "Who's there?" and you'd have to say a password. According to joke historian Charlie Orr, drunken patrons often had fun with this custom as the night wore on, and that's how the knock-knock joke was born. Orr claimed that the very first knock-knock joke was told in the restroom of a Philadelphia hotel. The first guy said, "Knock-knock." His friend replied, "Who's there?" "Ranger." "Ranger who?" "Ranger clothes before you leave here!"

TOM SWIFTIES

Uncle John's favorite type of pun consists of a made-up quotation followed by a clever attribute that reinforces what was said:

• "I feel like raising the dead," said Tom cryptically.

• "That's the last time I stick my arm in a lion's mouth," said Tom off-handedly.

These puns parody the writing style in the Tom Swift book series. Created in 1910 by Edward Stratemeyer (who also created the Hardy Boys and Nancy Drew), Tom Swift is a teenaged hero who uses his wits to thwart bad guys. Stratemeyer used clever wordplay, such as, "'We must hurry,' said Tom swiftly." The pun style was originally called Tom Swiftly, later shortened to Tom Swifty.

POLISH JOKES

Blame Adolf Hitler for these. In his quest to conquer Poland in the 1930s, Hitler pushed the racist "dumb Polack" stereotype so the rest of Europe wouldn't sympathize with the country's fate. The Nazi propaganda machine claimed, among other things, that Polish soldiers on horseback had once attacked German tanks with swords. That stereotype spread to

---

Real headline: HERMAPHRODITIC DEER WITH SEVEN LEGS 'TASTY'

the U.S. after the war, and by the 1960s, Poles had become a punch line. The TV show *Laugh-in* (1967–73) featured a regular segment dedicated to Polish jokes. Books of Polish jokes followed over the next decade. The perception began to change in 1978 when Cardinal Karol Wojtyla became the first Polish pope (John Paul II). The fad tapered off after the fall of the Soviet Union in 1991.

YO' MAMA

These jokes became popular in the 1960s in inner cities as part of a trash-talking game called the Dozens. Two African Americans would trade insults until one of them couldn't think of a comeback. The Dozens, which is considered a progenitor of freestyle rap music, goes back centuries. According to Mona Lisa Saloy's book, *Still Laughing to Keep from Crying*, "The Dozens has its origins in the slave trade of New Orleans, where deformed slaves—punished with dismemberment for disobedience—were grouped in lots of a 'cheap dozen.' To be sold as part of the 'dozens' was the lowest blow possible." And in the insult game that came out of it, there is no lower blow than one directed at your opponent's mama:

- Yo' mama so hairy, Bigfoot was taking her picture!
- Yo' mama so stupid, she cooks with Old Spice!
- Yo' Mama so fat, she went to the movies and sat next to everyone!

MORE CLASSIC JOKES

- **The Chicken Joke:** First appeared in print in 1847 in a New York magazine called *The Knickerbocker*, on a page titled "Gossip with Readers and Correspondents." A reader wrote in: "There are 'quips and quillets' which seem actual conundrums, but yet are none. Of such is this: 'Why does a chicken cross the street?' Are you 'out of town?' Do you 'give it up?' Well, then: 'Because it wants to get on the other side!'"

- **The Newspaper Joke:** What's black and white and red all over? A newspaper, of course. The joke first appeared in an American humor anthology in 1917.

- **Elephant Jokes:** How do you get six elephants in a Volkswagen? Three in the front and three in the back. This fad began in 1960, when Wisconsin toymaker L.M. Becker Co. released a set of 50 elephant-joke trading cards. (That one is card #12.)

While president, Ulysses S. Grant was arrested for riding his horse too fast and was fined $20.

TOM SWIFTIES

"If you read the previous article about this classic style of pun, you'll know it was invented a century ago," said Tom go-back-two-pagesly.

"I'm taller than I was yesterday," said Tom gruesomely.

"Well, that certainly took the wind out of my sails," said Tom disgustedly.

"I'm waiting to see the doctor," said Tom patiently.

"I have no idea," said Tom thoughtlessly.

"I have diamonds, clubs, and spades," said Tom heartlessly.

"I can't walk. My leg hurts too much," reported Tom lamely.

"I wonder if there's a number between seven and nine," said Tom considerately.

"I'm the butcher's assistant," said Tom cuttingly.

"I can't remember anything from the last 24 hours," said Tom lackadaisically.

"I love the taste of orange peels," said Tom zestfully.

"Don't you have any oranges?" Tom asked fruitlessly.

"Your Honor, you're crazy!" said Tom judgmentally.

"Elvis is dead," reported Tom expressly.

"I can take photographs if I want to!" Tom snapped.

"Congratulations, you graduated," said Tom diplomatically.

"I love mustard on my hot dogs," said Tom with relish.

"I hate this Chardonnay," Tom whined.

"Has my magazine arrived?" Tom asked periodically.

"I think that wasp is in pain," Tom bemoaned.

"Look! Here comes a big, black bird," Tom crowed.

"Someday, I want to teach at a university," Tom professed.

"I've only enough carpet for the hall and landing," said Tom with a blank stare.

"Stop, horse! Stop!" cried Tom woefully.

Uncle John is a *paronomasiac*—one who is addicted to puns and wordplay.

CELEBRITY GOSSIP

Here's where we laugh at famous people.

DADDY I$$UES
Famous investor Warren Buffett's largest-ever purchase was a $26 billion acquisition of the Burlington Northern Santa Fe Railroad in 2010. Why'd he buy it? "Because my father didn't buy me a train set as a kid," said Buffett.

MORE DEGREES OF SEPARATION, PLEASE
Whenever he attends a wedding reception, Kevin Bacon bribes the DJ with $20 to *not* play Kenny Loggins's title song from the 1984 movie *Footloose*, in which Bacon starred. Reason: Whenever the song is played, guests form a circle around the actor and expect him to dance.

IT IS UNUSUAL
Trying to maintain a hip image, 65-year-old crooner Tom Jones recently returned to wearing his trademark tight leather pants and open shirt on stage. But his son (and manager) Mark Woodward told him: "Dress your age." Fearing that fans may have stopped taking the Welsh singer seriously, Woodward banned his father's new outfit. Also on the "Don't do that anymore" list: picking up women's panties that are thrown onto the stage.

KIDS SAY THE DARNEDEST THINGS
New York Yankees Hall-of-Famer Mickey Mantle recalled this story about a poignant moment after a game in which he struck out three times in a row: "When I got back to the clubhouse, I just sat down on my stool and held my head in my hands, like I was going to start crying. I heard somebody come up to me, and it was little Timmy Berra, Yogi's boy, standing there next to me. He tapped me on the knee, nice and soft, and I figured he was going to say something nice to me—you know, like, 'You keep hanging in there,' or something like that. But all he did was look at me, and then he said in his little kid's voice, 'You stink!'"

HUMOR IN THE FORM OF A QUESTION

• Just prior to the "Ultimate Tournament of Champions" game in 2005, *Jeopardy!* host Alex Trebek was informed that the three finalists were nervous, so they all decided to play the game without wearing any pants, just to ease the tension. They requested that out of solidarity, Trebek do the same. So he walked out onto the stage in his boxer shorts, only to discover that the contestants—Brad Rutter, Ken Jennings, and Jerome Vered—*were* wearing pants...and big smiles. Trebek turned around, walked back to his dressing room, and put on his pants.

• When the *Jeopardy!* host was saying his vows at his wedding ceremony in 1990, the officiant asked if he would "take this woman as his lawfully wedded wife." Trebek replied, "The answer is...Yes!"

WAKE UP, LITTLE DOOGIE

In the 1988 movie *Naked Gun*, Lt. Frank Drebin (Leslie Nielsen) leaves a press conference to go to the restroom...forgetting that his lapel microphone is still on. Outside, everyone can hear him peeing while he sings to himself. Skip ahead to 2009 when that scene played out in real life: The cast of the sitcom *How I Met Your Mother* was doing a Q&A session for fans and reporters when Neil Patrick Harris, who plays Barney, got up to go to the bathroom...with his mic still on. His publicist could hear the shuffling sounds and ran in to tell Harris to turn it off, but not before everyone in the room heard the actor unzip and say to himself, "Wake up!"

THE CLASSIC EBERT TAKEDOWN

In February 2005, *Los Angeles Times* film critic Patrick Goldstein wrote about how the major movie studios had initially rejected many of the films that were nominated for that year's Academy Awards. Instead, said Goldstein, they chose "to bankroll hundreds of sequels, including a follow-up to *Deuce Bigalow: Male Gigolo*." Rob Schneider, the star of the Deuce Bigalow movies, responded by taking out full-page ads in *Variety* calling Goldstein unqualified to attack his movie—he'd never won any awards, particularly a Pulitzer Prize, "because they haven't invented a category for Best Third-Rate, Unfunny Pompous Reporter." In August 2005, in his review of *Deuce Bigalow: European Gigolo*, *Chicago Sun-Times* critic Roger Ebert noted the Schneider-Goldstein feud and said, "As chance would have it, I have won the Pulitzer Prize, and so I am qualified. Mr. Schneider, your movie sucks."

In 2011 a motorized sofa drove at 101 mph, setting a world record for "fastest sofa."

TO SEE THE SNOWMAN IS TO DISLIKE THE SNOWMAN

Two pages of why Roger Ebert (1942–2013) is our all-time favorite film critic.

"Vincent Gallo has put a curse on my colon and a hex on my prostate. He called me a 'fat pig' in the *New York Post* and told the *New York Observer* I have 'the physique of a slavetrader.' He is angry at me because I said his *The Brown Bunny* was the worst movie in the history of the Cannes Film Festival. It is true that I am fat, but one day I will be thin, and he will still be the director of *The Brown Bunny*."

"*Gone in 60 Seconds* is the kind of movie that ends up playing on the TV set over the bar in a better movie."

"Yes, I take notes during the movies. During a movie like *House of D*, I jot down words I think might be useful in the review. Peering now at my 3x5 cards, I read 'sappy,' 'inane,' 'cornball,' 'shameless,' and, my favorite, 'doofusoid.' I sigh. This film has not even inspired interesting adjectives, except for the one I made up myself."

"*Mr. Magoo* is a one-joke movie without the joke."

"*The Village* is so witless, in fact, that when we do discover the secret, we want to rewind the film so we don't know the secret anymore. And then keep on rewinding, and rewinding, until we're back at the beginning, and can get up from our seats and walk backward out of the theater and go down the up escalator and watch the money spring from the cash register into our pockets."

"I think the future of the Republic may depend on young audiences seeing more movies like *Whale Rider* and fewer movies like *Scooby-Doo 2*, but then that's just me."

"I have often asked myself, 'What would it look like if the characters in a movie were animatronic puppets created by aliens with an imperfect mastery of human behavior?' Now I know."

—Friends & Lovers

Q: What kind of coffee was served on the *Titanic*? A: Sanka.

"*Return to the Blue Lagoon* aspires to the soft-core porn achievements of the earlier film, but succeeds instead in creating a new genre, 'no-core porn.'"

"I hated this movie. Hated hated hated hated hated this movie. Hated it. Hated every simpering stupid vacant audience-insulting moment of it. Hated the sensibility that thought anyone would like it."

—*North*

"*Lake Placid* is the kind of movie that actors discuss in long, sad talks with their agents."

"I hope *Serendipity* never has a sequel, because Jon and Sara are destined to become the most boring married couple in history. For years to come, people at parties will be whispering, 'See that couple over there? The Tragers? Jon and Sara? Whatever you do, don't ask them how they met.'"

"*Mad Dog Time* is the first movie I have seen that does not improve on the sight of a blank screen viewed for the same length of time."

"There is always the moment when the killer is unmasked and spews out his bitterness and hate and vindictive triumph over his would-be victims. How about just once, at the crucial moment, the killer gets squished under a ton of canned soup, and we never do find out who he was?"

—*Saw*

"This movie doesn't have a brain in its three pretty little heads."

—*Charlie's Angels*

"*Jack Frost* could have been co-directed by Orson Welles and Steven Spielberg and still be unwatchable, because of that damned snowman…Never have I disliked a movie character more…the most repulsive single creature in the history of special effects…To see the snowman is to dislike the snowman. It doesn't look like a snowman, anyway. It looks like a cheap snowman suit…with a big, wide mouth that moves as if masticating Gummi Bears. And it's this kid's dad."

"*Battlefield Earth* is like taking a bus trip with someone who has needed a bath for a long time."

"If you, under any circumstances, see *Little Indian, Big City*, I will never let you read one of my reviews again."

JUST PLANE DUMB

*These days, it's not wise to make a plane-crashing joke on a plane,
especially if you're the pilot. Here's the harrowing tale of
a practical joke that almost went horribly wrong.*

CRASH COURSE

In 1947 an American Airlines pilot named Charles Sisto was in command of a propeller-driven DC-4 aircraft carrying 49 passengers from Dallas to Los Angeles. Along with Sisto were his copilot, Melvin Logan, and John Beck, a DC-3 pilot who was learning how to operate the more sophisticated DC-4. While cruising along at 8,000 feet, Captain Sisto invited Beck to take the controls. As Beck was settling into the captain's chair, Sisto thought he'd have a little fun at the rookie's expense—he fastened the gust lock, a device that locks up both the rudder and the elevator and is supposed to be used only on the ground.

Beck was obviously confused when the DC-4 started climbing... and climbing...and kept climbing, no matter what he did. Beck tried everything he could think of, but he couldn't level the plane out. Finally, suppressing his laughter, Captain Sisto decided that the joke had gone on long enough and unlocked the gust lock. Bad idea: While trying to correct the plane's altitude, Beck had left the controls set to an extreme position. Once the gust lock was turned off, the airplane went straight into a nose dive.

The sudden lurch threw Sisto and Beck, who were not strapped in, out of their seats. They hit the ceiling—which happened to be where the propeller controls were located—and shut off three of the four engines. This actually turned out to be a good thing, because shutting off the propellers slowed the plane's descent and allowed Logan, who *was* strapped in, to level the plane just 350 feet from the ground. They made an emergency landing in El Paso, Texas.

Many of the passengers were injured, but none seriously. At first, the three pilots claimed that the autopilot had failed, but after a lengthy investigation, Sisto finally confessed to his ill-conceived practical joke.

He was fired.

The "Pretend Cafe" in Tel Aviv served empty plates. Now they're closed (for real).

BALD TO THE BONE

This page is dedicated to Uncle John's hair…last seen in 1983.

"Balding African-American men look cool when they shave their heads, whereas balding white men look like giant thumbs."
—**Dave Barry**

"The most delightful advantage to being bald—one can hear snowflakes."
—**R. G. Daniels**

"Balding is God's way of showing you are only human…He takes the hair off your head and puts it in your ears."
—**Bruce Willis**

"Being baldplate is an unfailing sex magnet."
—**Telly Savalas**

"I've always wanted to be bald. Wouldn't it be great to be bald in the rain?"
—**Harrison Ford**

"Grass doesn't grow on a busy street."
—**William Hague**

"The tenderest spot in a man's makeup is sometimes the bald spot on top of his head."
—**Helen Rowland**

"I am not the archetypal leading man. This is mainly for one reason: as you may have noticed, I have no hair."
—**Patrick Stewart**

"People get real comfortable with their features. Nobody gets comfortable with their hair. Hair trauma. It's the universal thing."
—**Jamie Lee Curtis**

"There's one thing about baldness, it's neat."
—**Don Herold**

"I don't consider myself bald, I'm just taller than my hair."
—**Lucius Annaeus Seneca**

"A man can be short and dumpy and getting bald—but if he has fire, women will like him."
—**Mae West**

"Baldness may indicate masculinity, but it diminishes one's opportunity to find out."
—**Cecil Hardwicke**

"Better a bald head than no head at all."
—**Seamus MacManus**

In '94 NY EMTs rushed an abandoned bag of spaghetti to the hospital after mistaking it for a fetus.

COWABUNGA!

Cows just kind of do what they do; they stand in fields and graze and moo.
But they also do other things that make us stop and say, "Ooh!"

I'M OK, YOU'RE OK. BUT WHAT ABOUT THE COW?

One morning in 2005, traffic backed up on Interstate 4 near DeBary, Florida. The cause: A cow was standing in a swamp beside the road… and she appeared to be sinking. Concerned drivers called the Highway Patrol, who determined that the cow wasn't in danger, but was merely grazing in the two-foot-deep bog. The worried calls kept coming in, so police put up an electronic sign on the shoulder that read: "THE COW IS OK." Shortly after the officers left, however, the cow wandered off… but the sign remained. Now motorists were really confused: What cow was okay? Was this some kind of spiritual message, or news of some event they hadn't heard about? Those were just a few of the questions the Highway Patrol received over the next few hours. And as more and more drivers slowed down to look for the nonexistent cow, a second, larger traffic jam ensued. Officers eventually went back out and removed the sign.

A MOO-MOO HERE AND A ROAR-ROAR THERE

Jack McDonald had a cow. Her name is Apple. One day in 2008, a black bear wandered into Apple's field in Colorado and climbed up Apple's apple tree. Apple ran to the tree and mooed sternly at the bear. It climbed back to the ground and the two animals stared each other down—and even touched noses for a brief moment. Then Apple mooed loudly and chased the bear away. McDonald described the confrontation as "hilarious."

FIRE IN THE HOLE

A Dutch veterinarian was fined 600 guilders (about $240) for starting a fire that destroyed a farm near the town of Lichtenvoorde. The vet had been trying to demonstrate to a farmer that his cows were passing too much gas and, to make his point, he used a lighter to set fire to one of the cow's farts. The cow became, according to reports, a "four-legged flamethrower," as it ran around frantically, setting hay bales on fire. The flaming cow (which, amazingly, was unharmed) caused more than $80,000 in damage.

Q: What did the cat say to the elephant? A: Meow.

NOT-SO-EASY RIDERS

A rider is a the part of a performer's contract that includes a list of the artist's backstage demands. The promoter must provide these items, or else the performer might not go on. Here are some real excerpts from real riders.

Foo Fighters: Among the food items requested by the alternative rock band are "stinky cheese" and a vegetarian soup, because "meaty soups make roadies fart."

Cher: The singer requires a separate room, adjacent to her dressing room, for her wigs.

Clay Aiken: Nuts, shellfish, mushrooms, coffee, chocolate, and mint are banned from all backstage areas. The singer is severely allergic to them.

Metallica: Their 24-page rider states that it's "very important that bacon be available at every meal and during the day."

Prince: The artist demanded that all items in his dressing room be covered by clear plastic wrap, which may be removed by nobody other than Prince himself.

Coldplay: This British rock group won't perform unless there are eight "stamped, local postcards" in their dressing room.

Poison: Apparently, this hard rock band played a little too loud in the 1980s, because on recent tours, they've asked for a sign language interpreter to accompany them onstage.

50 Cent: A box of Cuban cigars—which are illegal.

The Wallflowers: In no press materials is singer Jakob Dylan (Bob Dylan's son) to be referred to as "Bob Dylan's son."

Ted Nugent: His dressing room must be stocked with tropical fruit-flavored Slim-Fast.

K.C. and the Sunshine Band: No strobe lights may be used during the band's performance. Why? A member of the group has epilepsy. If strobes are used, he could have a seizure, in which case the blame— and the hospital bills—would be given to the promoter.

Burt Bacharach: He requires a bottle of "first-class" red wine and some peanut butter.

Dionne Warwick: Most singers want to be picked up at the airport in a limo. Warwick demands a station wagon.

John Mayer: The singer requires several boxes of sugared cereal from which to choose…and four toothbrushes.

Razorlight: This British band requires a plate of cornbread and a selection of music magazines that feature articles about themselves.

Peter Gabriel: He requires promoters to provide a female masseuse to give him a massage, "hippie style."

Billy Idol: Backstage caterers must provide one large tub of I Can't Believe It's Not Butter.

Boy George: The 1980s pop star's performance requires a "crack oil machine," a primitive fog machine used in British theaters in the 19th century.

Iggy Pop: "No toy robots."

Johnny Cash: Not surprisingly, the late singer required a large American flag to wave while he was on stage.

Janet Jackson: Beverages for the singer are to be presented in "fresh, clean, crushed, or cubed ice," and never in "fish ice" (whatever that is).

Nine Inch Nails: Lead singer Trent Reznor needs two boxes of cornstarch (to help him squeeze into a tight pair of leather pants).

*   *   *

REAL (FUNNY) FLYERS

You see them on telephone poles and bulletin boards at the grocery store. Here are some lines we've collected from actual flyers.

"Do not take this flyer down. There is a very angry hornet hiding behind it who will sting you in the neck. See that bulge right there? That's him."

"Missing: my imaginary friend Steve."

"Found: a nice pile of dog poop. If you've lost a pile of dog poop and this photo looks like your dog's poop, then please come by and get it."

"Lost cloud. Last seen in the sky above my house. Looks white, fluffy, drifty. May or may not respond to 'Mr. Wispies.'"

"Missing unicorn. If you see it, you are probably high."

One in four British veterinarians say they've treated a drunken dog.

WORD PLAY

Words that contradict or complement each other—together on the same page!

OXYMORONS

More than a dumb ox…

- leisure suit
- minor catastrophe
- objective opinion
- wireless cable
- stand down
- preliminary conclusion
- anxious patient
- talk show
- now then
- passive-agressive
- ill health
- long shorts
- black light
- Congressional leadership

LOST YOUR JOB?

Lawyers are disbarred, and priests defrocked, so it should be true that…

- A banker is disinterested.
- A clerk is defiled.
- A cashier is distilled.
- A medium is dispirited.
- A rock climber is disinclined.
- An electrician is discharged.
- A civil rights leader is disintegrated.
- A jockey is derided.
- A gardener is deflowered.
- A drug dealer is disjointed.
- A senator is devoted.

"If you need directions, ask a man with one leg. If there's a shortcut, he knows it." —Dave Attell

PARK ON AN ANGEL

What's the difference between good and evil? Proofreading.
The following are excerpts from real church bulletins.

"The church office will be closed until opening. It will remain closed after opening. It will reopen Monday."

"When parking on the north side of the church, please remember to park on an angel."

"The cost for attending the Fasting and Prayer conference includes meals."

"Irving Benson and Jessie Carter were married on October 24 in the church. So ends a friendship that began in their school days."

"Place your donation in the envelope along with the deceased person you want remembered."

"There is a sign-up sheet for anyone wishing to be baptized on the table in the foyer."

"Please join us as we show our support for Amy and Alan in preparing for the girth of their first child."

"The third verse of 'Blessed Assurance' will be sung without musical accomplishment."

"The concert held in Fellowship Hall was a great success. Special thanks are due to the minister's daughter, who labored the whole evening at the piano, which as usual fell upon her."

"The visiting monster today is Rev. Jack Bains."

"The Sunday Night Men's Glee Club will meet on Saturday at the park, unless it rains. In that case they will meet at their regular Tuesday evening time."

"The class on prophecy has been canceled due to unforeseen circumstances."

"Jean will be leading a weight-management series Wednesday nights. She's used the program herself and has been growing like crazy!"

"Next Thursday there will be tryouts for the choir. They need all the help they can get."

"The sermon this morning: 'Jesus Walks on the Water.' The sermon tonight: 'Searching for Jesus.'"

APRIL FOOLS!

*It's not unusual to find odd-but-true stories in the news
these days. But if the date of the article is April 1, you
might want to think twice before assuming it's true.*

On April 1, 1998, Burger King ran a full-page advertisement in *USA Today* announcing the new Left-Handed Whopper. "The new left-handed sandwich will have all condiments rotated 180°, thereby reducing the amount of lettuce and other toppings from spilling out the right side of the burger."

• In 1993 a group calling itself "The Arm the Homeless Coalition" announced that volunteers dressed as Santa would be stationed outside local malls collecting donations to buy guns and ammo for the homeless citizens of Columbus, Ohio. "There are organizations that deal with food and jobs, but none that train homeless people to use firearms," a spokesperson told reporters. A few days later three Ohio State University students admitted they'd made the whole thing up.

• In 1959 the Indiana *Kokomo Tribune* announced that due to budget cuts, the city police department would now be closing each night from 6 p.m. to 6 a.m. Anyone who called the police after hours would have to leave a message on the answering machine, and in the morning a police officer would listen to the messages. "We will check the hospitals and the coroner, and if they don't have any trouble, we will know that nothing happened," the paper quoted a police department spokesperson as saying.

• In 1999, just four months after most of western Europe adopted the euro as a standard currency, England's BBC radio service announced that England was scrapping the national anthem, "God Save the Queen," in favor of a European anthem that would be sung in German. "There's too much nationalism," a spokesperson for the EU supposedly told the BBC. "We need to look for unity."

• In March 1998, the newsletter *New Mexicans for Science and Reason* published a story claiming that the Alabama state legislature had passed a bill changing the mathematical value of pi from 3.14159 to the "Biblical value" of 3.0. On April 1 a physicist named Mark Boslough came forward and admitted he wrote the article to parody legislative attacks on the teaching of the theory of evolution.

• At about the same time that Pepsi made a worldwide change from its traditional white soda cans to blue ones in 1996, England's Virgin Cola announced an "innovation" of its own: its red cans would turn blue when the cans passed their sell-by date. "Virgin strongly advises its customers to avoid ALL blue cans of cola," the company said in an April 1 newspaper ad. "They are clearly out of date."

• In 1996 America Online published a report that NASA's *Galileo* spacecraft had found life on Jupiter. The following day they admitted they made it up. "Yes, it is a hoax," an AOL representative told reporters, "but it's a good one, don't you think?"

• In 1993 the German radio station Westdeutsche Rundfunk in Cologne broadcast a report that the city had issued a new regulation requiring joggers to run no faster than 6 mph; running faster than that "could disturb the squirrels who were in the middle of their mating season."

• In 1981 the *Herald-News* in Roscommon, Michigan, printed a warning that scientists were preparing to release 2,000 "freshwater sharks" into three area lakes as part of a government-funded study.

• In 1980 the BBC broadcast a report that London's Big Ben was going to be remade into a digital clock and the clock hands would be offered for sale to the first listeners who called in. "Surprisingly, few people thought it was funny," a BBC spokesman told reporters.

• In 1993 San Diego's KGB-FM radio station announced that the space shuttle *Discovery* was being diverted from Edwards Air Force Base to a local airport called Montgomery Field. More than 1,000 people descended on the tiny airstrip, snarling traffic for miles. "I had to shoo them away," said airport manager Tom Raines. "A lot of them were really mad."

• In 1981 England's *Daily Mail* newspaper published a story about a Japanese entrant in the London Marathon named Kimo Nakajimi who, thanks to an error in translation, thought he had to run for 26 *days*—not 26 miles. The paper reported that there had been several recent sightings of Nakajimi, but that all attempts to flag him down had failed.

The "Don't" in "DONT WALK" signs is misspelled—the apostrophe is missing.

DUMB JOCKS

Playing sports is hard. Talking is harderer.

"I've been consistent in patches this season."
—**Theo Walcott, soccer player**

"They were numerically outnumbered."
—**Garry Birtles, soccer player**

"We may make a lot, but we spend a lot, too."
—**Patrick Ewing, NBA player, defending players' salaries**

"How can I play baseball if I'm stupid? If I was stupid I wouldn't have pitched in the World Series. I'd be playing ball in Mexico or Yugoslavia or on Pluto."
—**Joaquín Andújar, MLB player**

"I'm not talented enough to run and smile at the same time."
—**Emil Zatopek, runner, on why he frowns during races**

"I view this situation as one big lie...that I repeated a lot of times."
—**Lance Armstrong, cyclist, coming clean about his doping scandal**

"What I was always good at was letting things go through, like, through one ear and out the other, so to say."
—**Ryan Lochte, swimmer**

"I PRAISE YOU 24/7!!!!!! AND THIS HOW YOU DO ME!!!!! YOU EXPECT ME TO LEARN FROM THIS??? HOW??!! ILL NEVER FORGET THIS!! EVER!!! THX THO..."
—**Steve Johnson, NFL player, who, after dropping a pass, went on Twitter to blame God**

"I was dizzy from the middle of the first set and then I saw Snoopy and I thought, 'Wow Snoopy, that's weird.'"
—**Frank Dancevic, tennis player, after collapsing from the heat**

"People say I'll be drafted in the first round, maybe even higher."
—**Craig Heyward, college football player**

"If you don't believe you can win, there is no point in getting out of bed at the end of the day."
—**Neville Southall, soccer player**

Ancient Roman wrestling matches had only one rule: No eye gouging.

I TOLERATE LUCY

TV show titles are often misleading, so we're suggesting these new, 100% accurate titles.

42 Minutes, Plus Commercials

Dancing with the Recognizable Names

Deal or Yelling at Briefcases?

Why Aren't You Smarter Than a 5th Grader?

I Tolerate Lucy

Urkel Matters

How I Hung Out with My Friends for Years Before I Eventually Met Your Mother

Two and 3/4 Men

The Wildly Disparate States of Tara

Knight Driver

Who's the Boss? Angela, Because She Hired Tony

He Has a Camera Crew, so He's Not Exactly an Undercover Boss

My Only Martian

Not Very Good Times at All

Mindy Reacting to Mork

The Gray Girls

Saturday Night on a Seven-Second Delay, Taped for the West Coast

Sex in a City

Mission: Quite Possible

In-Need-of-a-Makeover-Is-All Betty

The Resident of Queens

Fairly Large House on the Prairie

With a Slight Trace

The Doesn't-Want-to-Be-a-Bachelor-Anymore

It's Always Misanthropic In Philadelphia

They Promised Cougars in This Town, but It's Just a Bunch of Humans

Major Stepdad

The Flirting and Bickering Boat

Makes sense: The first Charmin commercial was filmed in Flushing, New York.

TAIWAN'S
#2 RESTAURANT

When Uncle John read about this Taiwanese restaurant chain, he laughed a little, recoiled a little, and then said, "Why didn't I think of that?" (Then again, it's probably better that he didn't.)

POO-BOT

You've probably never heard of the Japanese comic-book character Arale Norimaki. She's a purple-haired robot teenager whose favorite hobby is "poking poop with a stick." Arale Norimaki has a huge following not just in Japan, but in other parts of Asia as well, including Taiwan. That's where, in 2004, a 26-year-old banker named Wang Zi-wei was inspired by Norimaki's poop-poking example to go into the soft-serve ice cream business. (If you're at all squeamish, you should probably stop reading right now and turn to another page.)

GENIUS AT WORK

Somehow, Wang came to the conclusion that if people liked watching cartoon robots poking at poop, they'd probably love eating soft serve ice cream that looks like poop, served in paper dishes that look like tiny toilets.

What's even stranger than the way Wang's mind works is the fact that his business instincts were dead-on. His human-waste ice cream stand was a big hit—customers not only lapped up all the "diarrhea with dried droppings" (chocolate ice cream with chocolate sprinkles), "bloody poop" (strawberry ice cream), and "green dysentery" (kiwi ice cream) he served, they pestered him to come up with more similarly themed treats.

After four months of working in the bank by day and selling his frozen fecal confections by night, Wang decided to expand. "The success with 'toilet ice cream' was a leap of faith for me to quit the stable, but boring, banking job and start my business, despite strong objections from my family," Wang said. In May 2004, he opened what would become the first location in the Modern Toilet restaurant chain.

Studies show: English speakers say "uh" before a short pause and "um" before a long pause.

LOOKS FAMILIAR

If you've never had an opportunity to dine in a Modern Toilet, it's pretty easy to conjure up a mental image of what one looks like.

Picture a large public restroom, say one at an airport or a shopping mall. See all those bathroom stalls? Take the stalls out...but leave the toilets, and then keep adding more toilets until you have about 100. Now arrange them tastefully around bathtubs and sinks that have been covered with glass tabletops. Now hang some showerheads and shower curtains from the ceiling, and install some urinals on the tiled walls to serve as light fixtures. Need a napkin? Help yourself to the toilet paper dispenser on your bathtub/table. That's pretty much what Modern Toilet restaurants look like—and as of 2013, there were 12 of them in Taiwan and Hong Kong, and more planned for cities in Macao, Malaysia, and mainland China.

IT GETS WORSE

"Go Pee-Pee or Go Poo-Poo?" That's the Modern Toilet way of directing you to the beverage (Pee-Pee) and food (Poo-Poo) sections of the menu. There are plenty of entrées to choose from; if Modern Toilet Beef Curry (served in a toilet-shaped bowl) doesn't strike your fancy, there's always the Japanese Milk Hot Pot, the Texan Chicken, or the No. 2 Double Surprise Banquet Combo (Korean beef and German smoked chicken with cream sauce), also served in little toilets. Appetizers, such as the Fun Platter (California potato fries, onion rings, and popcorn chicken), are served in tiny bathtubs.

BODILY FLUIDS

Wash your meal down with your choice of 18 different tea drinks, including Ice Cream Black Tea, Pudding Milk Tea, or Coffee Jelly Milk Tea, plus plenty of non-tea beverages, including Plum-and-Cola and Honey Lemon Juice. If you're feeling homesick (as opposed to just plain sick), Modern Toilet also serves Ovaltine.

If you prefer your beverage hot, it will be served in a plain mug. Too boring? Order your drink cold, and it will be served in your choice of either a plastic "urinal bottle" similar to those used by bedridden hospital patients, or in a miniature plastic urinal that looks disturbingly like the porcelain fixtures in the Modern Toilet men's room. Bonus: When you're finished with your meal, the urinal (or the urinal bottle) is yours to keep!

A person who removes armpit hair professionally is called an _alipile_.

Did you manage to keep your dinner down? Is there still room for dessert? The dessert menu has been expanded from soft-serve ice cream to include a dozen varieties of shaved ice. Yes, they even serve yellow snow.

A WORD OF ADVICE

As with any well-designed restaurant, the restrooms at Modern Toilet are clearly marked. But since the entire restaurant looks like a restroom, if nature calls be sure to ask for directions to the restroom and listen very carefully when they are given. If you have any doubts as to whether you really are in the restroom, as a courtesy to other diners, please confirm that you are where you think you are before using the toilet for its intended purpose.

*   *   *

HOW TO PLAY WITH "TOUNGE OF FROG"

The misspelled, mistranslated English instructions for a toy made in Taiwan.

• Frog. If it is thrown with full of your strenght, it will spit out the tounge, which is like the genuine one from the frog.

• A product has the stickness and is just like a soft rubber band with high contractility. It can be played to stick the remote objects.

• Inspite of it is sticky, it is never like the chewing guns which is glued tightly and cannot be separated.

• If the stickness is not good enough, it can be washed by soap. After it is dried, it can be used continously many times.

• The packing paper has printed the bug picture, which can be cut as per the black frame and placed on the table; then you can stick the picture with your tounge of frog.

CAUTIONS:

• Never throw out the other person's head.

• Inspite of it is non-toxic, it cannot be eaten.

• Never pull out tounge of frog hard, as it might be separated.

• Never put on surface of any object, shall keep in polybag.

• Its content has the oil, so if it touches on cloth, precious object or wall, the stains will remain if you don't care about it.

The hanging parts of a dog's lips are called *flews*. (No wonder the slobber flies.)

THE OBITS

These real death notices weren't written by journalists, but by the witty families of the dearly departed.

James Robert "Beef" Ward, 39, will be sadly and sorely missed by his loving family. Jimmy, who his family affectionately called "Pork" or "Bubba," was preceded in death by his mother, Barbara Jean "Buffalo Butt" Ward. Survived by his fiancée, Annie "Red" Callahan; father, J. Richard "Old Fart" Ward; sisters, Cathy "Funny Face" Graf, Karen "Turtle" Ward, and "Hamburger" Patty Ward.

—*Columbus Dispatch*

Edward "Bruce" Merritt. Born April 3, 1951 in North Carolina. His older sisters regularly beat him up, put him in dresses, and then forced him to walk to the drugstore to buy their cigarettes. Bruce never met a stranger, and in many ways was stranger than most. He is survived by one daughter, two grandchildren, two ex-wives, unpaid taxes, and many loyal loving friends.

—*Dallas Morning News*

Chuck P. Dimmick passed away suddenly on April 18, 2009 while attending a NASCAR race to watch his favorite driver, Jeff Gordon. Chuck was the Director of Marketing for the Lund Cadillac Group. We are sure he would still want all to know that 0.9% financing is still available on all new 2008 Hummer H2's.

—*Arizona Republic*

Theodore Roosevelt Heller, 88, was discharged from the U.S. Army during WWII due to service-related injuries, and then forced his way back into the Illinois National Guard insisting no one tells him when to serve his country. In lieu of flowers, please send acerbic letters to Republicans.

—*Chicago Tribune*

Arthur (Fred) Clark, who had tired of reading obituaries noting others' courageous battles with this or that disease, wanted it known that he lost his battle as a result of an automobile accident on June 18, 2006. During his life he excelled at mediocrity. He had lifelong love affairs with bacon, butter, cigars, and bourbon. His

---

The awful truth: The word *awful* originally meant "awesome."

sons said of Fred, "He was often wrong, but never in doubt." When his family was asked what they remembered about Fred, they fondly recalled how Fred never peed in the shower—on purpose.

—*Richmond Times Dispatch*

Ruth E. Rencevicz, born on August 28, 1927, passed away on September 7, 2008, due to complications resulting from her children making her old before her time. Ruth served her country as a covert spy for the CIA, where during the Cold War she was largely responsible for the breakup of the Soviet Union. At least, that's the way she told it.

Ruth was also very active as a volunteer known to selflessly give of her time by standing on her balcony yelling at kids for "playing that rap music" at all hours of the day and night.

—*Akron Beacon Journal*

Louis J. Casimir Jr. bought the farm Thursday, Feb. 5, 2004, having lived more than twice as long as he had expected and probably three or four times as long as he deserved. Although he was born into an impecunious family, in a backward and benighted part of the country at the beginning of the Great Depression, he never in his life suffered any real hardships. For more than six decades, he smoked, drank, and ate lots of animal fat, but never had a serious illness or injury. His last wish was that everyone could be as lucky as he had been, even though his demise was probably iatrogenic. Lou was a daredevil: his last words were "Watch this!"

—*The Daily Item (Pa.)*

Jack Balmer. As this is my auto-obituary, I'd like to write it in my own fashion! I was born in Vancouver on All Saints day, 1931. Apart from practicing dentistry for 30 years, I have also at one time or another been fairly adept as a skier, private pilot, race car driver, vintner, mechanic, model builder, marine aquarist, carpenter, photographer, plumber, scuba diver, writer, boat builder, Olympic team member (coach for a bronze medal), and a Canadian Coast Guard Auxiliary member. Since I've had a ball in life, with no regrets and nothing left still undone, and since our world seems to be quickly deteriorating, it's a good time for me to cash in. Goodbye, and good luck!

—*Vancouver Sun*

The average child can recognize over 200 company logos by the time he or she enters 1st grade.

THE MANHATTAN HOAX

If you believe this story, we've got a bridge we'd like to sell you.

WAIT A NEW YORK MINUTE!
Background: In 1824 a well-known, retired carpenter named Lozier stood on a soapbox in Manhattan's busy Centre Market and announced to the crowd that because of all the island's new buildings, the southern tip of Manhattan Island had become too heavy and was in danger of sinking. The solution, he said, was to saw the island off at the northern end, tow it out to sea, turn it 180 degrees around, and reattach it.

Lozier claimed that sawing Manhattan Island in half would be one of the biggest public works projects New York had ever seen, and that Mayor Stephen Allen had put him in charge of the project. The idea sounded preposterous to most of Lozier's listeners; but then again, so had the Erie Canal, and that wonder of the world was nearly finished, wasn't it? Besides, if it wasn't true, why would he publicly declare that the mayor had authorized him to handle the project?

What Happened: Lozier began signing up hundreds of laborers for the task, offering triple wages to anyone willing to saw underwater. He directed blacksmiths and carpenters to begin designing the 100-foot saws and 250-foot oars needed to saw the island and row it out to sea. He also arranged for the construction of barracks and a mess hall for his laborers, and the delivery of 500 cattle, 500 hogs, and 3,000 chickens, so his workers would have plenty to eat.

After two months of planning, the date arrived for construction to begin. Scores of laborers, carpenters, blacksmiths, butchers, and animals—as well as a marching band and hundreds of onlookers—arrived at Spring Street and Bowery to see the historic project get underway. About the only person who didn't show up was Lozier, who'd suddenly left town "on account of his health." He was actually hiding in Brooklyn, and although there was talk of having him arrested, he wasn't. Why? The authorities didn't want to admit they'd been duped.

Not too pious: Pope Pius II wrote an erotic novel.

TRUTH IS FUNNIER THAN FICTION

Because you just can't make this stuff up.

WON'T GIVE YOU THE TIME OF DAY

Yvan Arpa, CEO of the Swiss wristwatch company Romain Jerome, claims that two-thirds of wealthy people don't even use their watches for the intended purpose. "Anyone can buy a watch that tells time," Arpa explains, "but it takes a truly discerning customer to buy one that doesn't." That's the strange idea behind the company's "Day & Night" watch. It's intended to be more a status symbol than a timepiece, because it doesn't give the wearer the hour or even the minute—only whether it is currently daytime or nighttime. Cost: $300,000.

DON'T DRINK THE...

While surfing the Internet one day, a paralegal in Aliso Viejo, California, came across a website that warned in big, bright letters to be aware of the dangers of dihydrogen monoxide. "This odorless, colorless chemical can cause death if inhaled! Thousands have already died this year!" The paralegal forwarded the website to city officials, who held a special vote to ban dihydrogen monoxide. However, shortly before the law was passed, one of the council members remembered basic science: Dihydrogen monoxide is better known as H_2O, more commonly called...water. Apparently, they fell victim to an old prank, and nearly outlawed water within city limits.

STAMP OF DISAPPROVAL

In 2004 the U.S. Postal Service allowed Internet users to make their own postage stamps featuring pictures of anything they wanted. The program was a success: Two million stamps were printed in the first six weeks. Then it was terminated. Why? As a joke, some pranksters printed stamps with a picture of Ted Kaczynski (the "Unabomber"), the man who used the Post Office to mail letter bombs in the early 1990s. The USPS didn't think it was funny.

Nearly 33% of Taiwanese funerals include a stripper.

NO-BLOODED REPTILE

Responding to a call of an alligator threatening kids in an Independence, Missouri, neighborhood in June 2011, officers located the creature in a yard belonging to Rick Sheridan. With orders to shoot the animal on sight, an officer fired two rounds into it. That's when Sheridan came running outside, yelling, "What are you doing? It's made of concrete!" When asked why he had a concrete alligator in his yard, Sheridan explained that it works better than a "No Trespassing" sign.

USE THE FIRE EXTINGUISHER, LUKE!

In 2005 two die-hard *Star Wars* fans in England tried to stage (and film) their own lightsaber battle. The pair of wannabe Jedis, a 20-year-old male and his 17-year-old female friend, built their makeshift lightsabers out of two discarded fluorescent light tubes. Bad idea: They poured gasoline into the tubes and lit them on fire. Early on in the battle, their tubes collided and shattered—splattering them with glass and flames. Both were hospitalized with severe burns…just like Anakin Skywalker!

HOW NOT TO CLEANSE YOUR PALATE

Normally, when your waiter offers a round of schnapps on the house, it's a cause for celebration. But in Klagenfurt, Austria, it was the cause of something else: a trip to the emergency room. The fun began when the waiter announced to the dinner party he was serving that they were getting a free round of schnapps. He took a bottle from behind the bar, poured for his guests, everyone toasted, and slugged back the schnapps. This was followed by the reddening of faces, the gasping of air, and a lot of coughing and complaining (both of which sound very harsh in Austrian).

The waiter would hear none of it. He wouldn't serve them anything he wouldn't serve himself. To prove it, he poured himself a shot and drank it up…and spit it out…and coughed…and his face turned as red as his guests' faces. That's when they took the party to the hospital to all get treated for burns to their mouths and throats. So what happened? For some stupid reason, the bartender had poured clear cleaning detergent into the empty schnapps bottle and kept it behind the bar…where the waiter later found it. So the next time you're in Klagenfurt, Austria, and your waiter offers you a free drink, have him go first.

HOW TO SPOT A HIPSTER

Of all the creatures native to America, one of the most curious is the "hipster." Here's our guide to spotting one.

If you answer "yes" to at least three of these questions, you have, in fact, found a hipster. Proceed with caution—don't mention that you use a PC, and keep quiet about your love of instant coffee.

• Does he have a mustache that was grown "ironically" because mustaches are out of date and uncool if grown to look cool?

• Ask her about her favorite rock band. If you have heard of the band, this person is *not* a hipster.

• Is he rail-thin, and the only thing skinnier than him is the pair of skinny jeans he's wearing?

• Does she wear earmuffs, a fur cap, or a scarf when it's not winter?

• Does he have a job in either the arts or at an espresso bar?

• Is she perpetually staring at an iPhone, MacBook laptop, or iPad, which she uses to blog or post pictures of herself in fur caps on Instagram?

• Do a disproportionate number of her sentences begin with the words "This reminds me of something Malcolm Gladwell says"?

• Does she have bangs?

• Do her clothes look like they were purchased at Goodwill or a thrift store, but when you ask, you find out that her sweater cost $250?

• When you ask him what he watched on TV last night, does he respond, "I don't own a TV"?

• Does she participate in an adult league of a children's sport (such as kickball) or a retro sport (such as roller derby)?

Now that you know how to spot a hipster, join us in our next edition when we tell you how to cook and eat one!

Q: What does an educated owl say? A: "Whom."

FICTIONARY

The Washington Post runs an annual contest asking readers to come up with alternate meanings for various words. Here are some of the best (plus a few by the BRI).

Carcinoma (n.), a valley in California, notable for its heavy smog.

Abdicate (v.), to give up all hope of ever having a flat stomach.

Esplanade (v.), to attempt an explanation while drunk.

Unroll (n.), a breadstick.

Mortar (n.), what tobacco companies add to cigarettes.

Flabbergasted (adj.), appalled over how much weight you've gained.

Balderdash (n.), a rapidly receding hairline.

Innuendo (n.), an Italian suppository.

Semantics (n.), pranks conducted by young men studying for the priesthood.

Lymph (v.), to walk with a lisp.

Gargoyle (n.), an olive-flavored mouthwash.

Instigator (n.), do-it-yourself reptile kit. Just add water.

Laughingstock (n.), an amused herd of cattle.

Coffee (n.), one who is coughed upon.

Hexagon (n.), how a mathematician removes a curse.

Reincarnation (n.), the belief that you'll come back as a flower.

Paradox (n.), two physicians.

Prefix (n.), the act of completely breaking a partially broken object before calling a professional.

Atheism (n.), a non-prophet organization.

Rectitude (n.), the dignified demeanor assumed by a proctologist immediately before he examines you.

Flatulence (n.), emergency vehicle that transports the victims of steamroller accidents.

Eyedropper (n.), a clumsy optometrist.

Zebra (n.), ze garment which covers ze bosom.

CELLO WHAT?

*"Fiddler's neck" is a real ailment suffered by people who play the violin;
"flautist's chin" is a real ailment suffered by flute players. Here's
the strange story of two more strange musical maladies.*

LETTER TO THE EDITOR
In April 1974, the *British Medical Journal* published a letter from a
physician in southern England:

> SIR,
>
> I have recently seen three patients with
> traumatic *mastitis* [inflammation] of one breast.
> These were all girls between 8 and 10 and the
> mastitis consisted of a slightly inflamed cystic
> swelling about the base of the nipple. Questioning
> revealed that all three were learning to play the
> classical guitar, which requires close attention
> to the position of the instrument in relation to
> the body. In each case a full-sized guitar was used
> and the edge of the soundbox pressed against the
> nipple. Two of the patients were right-handed and
> consequently had a right-sided mastitis while the
> third was left-handed with a left-sided mastitis.
> When the guitar-playing was stopped the mastitis
> subsided spontaneously.
>
> I would be interested to know whether any other
> doctors have come across this condition.
>
> I am, etc.,
> P. Curtis,
> Winchester

Clearly, Dr. Curtis believed that the pressure of the guitar against the
children's chests caused an irritation that cleared up as soon as they
stopped playing the guitar. As was common practice at the time, the
British Medical Journal printed the letter as a courtesy to see if any other
doctors had seen such an ailment. The letter did attract responses from a
number of physicians, but none had ever seen a case of "guitar nipple," as
it came to be called.

Some doctors did, however, write in with helpful suggestions for the original sufferers: One wondered if the problem was caused by left-handed children playing guitars intended for right-handed adults, or vice versa. Another doctor suggested that if the irritation persisted, the children should get another guitar instructor.

HEADING SOUTH

But the most interesting response of all came from a J. M. Murphy, who had this to say:

> SIR,
>
> Though I have not come across "guitar nipple" as reported by Dr. P. Curtis, I did once come across a case of "cello scrotum" caused by irritation from the body of the cello. The patient in question was a professional musician and played in rehearsal, practice, or concert for several hours each day.
>
> I am, etc.,
> J. M. Murphy

As had been the case with "guitar nipple," "cello scrotum" attracted some interest from physicians, but no cases of other patients suffering from the condition were ever reported.

Instrument-induced ailments are not uncommon, especially among professional musicians who play their instruments day after day for hours on end. Overuse can cause injury all by itself, and the nickel, chromium, brass, and other materials used to make musical instruments can also cause irritation to sensitive skin. So not much notice was taken of "guitar nipple" and "cello scrotum" when they surfaced; they were just added to the list of music-related maladies that get written up in medical journals from time to time. Years passed before much thought was given to them again.

BODY OF EVIDENCE

Then in 1991 a Connecticut doctor named Philip Shapiro read about "cello scrotum" in the *Journal of the American Academy of Dermatology*. Shapiro knew from personal experience (he played the cello) that the intimate parts of the male anatomy never come in contact with the instrument—the large size of the cello and the position in which it must be held to be played made it almost impossible. The musician's crotch is at least six inches away from the cello at all times, and besides, most men play the cello while *wearing pants*.

Dr. Shapiro stated his case in a letter to the journal and included a photograph of himself playing the cello (with his crotch nowhere near the instrument) as supporting evidence. Even if some cellists do experience irritation in the aforementioned area, he argued, the *cellist*, not the cello, would be at fault: "Just as people sometimes scratch their heads repetitively, some also scratch their genitals," he wrote. The journal published Dr. Shapiro's letter; from then on whenever "cello scrotum" was mentioned in medical journals, it was accompanied with a caveat that the ailment's existence had been questioned on the grounds that getting it "would require an extremely awkward playing position."

OH, NUTS

Then in 2009, after "cello scrotum" was mentioned in yet another *British Medical Journal* article, Dr. Elaine Murphy, a former medical school professor serving in the British House of Lords, came forward and admitted that the ailment was a hoax. Dr. Murphy and her husband, John M. Murphy—the J. M. Murphy who signed the original letter—had gotten such a laugh out of Dr. P. Curtis's original "guitar nipple" letter in 1974 that they decided to try and top it. "Somewhat to our astonishment, our letter was published," she wrote. "Anyone who has ever watched a cello being played would realize the physical impossibility of our claim."

That clears up "cello scrotum"…but what about "guitar nipple"? After all, it's been written up in many prestigious publications, including the *British Medical Journal* (and *Uncle John's Fast-Acting Long-Lasting Bathroom Reader*). So, if you play the guitar, should you still be on guard against it? Probably not—Dr. Murphy says she and her husband had suspected back in 1974 that it, too, was a hoax. "The following Christmas we sent a card to Dr. Curtis of 'guitar nipple' fame, only to discover that he knew nothing about it," Dr. Murphy wrote. "Another joke, we suspect."

The seventh-inning stretch makes baseball the only sport where spectators do calisthenics.

I'VE GOT A CUNNING PLAN...

Un-genious schemes from un-genious people.

WHAT A PHONEHEAD
In January 2004, Jack Painter of Plainville, Connecticut, called 911 and reported a robbery in process at a Dairy Mart store. He then proceeded to rob a Dairy Mart on the *other* side of town. Only problem: He accidentally gave the dispatcher the address of the Dairy Mart he was robbing, not of the decoy one, as he'd planned. Police showed up and arrested him in the middle of the robbery.

NOT TOO SWIFT

Stewart and Cathryn Bromley of Manchester, England, got two camera-detected speeding tickets in 2005 totaling about $200. Not wanting to pay the tickets, they told authorities that a friend named Konstantin Koscov had been visiting from Bulgaria and he was driving the car at the time of the tickets. Police were suspicious and started investigating...so Cathryn flew 1,400 miles to Bulgaria and mailed a postcard from the "friend," thanking them for the use of their car. When police contacted Interpol to locate "Koscov," the couple finally admitted that they'd made the whole thing up. Instead of the original $200, they ended up paying more than $20,000 in fines and court costs (plus a flight to Bulgaria).

BY THE BOOK

In 2006 Asante Kahari was charged with several counts of fraud for bilking a Michigan woman out of $38,000. He'd met her in 2001 on an Internet dating site, befriended her, and convinced her to deposit several (forged) checks into her bank account. Then he got her to withdraw the money in cash, took it, and disappeared. When police caught up with Kahari, he pleaded innocent to the charges, but prosecutors were able to convince jurors of his guilt by reading excerpts of a novel they found on his website. The book, titled *The Birth of a Criminal* and billed as "the new autobiography from Asante Kahari," describes meeting a woman from Michigan on an Internet dating site, mailing her counterfeit checks worth about $38,000, going to meet her, getting her to withdraw the money in cash, taking it, and disappearing. He was convicted on six counts of fraud.

NO EXIT

When 30-year-old Larry Bynum of Fort Worth, Texas, decided to break into a liquor store in June 2006, he failed to take a couple of things into account. The first was how to get safely into the store. Bynum broke in through a ceiling ventilation hatch. A surveillance camera showed him crashing through the ceiling tiles and falling almost 20 feet to the floor. He remained on the floor, barely moving, for almost five minutes. He finally got up and emptied the cash register. The second thing he hadn't thought of was how to get *out* of the store. He tried to climb a display shelf back to the ceiling, but fell and broke the shelf. Then he tried bashing through the front door with a beer keg, but that didn't work, either—it was made of Plexiglas. Finally, after Bynum had spent more than an hour trying to escape from the store, a cop happened to drive by and see him. The surveillance video shows Bynum calmly sitting down on the beer keg and lighting a cigarette, waiting to be arrested.

✝   ✻   ✻

DOUGH-BITUARY

Veteran Pillsbury spokesman Pop N. Fresh died yesterday of a severe yeast infection. He was 71. Fresh was buried in a lightly greased coffin. Many celebrities turned out to pay their respects, including Mrs. Butterworth, Hungry Jack, the California Raisins, Betty Crocker, and the Hostess Twinkies. The grave was piled high with flours, as long-time friend Aunt Jemima delivered the eulogy, describing Fresh as a man who never knew how much he was kneaded. Fresh rose quickly in show business, though his later life was filled with turnovers. He was not considered a very smart cookie, wasting much of his dough on half-baked schemes. Even as a crusty old man, he was considered a roll model for millions. Fresh is survived by his wife. They have two children and one in the oven. He is also survived by his elderly father, Pop Tart. The funeral was held at 3:50 for about 20 minutes.

"There are many dying children whose last wish is to see me." —David Hasselhoff

DUBYA-ISMS

These quotes are even funnier when you read them out loud doing your best impression of George W. Bush.

"When I was young and irresponsible, I was young and irresponsible."

"It's clearly a budget. It's got a lot of numbers in it."

"Redefining the role of the United States from enablers to keep the peace to enablers to keep the peace from peacekeepers is going to be an assignment."

"You work three jobs? Uniquely American, isn't it? I mean, that is fantastic that you're doing that."

"I've changed my style somewhat, as you know. I'm less—I pontificate less…and I'm more interacting with people."

"The American people's expectations are that we will fail. Our mission is to exceed their expectations."

"We cannot let terrorists and rogue nations hold this nation hostile or hold our allies hostile."

"We want America to be a more literate and hopefuller country."

"He can't take the high horse and then claim the low road."

"Families is where our nation finds hope, where wings take dream."

"Now, we talked to the Hanovers. They are near retirement—retiring—in the process of retiring, meaning they're very smart, active, capable people who are retirement age and are retiring."

"Too many OB/GYNs aren't able to practice their love with women all across this country."

"I glance at the headlines just to get a flavor for what's moving. I rarely read the stories and get briefed by people who probably read the news themselves."

"I'm also not very analytical. You know I don't spend a lot of time thinking about myself, about why I do things."

"People sometimes have to correct my English. I knew I had a problem when Arnold Schwarzenegger started doing it."

A fork used for pitching dung is called a *yeevil*.

BEAT THE PRESS

The mark of a truly good phony news story:
People in high places fall for it.

KENNY ROGERS: ROASTED

The website Zug.com reported that a book signing by country music star Kenny Rogers had disintegrated into a riot in which 19 people were injured. According to the report, Rogers had refused to sign a female fan's unspecified body part; the fan turned violent and incited the crowd. Zug linked to a report on the website of WTF-TV, based in Hazelton, the location of the riot. MSNBC, ABC, and the Associated Press all carried the story. But they failed to verify all of the facts: WTF-TV isn't real (WTF is Internet shorthand for "What the f***?"), Hazelton isn't real, and there was no riot. Kenny Rogers hadn't even written a book. Zug and WTF's sites even had disclaimers telling readers the whole thing was a prank. Zug's intent: to point out that the news media often rushes to report stories without verifying their accuracy.

WE REFUSE TO RETRACT

In 2004 the Chinese newspaper *Beijing Evening News* reported that the United States Congress had threatened to move out of Washington, D.C., unless a new, modernized Capitol Building with a retractable roof was built. *Evening News* writer Huang Ke had copied, nearly word for word, the entire story from its source: *The Onion*. (Ke didn't know that *The Onion* is a satirical newspaper.) The *Evening News* refused to admit fault…until the story was proven to be untrue. A few days later the paper apologized, but blamed *The Onion* for the error, writing, "Some American newspapers frequently fabricate offbeat news to trick people into noticing them with the aim of making money."

HOOSIER DADDY

In 2003 the *Hoosier Gazette* ran an item on its website about an Indiana University study that found that 100 percent of parents irreversibly lose 12 to 20 IQ points upon the birth of their first child. That, according to lead researcher Hosung Lee, is why every parent thinks their kid is the world's

Ben & Jerry's mourned Jerry Garcia's death by putting black cherries in Cherry Garcia ice cream.

funniest, smartest, and cutest. Newspapers in England, Russia, and the Netherlands ran the report, and it was the lead story on Keith Olbermann's MSNBC talk show. The only problem: The *Hoosier Gazette* is a comic newspaper; the story and study were hoaxes. The next day, Olbermann apologized on air, saying, "So there's no survey showing that parenthood will cost you at least 12 IQ points. But did you hear about the one showing how many IQ points newscasters lose when they see a story they really want to run?"

IN OTHER NEWS: THE PRESIDENT IS NOT A NINJA

In 2002 two teenagers started the "Fake CNN News Generator" website to prank their friends with phony news stories that looked like they came from CNN. But then, without the teens even knowing it, word of mouth took over: After the site was mentioned on a morning radio show, two million visitors a day suddenly started generating "Fake CNN News" stories…and spreading them. Newspapers and TV stations ran dozens of stories they thought had originated with the real CNN, among them that rock star Dave Matthews had died of a drug overdose, and that the Olsen twins had decided to attend Miami University. (Matthews and Miami U. both had to issue public denials.) Most angered, though, was CNN. Only a week after the Fake CNN News Generator was inadvertently made public, the cable news channel sent a threatening "cease and desist" letter and shut the impostor down.

TERRORISTS WANT TO INTERRUPT YOUR DINNER

In 2002 Dan Nichols, a detective in Branch County, Michigan, read an article entitled "Al-Qaida Allegedly Engaging in Telemarketing." Nichols had been leading an investigation of scams that targeted the elderly, and he jumped on the story, using it as the basis for a press release. He warned the public that buying magazines, time shares, or long-distance service over the phone could be funding terrorist cells. Local and national news picked up the story…which was bogus. Nichols had read it in *The Onion*. Unaware that it was satire, Nichols says he got to the article via a link on the Michigan Attorney General's website. (The AG's office denies linking to *The Onion*—they're aware it's fake.) "I enjoy a good joke," Nichols said, "I just hate it when it's on me."

Sir Bark-a-lot: In medieval Europe, some dogs wore suits of armor.

LOONEY LORDS

Noblemen are usually dignified people who act with grace. Just as often, they're fools made insane by generations of blue-blooded inbreeding.

THE HERMIT OF NOTTINGHAMSHIRE

William John Cavendish Scott-Bentinck (1800–1879) was a member of England's Parliament before he was 30, and seemed destined for a serious career in politics. Then his uncle died in 1854 and Scott-Bentinck inherited the title of fifth Duke of Portland. Almost immediately, the new duke rejected public life, preferring to be alone—*very* alone. He moved into his newly inherited estate in Nottinghamshire and quickly rid the house of everything in it, tossing most of his family's priceless treasures into a huge pile in one empty room. Scott-Bentinck then dedicated five empty rooms of the house for his living quarters, and had the rest of the empty house painted pink. But apparently that wasn't secluded enough, so the duke commissioned the construction of a series of underground rooms connected by 15 miles of tunnels. Among the subterranean rooms were a 11,000-square-foot ballroom and a billiard room large enough to house 12 pool tables. But nobody ever saw them; no visitors were ever permitted. In fact, from 1854 until his death in 1879, Scott-Bentinck saw only one person—his valet.

THE AQUAMAN OF KENT

Matthew Robinson, the second Baron Rokeby (1713–1800), was from a Scottish noble family that lived in Kent, England. He inherited the title in his 40s and served in the House of Lords. Then Robinson took a vacation in the German spa-resort town of Aachen. When he returned to Kent, Robinson was suddenly and permanently obsessed with water. He started skipping work and spent most of his days swimming in the ocean at a private beach in Kent. Every day Robinson walked to and from the beach wearing tattered peasant clothes, and would then swim for so long and so strenuously that he'd faint, requiring a servant to drag him out of the sea. Robinson drank lots of water, too, and he had drinking fountains installed along the path to the beach. If commoners were caught using them, Robinson didn't punish them—he gave them a gold coin to reward "their good taste." Robinson's embarrassed family eventually talked him into installing a swimming pool at his home. He still spent most of the day swimming, but now tried to prevent fainting by eating a roast leg of veal…underwater.

THE DOG LOVER OF BRIDGEWATER

Francis Henry Egerton, the eighth Earl of Bridgewater (1756–1829), wasn't a hermit, but he didn't care much for the company of people. He liked dogs. Throughout his life he always had 12 of them, and he liked to dress them in tiny, specially made leather boots to protect their paws. Every day, six of the dogs would join him on a carriage ride, then the menagerie would return home for dinner. At a long dinner table, all 12 dogs—and Egerton—would eat off of silver with white linen napkins tied around their necks. Egerton liked the dinners for the lively conversations he imagined he was having with the dogs. Egerton also liked his own shoes, wearing a new pair each day. At night he hung the used shoes on the wall as a makeshift calendar.

THE DUKE, DUKE, DUKE OF GIRL

Edward Hyde (1661–1723) was the third Earl of Clarendon and a cousin of Queen Anne of England. In 1701 Anne appointed Hyde to the position of governor of the American colonies of New York and New Jersey. Hyde took the task seriously and literally: He said that if he was governing the colonies on behalf of a woman, he should dress the part. So at the opening of the New York Assembly in 1702, Hyde attended wearing a blue silk gown and satin shoes, waving his face with a fan. Outside of work, he was often spotted on the streets wearing a hoop skirt. By 1708 Hyde was forced to relinquish the governorship and return to England because he was deeply in debt from spending too much money on women's clothes.

*   *   *

BONK!

From the "News That Sounds Like Satire" Department: "Britain's first 'Safe Text' street has been created in London complete with padded lampposts to protect mobile phone users from getting hurt in street accidents while walking and texting."

—*Daily Mail,* 2008

What's a "combat emplacement evacuator"? Pentagon-speak for a…shovel.

"STICK AROUND."

One of the things we love about action movies is listening for the cheesy one-liner that the good guy delivers just as he kills the bad guy.

"Looks like you won't be attending that hat convention in July."
—**Bruce Willis,**
***Hudson Hawk,* while**
decapitating the bad guy

"He's in the car."
—**Kevin Costner,**
***The Untouchables*, after**
throwing the bad guy
off a roof onto a car

"You're fired."
—**Arnold Schwarzenegger,**
***True Lies,* launching a**
missile through a building
with the bad guy attached

"I think he got the point."
—**Sean Connery,**
***Thunderball*, impaling**
a bad guy with a spear gun

"How do you like your ribs?"
—**Carl Weathers,**
***Action Jackson,* burning the bad**
guy with a flamethrower

"Stick around."
—**Arnold Schwarzenegger,**
***Predator,* after pinning a bad**
guy to a wall with a knife
through the chest

"Consider that a divorce."
—**Arnold Schwarzenegger,**
***Total Recall,* after shooting**
his wife when he finds
out she's an evil spy

"He always did have an inflated opinion of himself."
—**Roger Moore,**
***Live and Let Die,* after**
making the bad guy's body
expand and then explode

"You need a bath."
—**Charles Bronson,**
Death Wish V,
pushing the bad guy
into a vat of molten plastic

"What a pain in the neck."
—**Arnold Schwarzenegger,**
The Running Man,
breaking a bad guy's neck

"Looks like they'll be importing oil this year."
—**Jason Gedrick,**
***Iron Eagle,* after blowing**
up an enemy's oil refinery

"It's just about time, anyway."
—**Chuck Norris,**
***The Hitman,* just**
before the bad guy gets
blown up by a time bomb

Humans and armadillos are the only animals that can get leprosy.

GROANERS

Sorry to pun-ish you. Get it? pun-ish?
It's a PUN! Oh, never mind.

A LITTLE GIRL FELL INTO a well, and although she cried for help, her brother stood by and did nothing. Finally the next-door neighbor came over and pulled the girl up.

"Why didn't you help her?" the neighbor asked the boy.

"How," he replied, "could I be her brother and assist her, too?"

A GUY GOES TO a psychiatrist. "Doc, I keep having these alternating recurring dreams. First, I'm a teepee; then I'm a wigwam; then I'm a teepee; then I'm a wigwam. It's driving me crazy. What's wrong with me?"

The doctor replies: "Calm down. You're two tents."

A DOCTOR MADE it his regular habit to stop off at a bar for a hazelnut daiquiri on his way home, and the bartender would always have the drink waiting at precisely 5:03 p.m.

One afternoon, as the end of the workday approached, the bartender was dismayed to find that he was out of hazelnuts. Thinking quickly, he threw together a daiquiri made with hickory nuts and set it on the bar. The doctor came in at his regular time, took one sip of the drink and exclaimed, "This isn't a hazelnut daiquiri!"

"No," replied the bartender, "it's a hickory daiquiri, doc."

A PSYCHIATRIST'S RECEPTIONIST alerted the doctor: "A man is out here who says he is invisible."

"Tell him I can't see him right now," said the doctor.

IT IS WELL KNOWN THROUGHOUT central Europe that members of William Tell's family were early devotees of league bowling. They had sponsors and everything. According to historians, though, the records have been lost, so nobody knows for whom the Tells bowled.

Lawrence Welk's vanity license plate: A1 AND A2.

A GROUP OF CHESS ENTHUSIASTS checked into a hotel and were standing in the lobby discussing their recent tournament victories. After about an hour, the manager came out of the office and asked them to disperse. "But why?" they asked.

"Because," he said, "I can't stand chess nuts boasting in an open foyer."

TRUE STORY: UNCLE JOHN HAD an old telephone booth in his living room. The phone didn't work, but it was quite a conversation piece.

THIS GUY GOES TO A COSTUME party with a girl on his back. "What the heck are you?" asks the host. "I'm a snail," says the guy. "But, you have a girl on your back," replies the host. "Yeah," he says, "that's Michelle."

THERE'S A NUDIST COLONY for communists. Two old men are sitting on the front porch. One turns to the other and says, "I say, old boy, have you read Marx?" And the other says, "Yes. It's these wicker chairs."

THERE WAS THIS HOUSE PAINTER who was always looking for a way to save a buck, so he would often thin his paint to make it go further—and he usually got away with it. When a local church decided to do a big restoration, this fellow put in a bid, and because his price was so competitive, he got the job.

One day, just as the job was nearly done, he was up on the scaffold, painting away, when suddenly there was a horrendous clap of thunder. The sky opened and the rain poured down, washing the thin paint off the church and knocking the painter down onto the lawn, surrounded by puddles of the thinned and useless paint.

Fearing this was a judgment from the Almighty, he fell down on his knees and cried, "Oh, God! Forgive me! What should I do?"

And from the thunder, a mighty voice spoke, "Repaint! Repaint and thin no more!"

A FAMOUS VIKING EXPLORER returned home from a voyage and found his name missing from the town register. His wife insisted on complaining to the local civic official, who apologized profusely, saying, "I must have taken Leif off my census."

Bubble gum was invented in 1906. It's original name: "Blibber-Blubber."

WEIRD GAME SHOWS

Game show designers should be forced to play their own games.

TV *Champions* (Japan). A different, bizarre contest each week. One week contestants chug rancid, evil-smelling soy bean gruel, another week they allow themselves to be locked in cages and sworn at.

The Game of the Goose (Spain). Contestants move around a game board; each space represents a different challenge. One challenge: Release a semi-nude model from an exploding bed. Another: Try to escape from a box that's slowly filling with sand.

Dream House (U.S.). Young, married couples move from room to room, competing to win furniture. Grand prize: An entire mobile home, "put anywhere in the USA."

Finders Keepers (U.S.). Each day, the show is filmed on location at a different contestant's house. The film crew hides a prize in the contestant's living room, sets up cameras, and then lets viewers watch the contestant tear the room apart looking for it.

Italian Stripping Housewives (Italy). A strange game show takeoff on strip poker. Wives strip while their husbands gamble.

100 Grand (U.S.). Hollywood's response to the quiz show scandals of the 1950s: Contestants spend part of the show in an isolation booth writing their own questions. Amazingly, the first time the show aired, one contestant missed every single question. *100 Grand* aired twice.

Gonzo Games (U.S.). A precursor to *Fear Factor*, this game show from the early 1990s was hosted by Mark A. Walberg (*Antiques Roadshow*). In one event, each contestant had to see how many clothespins they could stick on their face. In another, they were forced to stand on a hot barbecue grill until the pain was too unbearable to continue.

Endurance (Japan). You think *Gonzo Games* was harsh? *Endurance* literally tortures its contestants. In one "game," they're dragged across pavement until they're bloodied up. Another game has them navigating a cage full of scorpions. When someone quits, the studio audience shouts, "Go Home!"

Survey result: 35% of people watching TV yell at it.

KEEP YOUR EYE ON THE GOAT CARCASS

Other cultures' sports and games may seem weird, but keep in mind that those same people might find the idea of a warlike game where 300-pound athletes crash into each other to move an oblong ball a few inches just as absurd.

BUZKASHI. Popular in the central Asian countries of Afghanistan and Kyrgyzstan, buzkashi is similar to polo: Teams of men on horseback have to move an object past a goal line to score. But instead of a ball, buzkashi is played with a headless, limbless, sandweighted goat carcass, which players must toss over the goal line. To steal the carcass from the other team, players are permitted to trip horses or whip their opponents.

HASHING. British colonists created this game in Malaysia in the 1930s, and it's still played by locals. Hashing involves a lot of running, but it's not really a race. Participants start the event drunk, and then run through a five-mile maze. Every quarter mile there's a checkpoint where more booze is consumed and the course branches out into three or four possible routes, with only one being correct. It doesn't even matter who wins—just who is able to finish and tell his story after the race, which traditionally takes place at a bar.

TRISKELION. A complicated version of soccer played by three teams on a triangular field. (It was invented by Green Party chairman Steve Kramer.)

CHESSBOXING. Inspired by a Serbian comic book, chessboxing is now played by small groups across Europe. It's exactly what the name implies: chess *and* boxing. Opponents box for one round, then sit at a table adjacent to the ring and play a four-minute round of chess. Then they go back to the boxing, then the chess, until a winner is determined in either one event or the other.

When John Lithgow won an Emmy for Showtime's *Dexter*, he accidentally thanked HBO.

POOH STICK RACING. This Japanese game is not what you think. Inspired by a game played by Winnie-the-Pooh in A. A. Milne's classic books, pooh stick racing involves finding sticks, dropping them into a river, and seeing which stick floats across the finish line first.

BOSSABALL. An instant sensation in Spain where it was created in 2006, bossaball combines volleyball…and bouncy castles. The net is very high; the field of play is one of those inflatable castles you see at kids' parties. Players can touch the ball with their hands or feet, but to make the game harder, the castle is set on top of large, bouncy, unstable, inflatable tubes. And to make it even *harder*, a "joker" from each team bounces on a trampoline next to the castle, trying to sabotage the other team by knocking the ball away.

KURLBOLLEN. Known as "feather bowling" in English, this sport originated in Belgium. Wooden balls shaped like large wheels of cheese are rolled down a dirt alley in the direction of a feather sticking out of the ground. The goal is to get the "ball" close to the feather without running over it. Each team gets 12 attempts; the side with the most balls closest to the feather wins.

CONGER CUDDLING. Since 1974, fans have flocked to the English village of Lyme Regis to watch two nine-man teams try to knock each off of a wooden platform…by swinging five-foot dead eels at each other. (A conger is a type of eel.) In 2006 the contest was almost canceled when animal-rights activists protested the event because "it's disgraceful to the memory of the eel." The contest was held—with rubber boat fenders instead of dead eels.

COLEO. This sport is popular in Venezuela. Four men on horseback chase a bull down a narrow pen, trying to pull its tail to make it fall over. Each successful tipping earns a point. After the bull falls over, the game must continue, so the men try to get the bull back on its feet by twisting or biting its tail or shocking it with an electric prod. (Interestingly, these tactics are similar to the way Uncle John manages his writers.)

HERE SPEECHING AMERICAN

*Let's face it: English can be pretty tough to grasp, especially
if it's not your first language. Uncle John gives the
authors of these signs and labels an "A" for affort.*

In an Austrian ski lodge: Not to
perambulate the corridors in the
house of repose in the boots of
ascension.

In a Japanese hotel room: Please
to Bathe inside the tub.

**From a chopstick wrapper in a
Chinese restaurant:**
Can you eat with chopsticks
Doctor told us / Be intell / eat by
using chopsticks / Lots of people
use chopsticks / So try eat your
chopsticks / Right Now!

**Air conditioner directions in a
Japanese hotel room:** Cooles and
Heates: If you want just condition
of warm in your room, please
control yourself.

Outside a Russian monastery:
You are welcome to visit the
cemetery where famous Russian
and Soviet composers, artists, and
writers are buried daily except
Thursday.

In a Finnish hostel: If you
cannot reach a fire exit, close the
door and expose yourself at the
window.

In a Copenhagen airport: We
take your bags and send them in
all directions.

From a Spanish shop entrance:
Here speeching American.

**Warning label on Chinese
lint-cleaning roller:**
1. Do not use this roller to the
floorings that made of wood and
plastic.
2. Do not use this roller to clean
the stuffs that dangerous to your
hands such as glass and chinaware.
3. Do not use the roller to
people's head, it is dangerous that
hair could be sticked up to cause
unexpected suffering.

In a Nairobi restaurant:
Customers who find our waitresses
rude ought to see the manager.

Ty Cobb once cheated at an old-timers baseball game.

MAN'S BEST FRIEND

…or worst nightmare?

BOUNCY DOG. A family in York, England, reported their bull terrier Harvey missing. At first, they had no idea how he'd escaped—there were no signs of him digging his way under the fence or finding a hole in it. They finally figured out that Harvey had bounced onto the trampoline in the backyard, over the backyard fence, into the neighbor's yard, and away.

STICKY DOG. One day, Pamela Panting was playing fetch with Hector, her Great Dane puppy. The game ended when Hector lost sight of the two-foot-long tree branch Panting had thrown. The next morning, Hector wouldn't eat and was drooling excessively, so Panting took him to a veterinarian. An X-ray revealed the problem: Hector hadn't lost the two-foot-long stick, he'd swallowed it. Cost to remove the branch: $4,000.

CRIME DOG. In 2000 a drug-sniffing German Shepherd police dog named Officer Nutz broke out of his kennel in Waukesha, Wisconsin, ran to a nearby supermarket, trotted through the automatic doors and into the store, grabbed a package of prime rib, and ran back outside…where he proceeded to attack the raw meat. Officer Nutz was captured on store security cameras; the police department placed him on administrative leave.

EMBARRASSING DOG. The Milner family of Dorset, England, was playing around with Google Earth, an Internet service that displays satellite photos of nearly any location on the planet. They looked up their home and saw a mysterious brown blob on their front lawn. The Milners finally came to realize what that brown lump was: Boris, their bull mastiff. At 200 pounds, the dog was so overweight that he could be seen from outer space.

TRAITOR DOGS. Police in Marion Oaks, Florida, went to the home of Wayne Huff to arrest him on wire fraud charges. Huff came to the door with his two dogs and resisted arrest, so the police used force. The struggle continued as the cops dragged Huff into his front yard. Both of Huff's dogs then attacked him, biting him on his arm, back, leg, and ear. The bites subdued him enough to be peaceably taken away by the police.

A Swede named Roger Tullgren receives disability benefits for his "heavy metal addiction."

QUIPPY COMEBACKS

How cool is it when someone asks you a question and you come up with a smart-aleck response right on the spot? These people know.

John Lennon, *in a late-1960s interview:*

Q: "John, do you think Ringo is the best drummer in the world?"

A: "The world? He's not even the best drummer in the Beatles!"

Pope John XXIII *during an interview in the 1950s:*

Q: "How many people work in the Vatican?"

A: "About half."

NASCAR pit crew member **Jeff Clark**, *speaking to his driver,* **Dale Earnhardt Jr.**, *over the radio during a race:*

Q: "How do the gauges look?"

A: "Nice. They're silver and they all have nice little red needles."

In the Georgia state congress, Rep. **Anne Mueller**'s *microphone wasn't working. So she asked Speaker* **Tom Murphy** *for assistance:*

Q: "Mr. Speaker, will you please turn me on?"

A: "Thirty years ago, I would have tried."

During **Adlai Stevenson**'s *1956 presidential campaign, a woman called out to him:*

Woman: "Senator, know that you have the vote of every thinking person!"

Stevenson: "That's not enough, madam, we need a majority."

An interviewer asked aging socialite **Zsa Zsa Gabor** *how many husbands she'd had. Her response:*

"You mean, other than my own?"

Jay Leno: "How do you feel being treated like a movie star?"

Al Gore: "Well, it's not all easy. For example, I'm in this huge feud with Lindsay Lohan now."

Leno: "Really? Can you give us a little more?"

Gore: "No, she knows what she did."

B-movie star **Bruce Campbell**, *when asked what he would want with him if marooned on a deserted island:*

"A continent."

The scientific name for stinky armpits: *tragomaschalia.*

LOVE IS STRANGE

We have a weird desire to name a future edition Uncle John's Monkey-Loving Bathroom Reader. *But we would never, ever do that for a bunch of really good reasons. However, if we did, the third entry below would fit in perfectly.*

BACKGROUND: In 2002 Jian Feng of Hegang, China, got married. Two years later his wife had a baby.

LOVE IS STRANGE: Jian accused his wife of having an affair—because she was so beautiful and the baby was "so ugly." His wife finally confessed: She hadn't had an affair—she'd had plastic surgery before they met. She showed him a pre-surgery photograph of herself to prove it. Jian immediately filed for divorce and sued for deceit.

OUTCOME: He won, and was awarded $99,700 for his wife's ugly past.

BACKGROUND: Romanian Nicolae Popa couldn't take his wife Maria's nagging every single night when he got home from work. "My business is going well but it takes all my energy," he said. "So when I get home in the evening I am so tired I just want to go to bed."

LOVE IS STRANGE: Popa made a deal with his wife: He bought her silence: "I pay her $500 a month as long as she doesn't nag me."

OUTCOME: Maria agreed to the deal, and the couple announced plans to start a family. But Mrs. Popa said that her husband will have to double her salary to keep the children quiet.

BACKGROUND: In 2003 German singer Werner Boehm, 62, made a music video which happened to feature a female baboon.

LOVE IS STRANGE: Boehm brought the animal home and "it was love at first sight," he said. "We're on the same wavelength." Boehm's wife Susanne, 31, wasn't amused. She soon left the singer, telling reporters, "I gave him the choice: the monkey or me. He chose the monkey."

OUTCOME: After complaints from animal-rights groups, police removed the baboon from Boehm's home and put it in a zoo. Then he asked his wife to come back. "I didn't want to," said Susanne, "but Werner assured me I feel much nicer in bed than the monkey did."

Christopher Walken once worked as an assistant lion tamer in a circus.

HOST WITH THE MOST

The Academy Awards is showbiz's premier event. Almost as important as selecting the nominees is selecting a celebrity host who can make or break the entire evening.

THE WRITE STUFF

The host of the Academy Awards is expected to be perfect. He's supposed to be smooth and gracious, funny but not too irreverent; ready with a witty ad-lib if something goes wrong, and most importantly, properly respectful of the evening's events. And he's supposed to do it all on live television in front of millions of people. It may look easy from the audience, but it takes *a lot* of preparation.

When Steve Martin was asked to host the 2003 Academy Awards, he assembled a team of top-notch comedy writers six months in advance of the event. They met at his home in Los Angeles eight times before the big night to prepare "the greatest opening monologue ever." Martin had a list of nominees, presenters, and stars who might be attending the ceremonies. At each meeting he sat at his laptop while the team of seven jokesmiths tossed out ideas. So who made the team?

• **Dave Barry,** Pulitzer Prize–winning columnist for the *Miami Herald* since 1983. He has written 24 best-selling humor books and is the subject of the CBS TV show *Dave's World.*

• **Bruce Vilanch,** *Hollywood Squares* regular and award-winning writer for the Oscar, Emmy, Tony, and Grammy shows as well as for Bette Midler and Whoopi Goldberg.

• **Rita Rudner,** stand-up comic and TV host.

• **Dave Boone,** head writer for *Hollywood Squares.* An Academy Award veteran, he also wrote material for Billy Crystal and Whoopi Goldberg.

• **Andy Breckman,** writer for David Letterman and *Saturday Night Live.* He also created the TV show *Monk.*

• **Beth Armogida,** joke writer for Jay Leno and for Drew Carey on *Whose Line Is It Anyway?*

• **Jon Macks,** staff writer for *The Tonight Show with Jay Leno* and an Academy Award veteran.

The Finnish language has no future tense.

THE BIG NIGHT

On Oscar night, while Martin stood at the microphone onstage, his comedy advisors were gathered in a small room, just offstage. As he delivered lines like, "A movie star is many things: tall, short, thin, or skinny," they sat in a semicircle facing a wall of television screens that showed the audience and the stage. Martin would introduce a presenter and then run to join the team for instant feedback and new jokes. When something unusual happened during the presentation, the writers wrote a few funny lines about it and Martin delivered them seconds later. For example, when Sean Connery appeared in a tuxedo accented with a frilly white front, Martin quipped, "So many people here tonight are wearing Armani but Sean is wearing Red Lobster."

Martin's team even handled the most controversial moment of the night with ease. When the outspoken filmmaker Michael Moore accepted his Oscar for *Bowling for Columbine*, Martin hurried to join his writers backstage. As Moore criticized President Bush for his handling of the war in Iraq, drawing cheers and catcalls in equal measure, the backstage writers went to work. From a list of possible jokes, the writers picked one, refined it, and sent Martin back onstage to ease the tension: "Backstage, it's so sweet. The Teamsters are helping Michael Moore into the trunk of his limo."

*   *   *

REEL FUNNY

Colonel Mustard doesn't have a clue.

Colonel Mustard: "Wadsworth, am I right in thinking there is nobody else in this house?"

Wadsworth the Butler: "Ummm, no."

Colonel Mustard: "Then there is someone else in this house?"

Wadsworth: "No, sorry. I said no meaning yes."

Colonel Mustard: "No meaning yes? Look, I want a straight answer. Is there someone else, or isn't there? Yes or no?"

Wadsworth: "Ummm, no."

Colonel Mustard: "No there is, or no there isn't?"

Wadsworth: "Yes."

—**Martin Mull and Tim Curry,** *Clue* **(1985)**

A "pregnant" GM crash test-dummy is called...

IRONIC, ISN'T IT?

There's something about a good irony that's so satisfying to read about. Perhaps it's because you're witnessing a cosmic joke being played out...on someone else.

IRONY THAT WON'T STAY DOWN

More than 100 food-safety experts who attended the 2014 Food Safety Summit in Baltimore, Maryland, got sick from food poisoning after eating the food in the convention center.

IRONY THAT DOES NOT COMPUTE

• Ben Bernanke applied for a loan to refinance his mortgage, but the bank's computerized approval system denied the loan because he'd recently changed jobs, which automatically puts up a "red flag." The job Bernanke left: he was the chairman of the Federal Reserve, the central banking system for the United States, which determines interest rates for banks.

• In February 2015, 800 graduate school applicants received acceptance e-mails from Carnegie Mellon University in Pittsburgh, Pennsylvania, a school "recognized around the world as a leader in all facets of computer science." Later that day, those same applicants received a second e-mail informing them that the first e-mail was a mistake. A school spokesperson blamed the goof on a "computer error."

STUPID @$%& IRONY

One of the most frustrating things in life: struggling to open stubborn plastic packaging. But now there's an As Seen on TV product called OpenX, with a "dual blade opener" that cuts plastic "like butter" so you can "stop struggling with stubborn plastic packages!" Only problem: you might need an OpenX to open OpenX because it comes in one of those "stubborn plastic packages."

ACCIDENTAL IRONY

• A newspaper truck for the *Republican*, based in Massachusetts, crashed into a home in 2010. Printed in big letters on the side of the truck were the words "Where News Hits Home."

• In 2014 a semitrailer driver for Halfords, a U.K.-based auto parts retailer, was driving through London when his 17-foot-tall trailer became wedged underneath a 15-foot bridge. Printed on the back of the trailer was the slogan "We Fit." (They didn't.) Underneath that was another slogan: "We Go the Extra Mile," which prompted a London Fire Brigade official to quip, "Going the 'extra mile' might have been the better option rather than trying to fit under a bridge."

OPERATIONAL IRONY

In 1964 a University of Illinois industrial design student named John Spinello got an assignment: create an electronic game in which players try to insert a metal rod into a hole without setting off a buzzer. He got to work and decided on a surgery theme. Good news: Spinello got an A! Bad news: he sold the rights of the game for $500 to the Milton Bradley Company, which turned it into Operation. Spinello's invention became one of the 20th century's most popular board games, but Spinello never made another cent off it. That could be why, in 2014, the 77-year-old couldn't come up with the $25,000 he needed for…an operation. (He had dental problems that required oral surgery.) Thanks to a crowd-funding site started by fans of Operation, along with a generous offer by Hasbro to purchase Spinello's original prototype (Hasbro bought Milton Bradley in 1984), he was able to pay for his operation.

THE GREAT CHICAGO FIRONY

In 2015 a Chicago building caught fire. More than 150 firefighters battled the blaze, but they couldn't save the structure because of a lack of water nearby. The building, by the way, housed a factory that manufactures fire extinguishers.

IRONY CUT SHORT

A British Royal Marine named Andy Grant had a tattoo on his leg that read "You'll Never Walk Alone," which is the motto of his favorite soccer team, Liverpool FC. Sadly, while serving in Afghanistan in 2009, Grant stepped on an IED that exploded, causing him to lose part of his leg. When his surgeon removed the bandage, Grant discovered that he'd lost part of the tattoo as well. Now it reads "You'll Never Walk."

Update: Not only did Grant walk again thanks to a prosthetic lower leg, but he's become a Paralympic athlete and has won several races. He now works as a motivational speaker. "The tattoo is bizarre and I just laugh about it," he said, adding that, ironically, the injury has "given me more of a life than I probably would have had."

What's the anatomical juxtaposition of two *orbicularis oris* muscles in contraction? A kiss.

TECHNOLOGICAL DIFFICULTIES

Man created technology in his own image…which is why it's so weird.

ROBOTS: NOW WITH A TASTE FOR FLESH. Scientists at NEC System Technologies in Japan have invented a robot that can taste and identify dozens of wines, as well as some types of food. The green-and-white tabletop robot has a swiveling head, eyes, and a mouth that speaks in a child's voice. To identify a wine, the unopened bottle is placed in front of the robot's left arm. An infrared beam scans the wine—through the glass bottle—and determines its chemical composition. The robot then names the variety of wine, describes its taste, and recommends foods to pair it with. Scientists are still working out the kinks: At a press conference, a reporter and a cameraman put their hands in front of the robot's infrared beam. According to the robot, the reporter tasted like ham, and the cameraman tasted like bacon.

WORST APP EVER. There are thousands of apps for Apple's iPhone, but none drew more complaints than the "Baby Shaker": a video game in which the player shakes the iPhone until a virtual baby stops crying (then two red X's appear over its eyes). The app was only available for download for two days in 2009 before Apple removed it. The company explained that it should have been rejected before it was added, but someone must have "missed it." Alex Talbot, the app's designer, admitted, "Yes, the Baby Shaker was a bad idea."

HOW TO GET ON THE NEWS. Say, what's that suspicious-looking device? It's the "Suspicious Looking Device!" This real product you can purchase is a darkly humorous response to the increased fears of terrorism in recent years. What is the SLD? It's a red metal box with dotted lights, a small screen, a buzzer, and whirring motor. What does it do? Nothing. It's just supposed to *appear* suspicious. So if you want to see your name in the headlines, just place the SLD in front of your local police station.

Say it out loud: "It looks like boogers but it's not."

SHOT SELF IN NOSE

What's worse than a trip to the emergency room? A trip to the ER for something really humiliating. These are real-life ER reports.

"40-year-old female using toothbrush to make herself gag, accidentally swallowed toothbrush."

"Abdominal pain. Diagnosis: tight pants and belt."

"Forehead pain: Patient shot self in nose with BB gun."

"Head injury: Rolled off couch and hit telephone."

"Patient stuffed ear with toilet paper so roach wouldn't crawl in, now unable to remove."

"Patient missed punching bag, hit metal safe."

"Concussion, severe headache: Patient being pulled on a sled behind golf cart, struck a bump, launched in air."

"Pulled groin while riding mechanical bull."

"Bruised shoulder: Husband was throwing cell phone at cat, missed cat."

"Patient, 23, used a sword to cut a piece of paper. Laceration left arm."

"Accidentally swallowed guitar pick."

"Patient, 31, was playing sex games with wife, had belt around neck, jumped over something and got hung up. Also fell down stairs."

"Ankle injury from falling off stage doing karaoke."

"Swallowed toothpick while eating cabbage."

"Fell off monkey bars at police academy."

"Patient playing with pillow case, buddy put a rock in it."

"Insect bites on lips while riding a go-kart."

"Generalized body rash after being in pool and hot tub at hotel."

"Pain, swelling, blister on palm: Patient, 15, was playing video games, woke next day with swollen hand. Pain and swelling getting worse."

"Patient has wrist pain after sex and bowling."

"A big laugh is a really loud noise from the soul saying, 'Ain't that the truth.'" —Quincy Jones

THE LIMBURGER CHEESE WAR

*From our "Dustbin of History" files, here's the pungent
tale of two Midwestern states whose pride and honor
were once challenged...by a slab of stinky cheese.*

IT AIN'T EASY BEING CHEESY

It began in the winter of 1935 when a doctor in Independence, Iowa, prescribed an odd medicine to an ailing farm wife: Limburger cheese. The doctor figured the heavily aromatic cheese would help clear the woman's clogged sinuses. (If you don't know what Limburger smells like, give it a whiff the next time you're at the supermarket.) So the order was put through to Monroe, Wisconsin, to send some Limburger cheese—post haste.

Why Monroe? Swiss cheesemakers first arrived there in 1845. At the time, Wisconsin was in the depths of an economic depression and cheese helped pull them out of it. By 1910, Wisconsin had become the cheese-making capital of the United States, producing more cheese than any other state. And Monroe was the Limburger capital of Wisconsin.

THE BATTLE LINES ARE DRAWN

Monroe's postmaster, John Burkhard, approved the delivery and sent it on its way. But the mail carrier in Independence, Iowa, who delivered the Limburger was so offended by the stench wafting through his roadster that he refused to deliver it, citing a postal rule that said mail would only be delivered if it "did not smell objectionable."

Independence's postmaster, Warren Miller, concurred without examining or even smelling the cheese. He had it sent back to Monroe on the grounds that it could "fell an ox at twenty paces."

Burkhard took it personally; to insult Limburger is to insult not just Monroe, but all of Wisconsin and its proud cheese heritage. So Burkhard rewrapped the package and sent it back to Iowa. Miller promptly returned it to Wisconsin. War was brewing.

THE BATTLE OF DUBUQUE

Burkhard took his gripe all the way to the U.S. postmaster general in Washington, D.C. At first, he couldn't understand what all of the fuss was about. So Burkhard sent him some Limburger. The postmaster general then decided that, yes, the cheese smelled bad, but no, it wasn't hazardous. And the war was over, right? Wrong.

By this time the press had sniffed out the story. At a time when the nation was mired in the Great Depression and Hitler was rising to power in Germany, a story about smelly cheese was a breath of fresh air. And unwilling to give in, Burkhard challenged Miller to a "cheese-sniffing duel"—if Miller could sit at a table and not retch from the stench of freshly cut Limburger, then he would never again raise a stink about Wisconsin or its cheese. Miller accepted. Dozens of people from each town—as well as a throng of reporters—showed up at the Julien Hotel in Dubuque, Iowa, on the cold afternoon of March 8, 1935, to witness the standoff.

A DUEL TO THE BREATH

The two men sat across from each other at a table. While flashbulbs flickered and onlookers whispered, Burkhard placed a box on the table, unwrapped it, and produced a very strong sample of his state's pride and joy, praising not only its medicinal qualities, but boasting that nothing on Earth tasted better with beer. The tension was so thick that you could cut it with a knife. Famed *Milwaukee Journal* reporter Richard S. Davis sent out a dispatch calling it a "duel to the breath."

As Burkhard prepared to push the slab of cheese over to Miller, he offered Miller a clothespin and a gas mask. But Miller just shook his head and meekly surrendered. "I won't need that clothespin," he lamented, "I haven't any sense of smell."

The crowd gasped. The battle was over before it began. Burkhard was immediately declared the winner and Miller had to agree to allow any and all Wisconsin cheese safe passage throughout Iowa's postal routes. The next day newspapers in 30 states ran a picture of the olfactorily challenged Miller looking bewildered next to a piece of steaming Limburger. And *now* the war was over, right? Wrong. The final battle was yet to come.

A glitch in Apple's iTunes store called the "Dick Van Dyke Song" the "D**k Van D**e Song."

THE BATTLE OF BEAVER DAM

While Burkhard was basking in victory, something he'd said about Limburger at that table in Dubuque—that nothing tasted better with beer—was churning through Miller's head. Every good Iowan knew that the best food to eat with beer is smoked whitefish, not some stinky piece of cheese. Miller just couldn't let it go. So he challenged Burkhard to another contest: a fight for the title of "Best *Snack* in the World." Once again the press got a whiff of the food feud, and they convened at a neutral site chosen for the contest: the American Legion hall in Beaver Dam, Wisconsin.

This confrontation was even more serious than the first—now there were judges. And with so much at stake, both sides used underhanded tactics: They bribed the judges with beer. The fish-heads bought a round, then the cheese-heads. And once all palates were properly whetted, the showdown began.

CARNAGE

First came the sliced Limburger with beer. Then the Iowans gave the judges smoked whitefish…and more beer. The battle raged on: Limburger and beer, whitefish and beer. Limburger and beer, whitefish and beer. Finally, when the judges could eat or drink no more, they sent the least-inebriated member of their panel to the podium: "The judgeth have reached a dethision. It was unamus…unans…they all said the same darned thing! Cheese'n beer s'wunnerful. Fishes'n beer s'wunnerful too. But when you have Limburger cheese *and* smoked whitefish and beer, heck, it don't get no better'n that!"

Both sides were declared victorious, Burkhard and Miller retained their respective states' honor, and Limburger cheese had risen from being referred to as "hazardous material" to holding the joint title of "Best Snack in the World."

VICTORY PARADE

That October, Monroe, Wisconsin, held its annual Cheese Day parade. All of the press coverage from the Limburger cheese war made it the biggest Cheese Day ever. Fifty thousand people showed up to bask in the glory—including the farmer's wife (who had healed quite nicely). Warren Miller came all the way from Iowa and was given a place of honor in the parade—right next to his friend John Burkhard.

Tongue twister: I slit the sheet, the sheet I slit, and on the slitted sheet I sit.

THE CHAUCER OF CHEESE

Have you heard of one James McIntyre?
His unusual verses set the world afire.
Think of this while eating your Cheerios:
In the 1800s, he was the bard of southwestern Ontario.
His work is published this day still,
If you read his poems, they'll make you ill.

A BARD IS BORN

James McIntyre (1827–1906), known to his admirers as the "Chaucer of Cheese," was born in the Scottish village of Forres. He moved to Canada when he was 14 and lived most of his life in Ingersoll, a small town in Ontario, where he worked as a furniture and coffin maker. But what earned him his reputation was his hobby—writing poetry. McIntyre wrote poems on a variety of topics: He described Ontario towns, saluted his favorite authors, and sang the praises of farming and country life. He even composed tributes to his furniture.

WHAT RHYMES WITH GOUDA?

Most famously, he wrote poems to promote the local economy. And in the mid-1800s, the economy of southwestern Ontario was cheese. In 1866, for example, Ontario dairy farmers produced what was then the world's largest block of cheese—it measured more than 21 feet across and weighed 7,300 pounds. The giant inspired two of McIntyre's best-known poems: "Ode on the Mammoth Cheese" and "Prophesy of a Ten Ton Cheese."

When the *Toronto Globe* printed some of his work, including such poems as "Oxford Cheese Ode," "Hints to Cheesemakers," "Dairy Ode," and "Father Ranney, the Cheese Pioneer," his fame spread across Canada and then around the world. What makes McIntyre's poetry fun to read isn't just his choice of subject matter (cheese) or his weird rhymes (pairing "fodder" with "cheddar," or "shoes Norwegian" with "narrow toboggan"). "If you read his poetry, what comes out is his enthusiasm," said Michael Hennessy,

---

Aloha, good-lookin'! The hula was originally performed as a fertility rite.

mayor of Ingersoll. "People might say they are terrible poems, but McIntyre was a trier, and that is a great quality in a writer."

WHO IS THE WORST?

Giving new meaning to the term *cheesy*, many of McIntyre's admirers argue that he, not Scotland's infamous William McGonagall, deserves the title of World's Worst Poet. But McGonagall's fans steadfastly disagree. "McGonagall is by far the worst poet in the English language," said Scottish poet Don Paterson. "He could write a bad poem about anything. This cheese guy may be a bad poet, but it seems he could write bad poetry about only one subject."

A MCINTYRE SAMPLER

A few excerpts from our favorite McIntyre poems:

"Hints to Cheesemakers"

All those who quality do prize
Must study color,
taste and size,
And keep their dishes
clean and sweet,
And all things round
their factories neat,
For dairymen insist that these
Are all important points
in cheese.

Grant has here a
famous work
Devoted to the cure of pork,
For dairymen find it doth pay
To fatten pigs
upon the whey,
For there is money
raising grease
As well as in the
making cheese.

"Dairy Ode"

Our muse it doth
refuse to sing
Of cheese made
early in the spring.
When cows give milk
from spring fodder
You cannot make
a good cheddar.

The quality is often vile
Of cheese that is
made in April,
Therefore we
think for that reason
You should make cheese
later in the season.

Cheese making
you should delay
Until about the first of May.
Then cows do feed
on grassy field
And rich milk they
abundant yield.

In scientific circles, the collision that formed the moon is known as the Big Whack.

Utensils must be
clean and sweet
So cheese with first class can
compete,
And daily polish up
milk pans,
Take pains with vats
and with milk cans.

And it is important matter
To allow no stagnant water,
But water from
pure well or stream
The cow must drink
to give pure cream.

Though 'gainst spring cheese
some do mutter,
Yet spring milk also makes
bad butter,
Then there doth arise the query
How to utilize it in the dairy.

"Oxford Cheese Ode"

The ancient poets
ne'er did dream
That Canada was
land of cream
They ne'er imagined
it could flow
In this cold land
of ice and snow,
Where everything
did solid freeze,
They ne'er hoped or
looked for cheese.

"Ode on the Mammoth Cheese"

We have seen thee,
queen of cheese,
Lying quietly at your ease,
Gently fanned by evening breeze,
Thy fair form no flies dare seize.

All gaily dressed soon you'll go
To the great Provincial show,
To be admired by many a beau
In the city of Toronto.

Cows as numerous
as a swarm of bees
Or as the leaves upon the trees,
It did require to
make thee please,
And stand unrivalled,
queen of cheese.

May you not receive a scar as
We have heard that Mr. Harris
Intends to send you off as far as
The great world's show at Paris.

Of the youth beware of these,
For some of them might
rudely squeeze
And bite your cheek,
then songs or glees
We could not sing, oh!
queen of cheese.

We'rt thou suspended
from balloon,
You'd cast a shade even at noon,
Folks would think
it was the moon,
About to fall
and crush them soon.

What is the only type of cheese that is made backward? Edam. (It's "made" backward.)

CELEBRITY BLOWHARDS

Blah, blah, blah. Ain't I great?

"I've got a talent to act. No matter what any newspaper says about me, I am one of the most sensitive human beings on Earth, and I know it."

—**Jean-Claude Van Damme**

"I considered myself and still consider myself the hippest man on the planet."

—**Barry Manilow**

"A select group of my classmates thought I was more interesting than anything in the classroom."

—**Bruce Willis**

"I am a great mayor; I am an upstanding Christian man; I am an intelligent man; I am a deeply educated man; I am a humble man."

—**Marion Barry**

"The guy I was reading with got lost because he was so busy watching me."

—**Samuel L. Jackson, describing his audition for *Pulp Fiction***

"I consider Madonna a good friend, and she sure knows how to work that publicity machine. Of course, I don't have breasts. If I did, I'd be in the number one spot over Madonna."

—**Spike Lee**

"Gingrich—primary mission: Advocate of civilization, Teacher of the rules of civilization, Leader of the civilizing forces."

—**Newt Gingrich**

"We've never been intimate—but maybe we do have a few things in common."

—**Noel Coward, on God**

"When I'm doing well, I like to think I'm doing God's work."

—**Faye Dunaway**

"I don't know what my calling is, but I want to be here for a bigger reason. I strive to be like the greatest people who have ever lived. Like Jesus."

—**Will Smith**

FOOLING SMART PEOPLE

That's what they get for using their brains all the time.

THE AMAZING TOMATO-WHEAT-COW

In September 1984, *Omni* magazine ran a story about "an amazing tomato-wheat-cow," a single plant-animal hybrid that had been created by two biologists at the University of Hamburg in West Germany. "With all the characteristics of a giant stalk of wheat," *Omni* wrote, "the skin can be tanned and used as leather, and several udder blossoms provide the grower with a steady supply of tomato juice." *Omni* attributed the genetic breakthrough to "Dr. Barry MacDonald and William Wimpey of the Department of Biology at the University of Hamburg."

It turned out that *Omni* got the story from the April issue of *New Scientist* magazine…which turned out to be the April Fool's issue. The "cow" was an obvious hoax—Wimpey's and McDonald's are the two largest hamburger chains in England—but *Omni* somehow missed the joke. According to one account, "Fact-checking for the article was limited to leaving a message for Wimpey and MacDonald at the University of Hamburg. The message was not returned."

THE FAMOUS UBIQUITOUS ALGORITHM HOAX

In 2005 Massachusetts Institute of Technology student Jeremy Stribling submitted an academic paper to a leading technology conference. The paper, entitled "Rooter: A Methodology for the Typical Unification of Access Points and Redundancy," was accepted, and he was invited to speak at the World Multiconference on Systemics, Cybernetics and Informatics in Orlando, Florida. One problem: The paper was nothing but gibberish. Generated by a computer program written by Stribling, it was sentence after sentence of random important-sounding nonsense, such as: "We can disconfirm that expert systems can be made amphibious" and "We concentrate our efforts on showing that the famous ubiquitous algorithm for the exploration of robots by Sato et al. runs in $\Omega((n + \log n))$ time [22]." So why'd he do it? Because he was tired of all spam e-mails soliciting research papers for the conference. When the ruse was discovered, Stibling's conference credentials were revoked.

Apes laugh when you tickle them.

GIVE ME A SIGN!

*Church reader boards are a great source of humor and wisdom.
Here are some real signs that we've collected.*

"God didn't create anything without a purpose. But mosquitoes come close."

"At Jesus Way, take the right turn. Others go to Hell."

"Jesus would so-o-o smack you in the head!"

"Blessing of pets. Bring your dog or cat or whatever and lawnchair."

"Whoever is praying for snow, please stop."

"Watch your tongue. It's wet and slips easily."

"Bored? Try a missionary position."

"Triumph is umph added to try."

"You may party in Hell, but you will be the BBQ!"

"Christmas: Easier to spell than Hannukah."

"He who farts in church sits in own pew."

"To err is human, to arrrr is pirate."

"Do you know what Hell is? Come hear our preacher."

"The class on prophesy has been cancelled due to unforeseen circumstances."

"What part of 'Thou Shalt Not' don't you understand?"

"Honk if you love Jesus. Text while driving if you want to meet him."

"Changing churches? What difference does it make which one you stay home from?"

"How will you spend eternity? Smoking or non-smoking?"

"Get behind me, Satin."

"Whoever stole our AC units keep one. It is hot where you're going."

"Hate corny church signs? Amen!"

Why? In Quitman, Georgia, it is illegal for a chicken to cross the road.

CRAZY WORLD RECORDS

Uncle John holds the world record for the most pages ever read on the throne (577,819 and counting). Here are some other dubious achievements.

• Christian Adam of Germany set the distance record for riding a bicycle backward while playing the violin: 37.5 miles. It took him a little more than five hours. He played J. S. Back…er, Bach.

• For 20 minutes of "every waking hour" for 16 years, Australian Les Stewart spelled out every number from one to one million on his typewriter. He went through seven typewriters and 1,000 ink ribbons. He not only owned a world record but a 19,890-page book consisting of every spelled-out number up to one million.

• On May 6, 2009, Eric "No Class" Matyjasik of Arizona unzipped his pants 162 times in 30 seconds, breaking the old record by 27 zips.

• Artist Maria Reidelbach built the world's largest garden gnome as of 2006. It stands 13 feet, 6 inches, and lives on a miniature golf course in Kerhonkson, New York. The gnome's name: Gnome Chomsky, a play on the name of linguist and philosopher Noam Chomsky (who is only about half as tall as Gnome Chomsky).

• The unofficial world record for staying awake: 18 days, 17 hours, set by Maureen Weston of England while participating in a rocking-chair marathon. Although she hallucinated quite a bit, she says she hasn't suffered any long-term health effects.

• An exotic dancer who goes by the name Maxi Mounds is the proud owner of the world's largest augmented breasts. Each of Mounds's mounds weighs 20 pounds; her bust measurement is about 60 inches.

• Naya Ganj of India had the world's longest ear hair. "Making it into *Guinness* is special for my family! God has been very kind to me!" said the guy with 5.25 inches of hair growing from his ears. Anthony Victor broke the record in 2007, with 7.12 inches of ear hair.

Monty Python's *Life of Brian* was marketed in Sweden as "so funny it was banned in Norway."

THE IG NOBEL PRIZES

Here's a look at one of our favorite annual awards, the Ig Nobel Prizes, created in 1991 by the scientific humor magazine Annals of Improbable Research. *Its mission: to honor scientific discoveries "that cannot, or should not, be reproduced." Here are some recent winners.*

Ig Nobel Prize: Physics (2003)

Topic: "An Analysis of the Forces Required to Drag Sheep Over Various Surfaces," by Jack Harvey of the University of Ballarat, Australia

Results: "Sheep shearing is an arduous occupation involving a range of physically demanding tasks.... Many shearers suffer back injuries during sheep dragging."

• "The texture with the lowest mean dragging force was wooden boards laid parallel to the drag.... This orientation is also favored by shearers for another reason. Sheep catch their toes much less in the 'parallel' floor than they do with steel mesh or with boards at right angles to the drag, resulting in a reduction in the effort expended in tipping sheep over."

Ig Nobel Prize: Medicine (2004)

Topic: "The Effect of Country Music on Suicide," by Steven Stack of Wayne State University, et al.

Results: "Country music is hypothesized to nurture a suicidal mood through its concerns with problems common in the suicidal population, such as marital discord, alcohol abuse, and alienation from work."

• "The results of a multiple regression analysis of 49 metropolitan areas show that the greater the airtime devoted to country music, the greater the whole suicide rate. The effect is independent of divorce, southernness, poverty, and gun availability."

Ig Nobel Prize: Chemistry (2002)

Topic: The Periodic Table Table. Theodore Gray of Champaign, Illinois, built a periodic table of the elements that doubles as a conference table, and stuffed it with samples of as many real elements as he could find. "One evening while reading *Uncle Tungsten* by Oliver Sacks, I became

---

In China, *World Wide Web* translates as "10,000 Dimensional Web in Heaven and Net on Earth."

momentarily confused. He begins a chapter with a description of a periodic table display he loved to visit in the Kensington Science Museum, and in misreading the paragraph, I thought it was a *table*, not the wall display it actually is. When I found out there wasn't a periodic table in the British Museum, it left a hole I felt I had to fill."

Results: "Each element group (e.g., alkali metals, noble gases, etc.) is represented by a different type of wood. Then of course there's the whole question of collecting elements! You'd be surprised how many are available at Walmart."

Ig Nobel Prize: Biology (2004)
Topic: "Sounds Produced by Herring Bubble Release," by Ben Wilson of the University of British Columbia
Result: "Herring apparently communicate by farting."

MORE WINNERS

• **Ornithology** (2006): "Woodpeckers and Head Injury" (a study of why woodpeckers don't get headaches)

• **Interdisciplinary Research** (2003): "Chickens Prefer Beautiful Humans"

• **Agricultural History** (2005): "The Significance of Mr. Richard Buckley's Exploding Trousers"

• **Physics** (2004): "Coordination Modes in the Multisegmental Dynamics of Hula Hooping"

• **Biology** (2003): "The First Case of Homosexual Necrophilia in the Mallard"

• **Medicine** (1994): Awarded in two parts to 1) "Patient X," who was bitten by his pet rattlesnake and tried to treat himself with electroshock therapy by applying sparkplug wires to his lips for five minutes while a friend revved his car up to 3,000 rpm; and 2) Dr. Richard C. Dart and Dr. Richard A. Gustafson, authors of the medical paper "Failure of Electric Shock Treatment for Rattlesnake Envenomation."

• **Medicine** (2006): "Termination of Intractable Hiccups with Digital Rectal Massage"

The funniest running foot in this book is on page 205.

ROYAL FLUSHERS

*Here at the BRI, Uncle John has to sit on the same piece of porcelain that
all of us underlings do. He often laments that if he were a king from
the days of ole, he could just go anywhere he damn well pleases.
We're relieved that he's not a king from the days of ole.*

King James I of England (reigned 1603–25) loved hunting so much
that he wouldn't leave the saddle, even to go to the bathroom.
The king just went in his pants and had his servants clean him up
after he got home.

King Henry IV of France tried to do something about repulsive toilet
habits. In 1606 he passed a law forbidding anyone to pee or poop in the
corners of his palace in Paris. His son, the **Dauphin (Louis XIII)**, issued a
similar warning—no one was allowed to pee or poop on the floors or under
stairways, either. But no one obeyed, including the prince. The very day
that he made his announcement, he was caught peeing against the wall of
his bedroom.

When **King Charles II of England** fled to Oxford in 1665 to escape the
plague, he really left his mark on the place. Historian Anthony Wood
wrote about the king and his entourage in his diary: "Although they were
neat in their apparel, they were nasty and beastly, leaving their excrement
in every corner; in chimneys, studies, coalhouses, and cellars."

King Louis XIV of France (1638–1715) thought that everything he did
was royally important—including going to the bathroom. One of his favorite things to do was greet guests while seated "on the throne." Some people
didn't mind doing business with the king while he was doing *his* business.
They even paid to see his bare bottom, seated on the royal pot. Others
were disgusted by it, especially foreign ambassadors. But that didn't stop
Louis. He even announced his engagement while sitting on the pot.

How things have changed: "The only time I worry about the press is when
I'm up at Balmoral fishing. When I'm standing in the river for hours, I
sometimes have a pee. I'm petrified some cameraman is going to catch me."

—**Prince Charles**

There is a British TV show called *Watching Paint Dry*. It shows paint drying.

THE ELVIS MOVIE GENERATOR

From 1956 to 1969, Elvis Presley made 31 movies with titles like Roustabout, Girls! Girls! Girls!, *and* Harum Scarum. *At a rate of more than two movies per year, they were by necessity low budget and formulaic, usually just a showcase for a handful of Elvis songs, a pretty girl, a chase scene, and a fight. Now you too can come up with your own Elvis movie plot... with Uncle John's patented Elvis Movie Generator.*

1) PICK A NAME FOR ELVIS'S CHARACTER

It should be something masculine, preferably one syllable.
Real examples: *Clint, Vince, Chad, Rick, Jess, Deke, Josh*
Or it can be playful and boyish, usually ending with the letter "y."
Real examples: *Jimmy, Johnny, Toby, Danny, Rusty, Lucky*

2) PICK A PROFESSION FOR ELVIS'S CHARACTER

He always has a job that requires lifting, throwing, and/or sweating. Extra points if it's dangerous or mildly threatening.
Real examples: *boxer, helicopter pilot, gambler, rodeo cowboy, lifeguard, crop duster, soldier, racecar driver, pro bono doctor, navy frogman, handyman*
Or it can be something a little more believable for Elvis.
Real examples: *rock 'n' roll singer, traveling singer, nightclub singer, coffeehouse singer, jazz singer, riverboat singer*

3) PICK A FUN-LOVING AND WHIMSICAL TITLE

It should contain one or more of the following: "Girls," "Love," "Rock," a city or state, an article of women's clothing, a nonsense word, two words that rhyme, or an exclamation point. Some examples we made up:
So Many Girls So Little Time, What a Night!, That Darn Girl, Gals-a-Poppin!, Wackity Schmackity, Howdy Denver!, Drive Faster!, What's a Feller to Do?, Too Many Bikinis, Say Hey, Once Upon a Time in the Islands, Aloha Mexico

"My way of joking is to tell the truth; it's the funniest joke in the world." —George Bernard Shaw

4) CREATE A PLOT BY FILLING IN THESE BLANKS

In (*title of the movie*), Elvis plays (*character's name*), a (*character's profession*) who needs to raise $5,000 by the end of the week to (*get into the big race, stay out of jail, buy his airplane back, fix his motorcycle, etc.*). Will he do it in time? And will he win the heart of (*Judy, Valerie, Cathy, Lily, etc.*) in the process? Here are a few we came up with:

• In *Stockholm Stockings*, Elvis plays **Dash**, a **lobster fisherman** who needs to raise $5,000 by the end of the week in order to **buy back his father's scuba business**. Will he do it in time? And will he win the heart of **Betty, the waitress in the local pie shop,** in the process?

• In *Racin'*, Elvis plays **Johnny**, a **motorcycle racer** who needs to raise $5,000 by the end of the week in order to **get enough money for the race entry fee**. Will he do it in time? And will he win the heart of **Sheree, the sheriff's daughter,** in the process?

• In *Turnpike*, Elvis plays **Lance**, a **singing truck driver** who needs to raise $5,000 by the end of the week in order to **buy a pony for the kids at the orphanage**. Will he do it in time? And will he win the heart of **Margie, the lady doctor who works in the orphanage,** in the process?

Your turn! See what kind of rockin', romantic, wacky, and manly plots you can think up for a future Elvis movie (should he be discovered alive somewhere).

* * *

CHEER UP, IT COULD BE WORSE

"Most people think life sucks, and then you die. Not me. I beg to differ. I think life sucks, then you get cancer, then your dog dies, your wife leaves you, the cancer goes into remission, you get a new dog, you get remarried, you owe ten million dollars in medical bills but you work hard for 35 years and you pay it back and then—one day—you have a massive stroke, your whole right side is paralyzed, you have to limp along the streets and speak out of the left side of your mouth and drool but you go into rehabilitation and regain the power to walk and the power to talk and then—one day—you step off a curb at 67th Street, and BANG you get hit by a city bus and then you die. Maybe."

—**Denis Leary**

Elvis once volunteered to be an FBI drug informant. (His services were refused.)

COME ON DOWN!

Deep thoughts from the highbrow world of television game shows.

Jack Barry: "What do you want to be when you grow up?"
Kid: "A game show host."
Jack: "Oh, you mean like me?"
Kid: "No, like Bob Barker."

—*Joker Joker Joker*

"It's not as easy as it looks, being on all the time. I mean, what happens if I'm in a bad mood?"

—**Vanna White**

Contestant: "I'd like to buy a vowel, Regis."
Regis Philbin: "I think you mean lifeline."
Contestant: "Yeah, that."

—*Who Wants to Be a Millionaire*

Anne Robinson: "Rob, do you still think I'm sexy?"
Rob Schneider: "Yes, I do."
Anne Robinson: "Good, because I still think you're stupid."

—*The Weakest Link*

"Lisa, from where I'm standing, you have some nice prizes."

—**Ken Ober,** *Remote Control*

Richard Dawson: "Name a fruit that begins with 'A.'"
Contestant: "Orange."

—*Family Feud*

Richard Dawson: "Name the first article of clothing that you take off when you get home from work."
Female Contestant: "My underwear."
Richard Dawson: "Next question, what time do you get off work?"

—*Family Feud*

"I'd like to buy an owl."

—**Contestant on** *Wheel of Fortune*

A contestant on *Wheel of Fortune* had gotten all of the letters but one in the following puzzle:

"_T TAKES ONE
TO KNOW ONE"

Contestant: "I'd like to solve."
Pat Sajak: "This shouldn't be too hard. Go ahead."
Contestant: "E.T. takes one to know one."
Pat Sajak: "Uhh…really?"

CODE BROWN

Actual abbreviations and terms used in the ER by doctors and nurses who—by necessity—have a morbid sense of humor.

TMB: Too Many Birthdays (suffering from old age)

FORD: Found On Road Dead

House Red: Blood

TRO: Time Ran Out

Frequent Flier: Someone who is regularly taken to the hospital in an ambulance, even though they aren't sick (because it's something to do)

Code Zero: Another name for a "Frequent Flyer." The real radio codes range from Code 1 (not serious) to Code 4 (emergency)

Code Yellow: A patient who has wet the bed

Code Brown: (You can guess this one yourself.)

FOOSH: Fell Onto Outstretched Hand (a broken wrist)

T&T Sign: Tattoos-and-teeth. (Strange but true: Patients with a lot of tattoos and missing teeth are more likely to survive major injuries.)

DFO: Done Fell Out (of bed)

MGM Syndrome: A "patient" who is faking illness and putting on a really good show

WNL: Will Not Listen

SYB: Save Your Breath, as in, "SYB, he WNL"

Insurance Pain: An inordinate amount of neck pain following a minor auto collision with a wealthy driver

ALP: Acute Lead Poisoning—a gunshot wound

ALP (A/C): Acute Lead Poisoning (Air Conditioning)— multiple gunshot wounds

Flower Sign: Lots of flowers at a patient's bedside (may indicate the patient is a good candidate for early discharge, since they have people who can care for them)

ART: Assuming Room Temperature (deceased)

Bagged and Tagged: A corpse ready for the morgue (it's in a body bag and has a toe tag)

AMF Yo Yo: Adios, Motherf@#*!, You're On Your Own

U.S. Patent #4,429,685 was granted for a "Method of Growing Unicorns."

CRAIGSLIST ODDITIES

A lot of newspapers are closing down in part due to revenue lost to Craigslist—more and more people are using the free online classified site to post their "room for rent," "for sale," and "help wanted" ads. It also tends to attract a lot of kooks. Here are some real Craigslist ads we found.

ROOMS FOR RENT

• "I have a bedroom available for a male or female roommate. The apartment is spacious and well lit. I work as a researcher and I'm also pursuing a Master's Degree. One more thing. On our bathroom door is a checklist. I like to keep a record of my bowel movements and I expect you to do the same."

• "I recently acquired a decommissioned Chinese nuclear submarine and am renting it out. The 'crew member' price is a low $120 per month and includes a bunk in the sleeping quarters, access to the mess hall, and a shared bathroom. Utilities included. We have enough uranium to power us through the 2060s."

FREE STUFF

• "Toilet: could be fixed up. A little dirty, and it leaked and overflowed last time it was used. My son stuffed an action figure down it, so if anyone picks this up and fixes it, can you drop the action figure back off at my house?"

• "One right New Balance shoe (never been worn). I broke my right foot and only used the left shoe, so now I have this new right shoe. Great gift for a one-footed person, or if you know anyone with a broken left foot."

• "Giving away absolutely free of charge, with no lien, mortgage, or other encumbrance of any sort, the undisputed world-record holder in the 'loudest vacuum cleaner on the face of the Earth' category! Act now to take advantage of this truly unique opportunity!"

• "Left-handed vintage air guitar for free. All that's needed is new strings and a good dusting."

According to *The New York Times Magazine,* Spam makes a good furniture polish.

FOR SALE

• "Fart Jar for sale: My hot girlfriend's fart in a mason jar. Need cash to pay the rent."

• "I have some banana slugs. I will lease them out for $1 per day. You just come and catch them, and keep sliding dollar bills under my front door. I am trying to save up for a flat screen TV."

• "I found four cockroaches in a box of Triscuits a few months back. I hate to have to get rid of them but I'm moving to a smaller place and won't really have the room for them anymore. Re-homing fee of $15 each or $50 for all four."

• "I have more than 1,300 pope hat replicas that I really need to get rid of. They are a little too small for most adult heads and are also irritating to the skin, so you would need to have long hair or wear a smaller hat underneath (just like the real pope). Dogs do not like to wear these pope hats, but maybe a large cat would wear one."

HELP WANTED

• "Looking for an assistant to help in texting duties—replies, deleting texts, alerting of new texts, reading texts, filtering texts. I get 40-50 texts an hour. I can't handle my workload plus texting responsibilities. My phone gets too full and needs to be deleted every couple of hours. This is a full-time position and you must be wherever I am, because my phone is always with me."

• "We have a complete business plan that aims to yield investors 1,000% returns within only a five-year period. We have all the pieces in place; the only missing piece is YOU! We are looking for a very motivated scientist who has experience in teleportation research and/or technology. Send a resume and any other information that may set you apart from other teleportation scientists."

• "I need someone to hide Easter eggs in my apartment when I am not there. They are small and filled with candy."

*   *   *

"We must laugh at man to avoid crying for him."

—**Napoleon Bonaparte**

A German study found that within a week, newborn babies begin to cry with an accent.

GOVERN-MENTAL

Strange but true tales from the public sector.

NAME RECOGNITION

In a January 2015 story in Maryland's *Frederick News-Post*, journalist Bethany Rodgers wrote, "Councilman Kirby Delauter has joined [former Commissioner Billy] Shreve in concern over parking for elected officials." After reading the article, Delauter went on his Facebook page to condemn Rodgers and her "unauthorized use" of his name. (Three months earlier, Rodgers had written an article about strained relations between Delauter and town officials, which the conservative councilman referred to as a "hit piece.") Rodgers replied that it was not only within the newspaper's rights to mention names of elected public officials—it was their responsibility. Delauter's response: "Use my name again unauthorized and you'll be paying for an Attorney. Your rights stop where mine start." Terry Headlee, the *Frederick News-Post's* managing editor, called the threat a "misguided attempt to intimidate and bully the press," with "an astonishing lack of understanding of the role of a public servant." The next day, the newspaper published an editorial titled "Kirby Delauter, Kirby Delauter, Kirby Delauter" that mentioned Delauter's name 30 times. After both the editorial and the Facebook post went viral, Delauter apologized: "I thought I had long ago learned the lesson of waiting 24 hours before I hit the send key."

THE ~~17TH~~ 48TH STATE

In 1953, while Ohio state officials were making preparations to celebrate the state's 150th anniversary, they made an alarming discovery: Ohio wasn't actually a state. The measure to declare it the nation's 17th state was submitted to Congress in 1803, but for reasons unknown, the lawmakers never got around to making it official. Once the error was discovered, Congress quickly passed a resolution making Ohio a state (and they backdated it to 1803).

STATE OF THE YAWNION

The president's annual State of the Union address can be an animated affair. Every time he says something even mildly inspirational, half the lawmakers—the ones in the president's party—stand up and cheer while the other half scowl from their seats. But that's not the case for members of the U.S. Supreme Court, who also attend but show no party affiliation. Traditionally, the nine robed justices sit stone-faced, showing no emotion at all. During the 2015 State of the Union address, Justice Ruth Bader Ginsburg showed even less emotion…because she fell asleep during President Barack Obama's speech. When asked about her nationally televised nap, Ginsburg, 81, explained that she would have stayed awake but, "I wasn't 100 percent sober."

WAS HE HIGH?

"States have their own official soft drinks and desserts," explained Missouri Rep. Courtney Allen Curtis (D). "Missouri even has an official dinosaur. But we do not have an official form of the most basic human interaction: greeting each other." So in January 2014, Allen submitted a bill that would make the high-five Missouri's official state greeting. "It's a form of celebration and promotes positivity among our citizens," he said. Unfortunately for Curtis, the reaction to his bill was not positive. It was derided by his fellow politicians, the media, and his constituents—many of whom complained that lawmakers should focus on the more pressing issues facing the state, like child poverty and racial tension. (And some people were concerned that all that high-fiving would spread germs.) The bill never even made it to a vote.

TREE-MAIL

As part of its goal to be "the most livable city in the world," the Australian city of Melbourne has given an ID number to every one of its 70,000 trees. Residents can now go to the city's website, choose a tree from an online map, and send an e-mail to it. And the tree will write back! (Obviously, trees can neither read nor type—City of Melbourne staffers write the replies.) Critics have accused the city of wasting taxpayer money that could be better spent actually trying to protect the trees from extended droughts, but Melbourne city councillor Arron Wood (that's really his name) defended the program: "The trees were always going to have individual ID numbers anyway. So it was only logical we'd assign the ID numbers to an e-mail which connects these trees to the community." A reporter at the *Guardian* newspaper decided to send a complimentary e-mail to a ginkgo tree near the city center. The reply: "Thank you for your lovely words. I am very well. Enjoy your day. Yours sincerely, Tree 1441724."

The perfume industry's annual awards are called the FiFis.

IT WASN'T MY FAULT!

Real—and really odd—excuses filed on car insurance claim forms.

"I pulled away from the side of the road, glanced at my mother-in-law, and headed over the embankment."

"I thought my window was down but I found it was up when I put my head through it."

"The other car collided with mine without giving me warning of its intention."

"To avoid hitting the bumper of the car in front I struck a pedestrian."

"I was sure the old fellow would never make it to the other side of the road when I struck him."

"Going to work at 7:00 this morning I drove out of my driveway straight into a bus. The bus was 5 minutes early."

"My car was legally parked as it backed into another vehicle."

"I told the police that I was not injured, but on removing my hat I found that I had a fractured skull."

"I didn't think the speed limit applied after midnight."

"Windshield broken. Cause unknown. Probably voodoo."

"I had been learning to drive with power steering. I turned the wheel to what I thought was enough and found myself in a different direction going the opposite way."

"I started to slow down, but the traffic was more stationary than I thought."

"I bumped into a lamppost which was obscured by human beings."

"I knew the dog was possessive about the car, but I would not have asked her to drive it if I thought there was any risk."

"First car stopped suddenly, second car hit first car, and a haggis ran into the rear of second car."

"No one was to blame for the accident but it would never have happened if the other driver had been alert."

What did the *Apollo 17* crew use to repair a fender on the lunar rover? Duct tape.

DOES THIS TASTE FUNNY?

Clever comedians and their culinary quips.

"I was making pancakes the other day and a fly flew into the kitchen. And that's when I realized that a spatula is a lot like a fly swatter. And a crushed fly is a lot like a blueberry. And a roommate is a lot like a fly eater."

—Demetri Martin

"I won't eat snails. I prefer fast food."

—Strange de Jim

"Pie can't compete with cake. Put candles in a cake, it's a birthday cake. Put candles in a pie, and somebody's drunk in the kitchen."

—Jim Gaffigan

"My mom made two dishes: Take It or Leave It."

—Steven Wright

"I believe that when life gives you lemons, you should make lemonade, and then find someone whose life has given them vodka, and have a party."

—Ron White

"A professor from the University of Wisconsin says he's found a way to take the bitterness out of cheddar cheese. Now, if he can only find a way to remove the arrogance from Wheat Thins."

—Tina Fey

"In Maine, scientists have made a hamburger out of blueberries. It's just like a regular hamburger, except it tastes awful."

—David Letterman

"Fun-sized Snickers? Who's this fun for? Not me. I need six or seven of these babies in a row to start having fun."

—Jeff Garlin

"I go running when I have to. When the ice cream truck is doing sixty."

—Wendy Liebman

"Sugar cookie? Every cookie is a sugar cookie. A cookie without sugar is a cracker."

—Gary Gulman

When cryptography is outlawed, bayl bhgynjf jvyy unir cevinpl.

"I'm a postmodern vegetarian; I eat meat ironically."
—**Bill Bailey**

"I bought a box of animal crackers, and it said on it, 'Do not eat if seal is broken.' So I opened up the box, and sure enough…"
—**Brian Kiley**

"At my lemonade stand I used to give away the first glass free and charge five dollars for the second glass. The refill contained the antidote."
—**Emo Philips**

"Fish—you have to wonder about a food that everybody agrees is great, except that sometimes it tastes like what it is."
—**P. J. O'Rourke**

"I order club sandwiches all the time and I'm not even a member. I don't know how I get away with it."
—**Mitch Hedberg**

"I'm the frosting on America's cake, and tonight I'm willing to let you lick the bowl."
—**Stephen Colbert**

*　　*　　*

A POX UPON THEE!

*May you never need a magical curse. But just in case…
here are a few of our favorites.*

- May the desert wind blow angry scorpions up your robe.
- May malevolent hedgehogs soil your cornflakes.
- May you be swallowed by a whale with bad breath.
- May the dog really eat your homework.
- May you be trapped in an elevator with the world farting champion.
- May a family of ferrets nest in your knickers.
- May the fleas of a thousand camels infest your armpits.
- May your gastric juices keep you from sleeping at night.
- May you grow like an onion…with your head in the ground.
- May no one tell you about the spinach between your teeth.
- May you be smitten with an itch where you cannot scratch.
- May you find a half-eaten worm in your apple…after you swallow.
- May the lumps in your oatmeal hide cockroaches.

The word most often misspelled in search engines: resturant…no, restauraunt…er, restaurant.

LANCE CUMSON, ESQ.

Why do soap opera characters always seem to have such fancy names? Because it's more dramatic to say "Your real father is…Alexander Channing!" than "Your real father is…Gus Lipshitz!" Here are some of our favorite soap names.

Bascombe Moody
(*One Life to Live*)

Lance Cumson (*Falcon Crest*)

Felicia Gallant (*Another World*)

Brock Hayden (*The Doctors*)

Meredith Lord Wolek
(*One Life to Live*)

Alexis Carrington Colby
(*Dynasty*)

**Abby Fairgate Cunningham
Ewing Sumner** (*Knots Landing*)

Quinn McCleary
(*Search for Tomorrow*)

Phoebe Tyler Wallingford
(*All My Children*)

Palmer Cortlandt
(*All My Children*)

**Maggie Fielding Van
Alen Powers** (*The Doctors*)

Claude Charbonneau
(*One Life to Live*)

Chase Kendall
(*Search for Tomorrow*)

Roland Saunders (*Falcon Crest*)

Greenlee Smythe
(*All My Children*)

Mortimer Bern (*One Life to Live*)

Gwendolyn Lord Abbott
(*One Life to Live*)

Margo Montgomery Hughes
(*As the World Turns*)

Clayton Boudreau
(*Guiding Light*)

Prunella Witherspoon
(*General Hospital*)

Edward Louis Quartermaine
(*General Hospital*)

Malcolm Scorpio
(*General Hospital*)

Therrese Lamonte
(*Another World*)

Brooke Logan Forrester
(*The Bold and the Beautiful*)

Penelope Hughes Cunningham
(*As the World Turns*)

Angelica Deveraux
(*Days of Our Lives*)

Real (odd) book title: *How Green Were the Nazis?*, by Franz-Josef Bruggemeier

JUST JOKES

Feel free to share.

The mayor wanted to get more townspeople to attend the city council meetings. One council member suggested bringing in a hypnotist. Everyone thought it was a great idea. A few weeks later, the town hall was packed, and the people sat fascinated as the hypnotist took out a pocket watch and began to chant, "Watch the watch, watch the watch, watch the watch..."

The crowd grew mesmerized as the watch swayed back and forth, back and forth, back and forth... suddenly the hypnotist's fingers slipped and the watch fell to the floor. "Crap!" said the hypnotist. It took three weeks to clean up the town hall.

An aspiring veterinarian put himself through veterinary school working nights as a taxidermist. When he graduated he decided he could combine the two occupations. On the door of his new business: "Dr. Boone, Veterinary Medicine and Taxidermy: Either way, you get your dog back!"

One day a man went to an auction to buy a parrot. He really wanted it but kept getting outbid. So he bid higher…and higher…and higher. Even though he had to bid way more than he intended, he finally won the bird! As he was paying for it, he said to the auctioneer, "I sure hope this parrot can talk. I'd hate to have paid this much to find out that he can't!"

"Don't worry," replied the auctioneer. "Who do you think kept bidding against you?"

Some race horses are having a conversation. One of them boasts, "In the last 15 races, I've won 8 of them!" Another horse breaks in, "Well, in the last 27 races, I've won 19!" "Oh, that's good, but in the last 36 races, I've won 28!" says another, flicking his tail.

At this point, a greyhound dog sitting nearby interrupts: "I don't mean to boast, but in my last 90 races, I've won 88 of them!"

The horses are clearly amazed. "Wow," says one, after a hushed silence. "A talking dog!"

To appear normal on black-and-white TV in the '40s, actors wore black lipstick and green makeup.

A man was flying home from a business trip when the flight attendant handed out brownies. He decided to save them for later, and he put them in the cleanest thing he could find—an unused vomit bag. After the plane landed, the man got up to leave and a flight attendant approached him. "Sir, would you like for me to dispose of that for you?"

"No thanks," he said. "I'm saving it for my kids."

Johnny was in the garden filling in a hole when his neighbor peered over the fence. "What are you up to there, Johnny?" the neighbor asked.

"My goldfish died," replied Johnny. "I've just buried him."

The neighbor saw the big mound of dirt and remarked, "That's an awfully big hole for a goldfish."

Johnny patted down the last heap of dirt and replied, "That's because he's inside your cat."

Two trucks loaded with thousands of copies of *Roget's Thesaurus* collided as they left a New York publishing house. Witnesses were stunned, startled, flabbergasted, surprised, taken aback, stupefied…

A man is trying on shoes. "So how do they feel?" the sales clerk asks.

"They're a little too tight," the man replies.

"Well, try pulling the tongue out," the clerk suggests.

"Hmmm," he says. "They thtill thfeel a bith thoo thight."

Seeking enlightenment, a young man made a long pilgrimage to a Buddhist monastery. There, the wisest monk told him: "In order to reach enlightenment, you must take a vow of silence for 10 years."

After 10 years of silent meditation, the monk said to the man, "You may now speak."

"My bed is too hard," he said.

"You have not yet reached enlightenment," replied the monk. "You must not speak again for 10 years." So the man remained silent for 10 more years, when the monk said, "You may now speak."

"The food is too cold," he said.

"You still have not yet reached enlightenment," said the monk.

So the man took another vow of silence. Ten years later, he was again allowed to speak.

"I quit," he said.

"Good," replied the monk. "All you do is complain, anyway."

Rats can find their way through a maze faster when Mozart's music is being played.

BRI'S FLATULENCE HALL OF FAME

*Here we honor people and institutions that
have made an art out of passing gas.*

Honoree: Caryn Johnson, a.k.a. Whoopi Goldberg
Notable Achievement: The first (and to our knowledge, only) Hollywood star named for their frequent farting habit
True Story: When she was just starting out in show business, Goldberg gained a somewhat dubious reputation for her frequent anal emissions. She explains, "People used to say to me, 'You're like a whoopee cushion.' And that's where the name 'Whoopi' came from." According to Goldberg's cohosts on *The View*, she still farts a lot.

Honoree: Taoism
Notable Achievement: Most interesting philosophy about farts
True Story: A 1996 BBC-TV program about the first Chinese emperor reported that "Chinese Taoists believe everyone is allotted a certain amount of air at birth which it is important to conserve. Belching and farting are considered to shorten one's life. Taoists therefore carefully control their diet, avoiding foods which lead to flatulence."

Honoree: King Ahmose of Egypt
Notable Achievement: Most effective use of a fart as a political statement
True Story: In 568 B.C., King Apries of Egypt sent a trusted general named Amasis to put down a mutiny among his troops. But when Amasis got there, the troops offered to make him their leader instead... and he accepted.

King Apries couldn't believe it. He sent a respected advisor named Patarbemis to bring Amasis back. Amasis responded to the king's entreaties by raising himself from his saddle and farting. Then he told Patarbemis to "carry that back to Apries." Unfortunately, the king was so enraged by the message that he had Patarbemis's nose and ears hacked off. Committing such a barbarous act against such a respectable man was the last straw for many Egyptians—they turned pro-Amasis. With their support, Amasis's troops attacked and defeated Apries's army.

Note: Amasis became King Ahmose and reigned for 44 years, from 569 to 525 B.C., which modern historians call one of Egypt's most prosperous periods.

Honoree: Richard Magpiong, a career criminal

Notable Achievement: The ultimate self-incriminating fart

True Story: In 1995 the residents of a home on Fire Island (near New York City) were awakened by a noise. They got up and looked around, but couldn't find anyone. They were about to go back to bed when, according to the *New York Daily News,* "they heard the sound of a muffled fart." Magpiong was discovered hiding in a closet and was held until the police arrived.

Honoree: Edward De Vere, the seventh Earl of Oxford and a courtier in Queen Elizabeth's court

Notable Achievement: Craziest overreaction to a fart

True Story: De Vere accidentally farted while bowing to the queen. He was so embarrassed that he left England and did not return for seven years. When he got back, the queen pooh-poohed the whole affair. "My Lord," she reportedly said, welcoming him back, "I had forgot the fart."

Honoree: Spike Jones and His City Slickers

Notable Achievement: Bestselling fart record

True Story: According to the book *Who Cut the Cheese?*: "During World War II, Bluebird Records released a disc called 'Der Fuehrer's Face' by Spike Jones and His City Slickers (an orchestra noted for parodying pop tunes), only a few months after the U.S. joined the war. Jones's band, armed with rubber razzers to create flabby farting noises, created a zany gas attack on Adolf Hitler: "And we'll Heil! *[fart!]* Heil! *[fart!]* right in der Fuehrer's face!" The record was a hit—it sold a million and a half copies in the U.S. and Great Britain.

Adolf Hitler's Mercedes had a false floor to make him look taller.

SEXY FINDING NEMO

In recent years, it's become popular for college-age women to wear "sexy" Halloween costumes like naughty nurses and French maids. Here are a few more costumes, proving that not everything can be sexed up (although somebody's clearly trying).

• **Sexy Freddy Krueger.** What's sexier than a child killer back from the dead who haunts your dreams? This costume consists of Freddy's striped sweater, lengthened into a short dress, along with a glove in the shape of the character's signature knife-fingers.

• **Sexy Cab Driver.** Because cab drivers don't generally wear uniforms, this costume looks more like a "sexy cab": a short, low-cut yellow jumpsuit with black-and-white checkered sides.

• **Sexy Little Bo Peep.** A short blue-and-white dress. The weird part is that it comes with a matching costume for a small dog.

• **Sexy Elvira.** The cable-TV and beer-commercial spokesperson (played by Cassandra Peterson) already wears a low-cut dress with a slit up the side. The "Sexy Elvira" costume has an even more plunging neckline and a higher leg slit, if that's possible.

• **Sexy *Finding Nemo*.** How did they make a child-age, lost, mildly disabled (one bad fin) clownfish into a sexy outfit? With a short orange-and-white dress and matching stockings.

• **Sexy Dora the Explorer.** The cartoon character aimed at preschoolers is a preschooler herself, and she wears a purple shirt and orange shorts. This costume gives Dora a low-cut shirt and short skirt instead.

• **Sexy Super Mario Bros.** The Nintendo video game characters Mario and Luigi are chubby, middle-aged, mustachioed, stereotypically Italian men who work as plumbers in Brooklyn. But they can be "sexy"…if you put short skirts on them.

• **Sexy Nun.** Short skirt, lots of cleavage, and a nun's habit. How sinful.

Hair is 70% easier to cut when soaked in warm water for 2 minutes. (Downside: You drown.)

OOPS!

*More stories of funny mishaps that are even funnier
because they happened to someone else.*

PICASSOOPS

Steve Wynn, a Las Vegas casino owner and real estate agent, owns the Pablo Picasso painting *The Dream*. In 2006 he arranged to sell the painting for $139 million, but before parting with it he had some friends over to his office to show it off. At the party, Wynn was waving his hands around as he told a friend a story. He lost his balance and fell backward into the painting, puncturing it with what one guest later called "a $40 million elbow." Wynn had to cancel the sale.

STAMP OF DISAPPROVAL

In 1999 the U.S. Postal Service printed up 100 million 60-cent "Grand Canyon" international stamps, but immediately had to scrap them. Why? The caption said "Grand Canyon, Colorado." It's located in Arizona.

IS GLORIOUS KAZAKHSTAN ANTHEM...NOT!

Kazakhstan's gold-medal winning sharpshooter Maria Dmitrienko was standing on the award platform at the Arab Shooting Championships in Kuwait in 2012 as Kazakhstan's national anthem began to play over the P.A. system. Only it wasn't the real anthem—it was a fake one written for the 2006 mockumentary *Borat: Cultural Learnings of America for Make Benefit Glorious Nation of Kazakhstan*. Sample lyrics: "Kazakhstan's prostitutes are the cleanest in the region, except, of course, for Turkmenistan's." (And dirtier lyrics that we can't print here.) The Kazakhstan government—which had banned Borat—demanded an apology. Kuwait blamed the goof on a staffer who downloaded the wrong anthem off the Internet.

IT'S ALL COMING BACK TO ME NOW

In 2000 Linda Lodadio was admitted to a hospital in Rochester, New York, with a severe case of botulism (from contaminated fish). She was completely paralyzed, unable to talk or open her eyes, but she could hear everything happening around her. Early in her stay, one of her friends told

In ancient Egypt, warm donkey droppings were prescribed to alleviate sore eyes.

a nurse that Lodadio loved Céline Dion. So the Canadian superstar's music was played in the hospital room 24/7 for several weeks while Lodadio lay motionless. When she finally regained her speech, the first thing she said was, "I hate Céline Dion!" The nurse rushed over and turned it off. "It was horrifying," she told reporters.

THREE'S COMPANY

In 2005 Melvyn Reed, 58, of Kettering, England, had an emergency heart bypass operation. His wife rushed in to see him. Then his wife rushed in to see him. Then his wife rushed in to see him. The three women, from different parts of England, quickly realized that their car-salesman husband had been living secret lives. He was sued for divorce (three times) and charged with bigamy (twice).

CAN'T PULL THE WOOL OVER THEIR EYES

Researchers in Britain sheepishly admitted that the findings of a five-year study to determine whether mad cow disease could be transmitted from cows to sheep had to be thrown out after they realized they'd been studying cows' brains the whole time, not sheep brains.

CONFESSIONS OF A NOT-SO-DANGEROUS MIND

Late one night in Louisiana a woman awoke to her phone ringing. As she placed the receiver against her ear, a man whose voice she didn't recognize exclaimed, "I've killed them all!" The woman immediately put down the phone and called police, who were able to trace the call to a man named Thomas Ballard. They barged into his apartment and questioned him about his "confession." After a little confusion, Ballard admitted that earlier that evening, he had killed "all the bad guys" in a video game and had intended to call his friend to brag...but accidentally dialed a wrong number.

ARE YOU KIDDING?

In 2008 a woman in Orem, Utah, called 911 to report that she was locked *inside* her luxury car. The battery was dead and the key chain's remote control would no longer open her door. When officers arrived, they tried to yell instructions through the closed window but the woman couldn't hear them, so they called her on her cell phone...and explained how to manually slide the locking mechanism located next to her on the door panel.

"The KKK adopted a highway. Joke's on them: It's black." —Jon Stewart

SURELY, YOU CAN'T BE SERIOUS

We are serious: Airplane! *is the funniest movie ever made. But don't take our word for it—it's science.*

DON'T CALL ME SHIRLEY
In 2012 the movie-subscription site LOVEFiLM asked its members to name their favorite comedy. After tallying up the entries, the staff screened the top ten, marking every time a line or a sight gag generated a laugh. Then, dividing that total by the film's length, they were able to calculate a "laughs per minute" rating. Topping the list, at an impressive 3 lpm: the 1980 disaster-movie spoof *Airplane!*, written and directed by Jim Abrahams, David Zucker, and Jerry Zucker; and starring Robert Hays, Julie Hagerty, and Leslie Neilson.

The plot: Former fighter pilot-turned-cabbie Ted Striker (Hays) boards a jetliner in L.A. bound for Chicago to win back his lost love, a pretty stewardess named Elaine (Hagerty). But when the pilots and most of the passengers get food poisoning, Striker must overcome his self-doubt to save the day and get the girl. Hilarity ensues...

Old lady passenger: "Nervous?"
Striker: "Yes."
Old lady: "First time?"
Striker: "No, I've been nervous lots of times."

Roger Murdoc: "We have clearance, Clarence."
Captain Oveur: "Roger, Roger. What's our vector, Victor?"

McCroskey: "Looks like I picked the wrong week to quit drinking."

Dr. Rumack: "Elaine, you're a member of this crew. Can you face some unpleasant facts?"
Elaine: "No."

Elaine, on the loudspeaker: "There's no reason to become alarmed, and we hope you'll enjoy the rest of your flight. By the way, is there anyone on board who knows how to fly a plane?"

McCroskey: "Looks like I picked the wrong week to quit smoking."

Millie the White House dog earned more than 4 times as much as President Bush in 1991.

Randy: "There's been a little problem in the cockpit."

Striker: "The cockpit—what is it?"

Randy: "It's the little room in the front of the plane where the pilots sit, but that's not important right now."

McCroskey: "I picked the wrong week to quit amphetamines."

Reporter: "What kind of plane is it?"

Johnny: "Oh, it's a big, pretty white plane with red stripes, curtains in the windows, and wheels, and it looks like a big Tylenol!"

Striker: "I flew single engine fighters in the Air Force, but this plane has four engines. It's an entirely different kind of flying altogether."

Dr. Rumack and Randy: "It's an entirely different kind of flying."

Striker (in a flashback): "My orders just came through. My squadron ships out tomorrow. We're bombing the storage depots at Daiquiri at 1800 hours. We're coming in from the north, below their radar."

Elaine: "When will you be back?"

Striker: "I can't tell you that. It's classified."

McCroskey: "I picked the wrong week to quit sniffing glue."

Newscaster: "They bought their tickets, they knew what they were getting into. I say—let 'em crash."

Dr. Rumack: "I won't deceive you, Mr. Striker. We're running out of time."

Striker: "Surely there must be something you can do."

Dr. Rumack: "I'm doing everything I can. And stop calling me Shirley."

*   *   *

THE LIST

Here's the entire list from LOVEFiLM's top-10 funniest movies, as determined by the number of laughs per minute: **1.** *Airplane!*, 3 lpm; **2.** *The Hangover*, 2.4 lpm, **3.** *The Naked Gun: From the Files of Police Squad!*, 2.3 lpm; **4.** *Superbad*, 1.9 lpm; **5.** *Borat: Cultural Learnings of America for Make Benefit Glorious Nation of Kazakhstan*, 1.7 lpm; **6.** *Anchorman: The Legend of Ron Burgundy*, 1.6 lpm; **7.** *American Pie*, 1.5 lpm; **8.** *Bridesmaids*, 1.4 lpm; **9.** *Shaun of the Dead*, 1.3 lpm; **10.** *Monty Python's Life of Brian*, 1.2 lpm.

In 1981 an L.A. man was arrested for hiding under tables and painting women's toenails.

SIT DOWN AND SHUT UP

In honor of Airplane!, *the funniest movie ever made (see page 119), here are some real-life quips uttered by flight attendants to passengers.*

"People, people! We're not picking out furniture here. Find a seat and get in it!"

"At the pointy end of the plane is our captain."

"We'll be coming through the cabin to make sure your seat belts are fastened and your shoes match your outfit."

"Ladies and gentlemen, if you wish to smoke, the smoking section on this airplane is on the wing. If you can light 'em, you can smoke 'em."

"In the event of a sudden loss of cabin pressure, oxygen masks will descend from the ceiling. Stop screaming, grab the mask, and pull it over your face. If you have a small child traveling with you, secure your mask before assisting with theirs. If you are traveling with two small children, decide now which one you love more."

"Please remain in your seats with your seat belts fastened while the captain taxis what's left of our airplane to the gate."

"Ladies and gentlemen, we will be turning down the cabin lights. This is for your comfort and to enhance the appearance of your flight attendants."

"The yellow button above your head is the reading light; the orange button releases the hounds."

"This aircraft is equipped with a video surveillance system that monitors the cabin during taxiing. Any passengers not remaining in their seats until the aircraft comes to a full and complete stop at the gate will be strip-searched as they leave the aircraft."

"Sit back and relax, or lean forward all twisted up; the choice is yours."

"Please remain in your seats until Captain Crash and the crew have brought the aircraft to a screeching halt up against the gate. And once the tire smoke has cleared and the warning bells are silenced, we'll open the door and you can pick your way through the wreckage to the terminal."

Surely you can't be serious: In the 19th century, Shirley was a popular name for boys.

PRANKSTERS

*We love a good prank here at the BRI, and these are
some of the cleverest ones we've heard about.*

FAKE PROPOSAL

In September 2007, Amir Blumenfeld learned that his friend Streeter Seidell was going to attend a New York Yankees game with his girlfriend, Sharon. So Blumenfeld called Yankee Stadium and paid $500 for a marriage proposal to be displayed on the stadium's Jumbotron—Seidell's proposal to Sharon. In the middle of the fifth inning, this message appeared on the huge screen in front of 57,000 people: "Dear Sharon, I love you forever. Will you marry me? Streety Bird." Sharon immediately burst into happy tears and jumped to her feet, shouting, "Yes!" Seidell, however, went into a panic. He denied he'd actually proposed, insisting it was a hoax. And when he said, "I don't wanna f***ing marry you," Sharon slapped him across the face and stormed out of the game. Blumenfeld, meanwhile, had enlisted some friends to sit near Seidell to videotape the proposal and its aftermath, and that video wound up being viewed by hundreds of thousands of people…because Blumenfeld and Seidell both worked for the Internet comedy site CollegeHumor.com.

FAKE RESTAURANT

Robin Goldstein is a wine critic and food writer. He's dined at many restaurants whose menus boasted the Award of Excellence from *Wine Spectator* magazine, despite having wine lists that Goldstein knew were populated with mediocre wines. Suspicious, he decided to try an experiment. In 2009 he invented a restaurant called Osteria l'Intrepido (Italian for "the fearless tavern") and typed up a menu of ordinary Italian dishes. Goldstein also included a wine list—the lowest-rated wines from the last 20 years of *Wine Spectator* magazine. Then he submitted his menu, along with the $250 fee, to *Wine Spectator* to apply for their Award of Excellence. Despite a list of wines *Wine Spectator* itself said were terrible, and despite the fact that his restaurant wasn't real, Osteria l'Intrepido was awarded the *Wine Spectator* Award of Excellence. Goldstein posted the story on his website, published it in a magazine, and shared it with the attendees of a wine conference. (And *Wine Spectator*'s reputation will never be the same.)

FAKE BEST BUY

A New York–based group called Improv Everywhere stages good-natured pranks with hundreds of volunteer operatives. Past pranks include a book signing at a Barnes and Noble with Russian playwright Anton Chekov (who died in 1904), a morning subway commute in which hundreds of people didn't wear pants, and another subway prank in which eight sets of twins rode around and performed every action in perfect unison. In April 2006, Improv Everywhere staged "Operation Best Buy." Eighty volunteers simultaneously entered a Best Buy electronics store, all wearing the same outfit—blue polo shirt and khaki pants. The goal: to look like Best Buy employees, who wear the same clothes (only with nametags and company logos). Improv Everywhere instructed the pranksters to be kind and even help customers find what they were looking for. The only motive behind the prank was silly amusement—to create, if only for an hour, a comically overstaffed electronics store.

FAKE TORCH

The 1956 Olympics were held in Melbourne, Australia. Nine University of Sydney students thought it was appalling that the Olympic torch relay—created by the Nazis for the 1936 Berlin Games—was elevating the torch to the level of a religious icon, with thousands of Australians lining the streets of Sydney wherever the relay passed through. So they devised a plan to protest the torch with a phony relay. In the real relay, cross-country athlete Harry Dillon was supposed to run through downtown Sydney and hand the torch to Mayor Pat Hills, who would then make a speech and give the torch to another runner. Moments before Dillon was to arrive, however, one of the protesters began running in the streets with a "torch"—a silver-painted chair leg topped with a flaming pair of underpants. The crowd laughed at the prank, but then the underwear fell off and the runner panicked and ran away. Another student took up the torch with a relit pair of underpants and continued to run the route...and police thought he was the real deal. They escorted him all the way to the town hall, where he presented the flaming underpants to Mayor Hills.

GARDY LOO!

Uncle John found a book called Slang and Euphemism, *by Richard Spears, with strange (and risqué) expressions from all over the world, some dating back centuries. Here are a few that we can print.*

Eruct: To belch

Gug: An unpleasant person

Have a jag on: Intoxicated

Woozle water: Whiskey

Tirliry-puffkin: A flighty woman

Fribble: A silly oaf

Ignatz: An ignoramus

Scrower: A drunkard

Wowser: A prudish person

Gaw-gaw: An oafish sailor

Yackum: Cow dung

Prep chapel: A toilet

Ethel: An effeminate male

Gooey: A gob of phlegm

Arse ropes: The intestines

Frogsch! Nonsense!

Bat house: An insane asylum

Dustman: A corpse

Joe-wad: Toilet paper

Ubble-gubble: Utter nonsense

Wretchcock: A puny or worthless person

Drain the bilge: To vomit

Tiger sweat: A strong alcoholic drink

Snow: Underwear

Rib-roast: A scolding from one's wife

Tattle water: Tea (because people gossip at tea parties)

Assteriors: Buttocks

Gardy loo! What a chambermaid yelled before dumping a chamber pot out of a window

Timber-headed: Stupid

Grubber: An unclean person

Alley apple: Horse manure

Pull a cluck: To die

Bingoed: Drunk

Hickus: A gadget

Make faces: Have children

Earth-bath: A grave

Q: How do you know if a cat burglar has been in your house? A: The cat is missing.

GROUCHO MARX, ATTORNEY AT LAW

Step back in time to 1933 for the radio adventures of Groucho and Chico Marx, from Five Star Theater.

Mrs. Brittenhouse: Is this a detective agency?

Groucho: A *detective* agency? Madam, if there's anything in it for me, this is Scotland Yard.

Mrs. Brittenhouse: This man told me he was taking me to a detective bureau.

Chico: You're cuckoo, I did not. You stop me in the hall. You say you want a detective. I say, you go see Flywheel. You say alright. Well, here's Flywheel.

Mrs. Brittenhouse: Sir, are you or aren't you a detective? My time is money.

Groucho: Your time is money? I wonder if you could lend me ten minutes for lunch, or maybe a half an hour for the rent?

Mrs. Brittenhouse: For the last time, are you a detective?

Groucho: Madam, for the first time I am a detective.

Mrs. Brittenhouse: You don't look much like a detective to me.

Groucho: That's the beauty of it. See? Had you fooled already.

Mrs. Brittenhouse: Is the man who brought me in a detective too?

Chico: Sure, I'm a detective. I prove it. Lady, you lose anything today?

Mrs. Brittenhouse: Why, I don't think so. Heavens! My handbag has disappeared.

Chico: Here it is.

Mrs. Brittenhouse: Where did you find it?

Chico: Right here in my pocket.

Groucho: Isn't he marvelous, madam? He has the nose of a bloodhound, and his other features aren't so good either.

Mrs. Brittenhouse: Well, you're the men I'm looking for.

Chico: You're looking for us? Hey, are you a detective?

Mrs. Brittenhouse: No, no. You misunderstand me. You see, my

The word *gullible* **is not in the dictionary.**

daughter is getting married this afternoon.

Groucho: Oh, your daughter's getting married? I love those old-fashioned girls.

Mrs. Brittenhouse: We're having a big wedding reception, and I want you two men to come out this afternoon and keep an eye on the wedding presents. They're very valuable, and I want to be sure that nothing is stolen.

Chico: How much you pay us? You know it's very hard work not to steal anything.

Mrs. Brittenhouse: I think fifty dollars would be adequate. But you understand, of course, that you're not to mingle with the guests.

Groucho: Well, if we don't have to mingle with the guests we'll do it for forty dollars.

Mrs. Brittenhouse: Dear, dear, I must hurry. My daughter can't get married unless I get her trousseau.

Chico: Trousseau? You mean Robinson Trousseau?

Groucho: Your daughter's marrying Robinson Crusoe today? Monday? Wouldn't she be better off if she'd marry the man Friday?

Mrs. Brittenhouse: Well, I must hurry along now. Good bye,

gentlemen. I'll be looking for you this afternoon.

Groucho: Well, why look for us this afternoon when we're here right now?

(*Later, at the Brittenhouse mansion*)

Mrs. Brittenhouse: Hello, Mr. Flywheel. Hives, our butler, will take care of you. Oh, I'm always so nervous at weddings. I'm really not myself today.

Groucho: You're not yourself, eh? Well, whoever you are, you're no bargain.

Hives: Now, on these two tables here, gentlemen, are the presents. Please watch them very carefully. I'll have to leave you now. (*Tap at the window.*)

Groucho: I think there's somebody at the window. You'd better let him in.

Chico: Hey, boss. He's a great big guy and he looks very tough.

(*Tap again.*)

Chico: Hey, who are you?

Man: Never mind who I am. Who are you guys?

Chico: We're a coupla detectives.

Man: Oh, you're a coupla detectives. Ha ha! That's a hot one!

Groucho: Well, I've heard better ones than that, but it's fairly good.

According to *Futurama*, in the year 3000 the major world religions are "voodoo and Oprahism."

Man: Hey, what are you guys supposed to do here?

Chico: I watch da presents. Flywheel, he watch me, but we got no one to watcha Flywheel.

Man: Well, you can clear outta here. I'll do the whole thing for you.

Groucho: Ravelli, that fellow certainly is a prince. I'm getting out of here before he changes his mind.

(*Opens and closes door. Footsteps*)

Mrs. Brittenhouse: Why, Mr. Flywheel, I thought you were supposed to stay in that room with the presents!

Groucho: Madam, I couldn't stand being alone in that room. I just had to have another look at you. And now that I've had that look, I can hardly wait to get back to the presents.

Mrs. Brittenhouse: Why, Mr. Flywheel!

Groucho: Don't call me Mr. Flywheel, just call me Sugar.

Mrs. Brittenhouse: Oh, Mr. Flywheel, I simply love the things you say.

Groucho: Oh, Mrs. Brittenhouse—I know you'll think me a sentimental old softie, but would you give me a lock of your hair?

Mrs. Brittenhouse: Why, Mr. Flywheel!

Groucho: I'm letting you off easy—I was going to ask you for the whole wig.

Mrs. Brittenhouse: Well, we'll discuss that later. It's too bad you can't join us now for refreshments, but maybe some evening you'd like to have me for dinner.

Groucho: Have you for dinner? Well, if there's nothing better to eat, I wouldn't mind, but personally, I'd prefer a can of salmon.

Hives: Mrs. Brittenhouse! Mrs. Brittenhouse!

Groucho: Is there no privacy here?

Mrs. Brittenhouse: Why Hives, what's the matter?

Hives: The presents! They're gone. We've been robbed!

Groucho: Robbed? Where's Ravelli? Quick, find Ravelli!

Chico: Here I am, boss. How you makin' out?

Groucho: Listen, Ravelli. I thought I told you to watch the presents.

Chico: That's what I was doing!

Groucho: There you are, Mrs. Brittenhouse. You have nothing to worry about.

Why did women shave their legs in the Middle Ages? To get rid of fleas and lice.

Hives: But, madam, the presents are gone!

Chico: Boss, I watch them just like a bloodhound. You remember that big fellow? He came in da room…well, I watch him…

All: YES…

Chico: He walked over and picked up da presents and I watch him…He took them outta da window! He put them on a truck and I watch him…

Chico: YES…

Chico: But when da truck drives away, I cannot watch no more.

Groucho: You're a genius. And now, Mrs. Brittenhouse, how about our fifty dollars?

*　　*　　*

AND NOW…DEEP THOUGHTS BY JACK HANDEY

• "The face of a child can say it all, especially the mouth part of the face."

• "For mad scientists who keep brains in jars, here's a tip: Why not add a slice of lemon to each jar, for freshness."

• "I wish I had a kryptonite cross, because then I could keep both Dracula and Superman away."

• "The crows were all calling to him, thought Caw."

• "Why do the caterpillar and the ant have to be enemies? One eats leaves, and the other eats caterpillars.…Oh, I see now."

• "Consider the daffodil. And while you're doing that, I'll be over here, looking through your stuff."

• "Instead of a seeing-eye dog, what about a gun? It's cheaper than a dog, plus if you walk around shooting all the time, people are going to get out of the way. Cars, too."

• "Dad always thought laughter was the best medicine, which I guess is why several of us died of tuberculosis."

• "If you're a horse, and someone gets on you, and falls off, and then gets right back on you, I think you should buck him off right away."

• "Can't the Marx brothers be arrested and maybe even tortured for all the confusion and problems they've caused?"

A Japanese company markets toupees for dogs.

ALCOHOL WAS A FACTOR

"O God, that men should put an enemy in their mouths to steal away their brains! That we should, with joy, pleasance, revel, and applause, transform ourselves into beasts!" —William Shakespeare, Othello

DEPARTMENT STORE COWBOYS

Clinton Evers and John Carelock decided to go shopping at the El Dorado, Arkansas, Walmart one day in 2009—on horseback. Sheriff's deputies tried to stop them after they rode into the parking lot, but the pair went inside the store—still on their horses—as the cops gave chase. The horses galloped through the food aisles, forcing customers to scatter. Police quickly reined in Carelock, but Evers galloped out of the store and into the woods before he was finally caught. According to police, "Alcohol was a factor."

GLASS HOLE

A homeowner in Buchanan, Wisconsin, woke up late one night in 2009 to the sound of breaking glass. He looked outside and saw that there was broken glass in the street. The next day, police investigators visited local auto-glass shops to see if anyone had come in needing a new car window— and found a customer named Andrew J. Burwitz, whose car police traced to the glass. When questioned, Burwitz admitted that he'd decided to do a drive-by shooting at the home of his ex-girlfriend's family…but he forgot to roll down his car window before firing his gun. Burwitz was arrested. According to police, "Alcohol was a factor."

ASSAULT AND WOMBAT-TERY

In March 2008, police in Motueka, New Zealand, received a bizarre call: "Help me!" a man was shouting. "I'm being raped by a wombat!" The officers found that strange, because wombats don't live in New Zealand (they live in Australia). They were about to race to the scene when the man called back and said, "No worries, mates. I'm all right now. He's gone." Police went there anyway, and found Arthur Cradock, 48, who told them it was a false alarm: "I'll retract the rape complaint from the wombat, because he's pulled out. Apart from speaking Australian now, I'm pretty all right, you know. I didn't hurt my bum at all!" The cops arrested Cradock for wasting their time. He was sentenced to 75 hours of community service. According to police, "Alcohol was a factor."

THAT'S NO WAY TO GO

A 28-year-old man (unnamed in press reports) went to a hospital in 1997, babbling that he wanted to kill himself; his head and chest were covered with bruises. The man told the doctors that he took several nitroglycerin pills and threw himself against a wall in an attempt to make the nitroglycerin explode. He also admitted that, along with the pills, he'd drunk a fifth of vodka. According to police, "Alcohol was definitely a factor."

YOU CAN DEPEND ON IT

In August 2008, Graham Nickerson, 27, was camping in Cape Sable Island, Nova Scotia. At some point in the night, he went to go pee in the woods, took off his pants, and then couldn't find them again. After searching the forest in a haze to find them, Nickerson broke into the home of a 92-year-old woman (who wasn't there) and found an adult diaper. He put it on and then passed out. The elderly woman returned home the next morning to find Nickerson still asleep on the floor…still wearing one of her diapers. The woman called the police and Nickerson was arrested. Say it with us: "Alcohol was a factor."

A WEE NIP

A few nights before Christmas in 2009, four-year-old Hayden Wright woke up at 1:00 a.m., snuck into the kitchen of his home in Chattanooga, Tennessee, and drank a beer (which can get a preschooler quite drunk). Then Hayden, beer in hand, wandered through the neighborhood, walked to a neighbor's house, found the door unlocked, went inside, found the Christmas tree, and started opening presents. When police finally found Hayden (empty beer can in hand), he was wearing one of the gifts: a brown dress. The boy was taken to a hospital, where his stomach was pumped. According to his mom, "He wants to get in trouble so he can go to jail because that's where his daddy is."

George Harrison's last letter: a note to Mike Myers…asking for a Mini-Me doll.

HOW TO BAMBOOZLE A TROLL

This article—from Uncle John's Enchanted Toilet Bathroom Reader
For Kids Only!*—is not talking about Internet trolls, but actual
mythological trolls. But if you encounter either one in real life,
these tricks are surprisingly effective for any type of troll.*

1. Trolls sometimes try to pass for human, but they sleep during the day
to avoid sunlight. When you come across a suspected troll napping, throw
open the blinds. Some trolls will immediately turn to stone. Others will
pull the bedcovers over their heads. If either of those things happen, you'll
know you're dealing with a troll.

2. Trolls love to build things. The next time one bugs you, give it the biggest LEGO set you can find. That will give you plenty of time to escape.

3. Many trolls have two or three heads. There's even a story about a troll
with 121 heads! If you need help with math homework, find a multiheaded
troll. Give each head a different problem to solve. The troll will be too
busy to bother you, and your homework will be done before you know it.
(*Warning:* Never give two heads the same problem to solve. They'll get
different answers and argue about which one is right.)

4. All trolls are compulsive and like to sort things into piles and stacks.
Next time your room's a mess, invite a troll to visit. It won't be able to
resist tidying up.

5. Think dogs like sticks? Trolls *love* them. You may think they want to hit
you over the head with those clubs they carry. They don't. They want you
to throw the clubs so they can chase them. (You know, like a dog would.)

6. Trolls have long, matted hair that covers everything but their noses. If
you need to escape from a troll, give it a hairbrush and a mirror. Then run!

You'll never sleep alone: There are more than 6 billion dust mites in your bed.

7. Like elves, trolls can be friendly or cruel. It all depends on how you treat them. If you want the trolls in your life to be nice, you have to be nice to them first. They will follow your lead.

8. Let's face it, trolls smell horrible. Cologne would help, but trolls *like* to smell bad, so they won't wear it. There's a simple solution: Give the troll a bottle of toilet water (*eau de toilette* if it's a French troll). Toilet water is actually watered-down cologne, but trolls don't know that. The troll will think it's water from the toilet, and it will sprinkle the stuff all over itself.

9. Want a surefire way to enjoy a troll-free life? Trolls hate being around people. So surround yourself with lots of (non-troll) friends.

*   *   *

A SWEET URBAN LEGEND

THE STORY: On a foggy November day, the California Highway Patrol finds the body of Stuart Bidasoe (called "Stu" by his friends) slumped over the wheel of his 1997 Saturn. He hit a fence post and the airbag deployed, but the accident was too minor to explain his death. So how did he die? Did he overdose on drugs? There aren't any drugs in the car—just a bag of Halloween candy on the passenger seat. The coroner solves the mystery when he pulls a lollipop out of Stu's throat.

Apparently he was eating the lollipop when he drove off the road and hit the fence post. The impact activated the airbag, which shoved the lollipop down Stu's windpipe. Tragically, he choked to death before help arrived. Moral of the story: Don't eat lollipops while driving.

HOW IT SPREAD: By e-mail and then word of mouth, starting in 2002. Fear of technology—airbags—helped the story spread, as did the abundance of details in the original e-mail: Stu Bidasoe is identified by name, as is Officer Benson (who found him), the make and model of Stu's car, the county in which the accident happened, and the precise date.

THE TRUTH: Is this a true story or an urban legend? Say "Stu Bidasoe" five times fast and decide for yourself.

The test atomic bomb dropped on Bikini Atoll had a pin-up photo of Rita Hayworth on it.

ME: BUXOM BLONDE

More humor from he funniest page in the newspaper: the personal ads.
(Sorry, comics page, but you haven't been that funny since you
lost The Far Side *and* Calvin & Hobbes.)

WOMEN SEEKING MEN

Me: buxom blonde with blue eyes. You: elderly, marriage-minded millionaire with bad heart.

I like driving around with my two cats, especially on the freeway. I make them wear little hats so that I can use the carpool lane. Way too much time on your hands too? Call me.

Lonely Christian woman has not sung Glory Hallelujah in a long time. Write soon!

Cute guy with snowplow sought by head-turnin', zany, brainy, late-30s Babe to share happy time in the big driveway of love. A rake for springtime a big plus!

Coldhearted, insensitive unconscionable, selfish, hedonistic, drunk liar seeks next gullible male without enough sense to stay away from me.

Gorgeous blonde model, tired of being patronized. Looking for sincere, understanding man. Must be willing to listen to stories of alien abduction.

MEN SEEKING WOMEN

Mentally Ill? Are you restrained in a straitjacket? Do you think you're a chicken? Did you kill and eat your last boyfriend? I don't mind. This tall, educated, professional SWM would like to meet an interesting woman!

I drink a lot of beer, smoke a lot of cigars, and watch football non-stop from September to January. I seek a woman, 18-32, to share this with.

If it takes a 3-legged elephant with 1 tusk 5 days to cross the Sahara, how many times do I have to put an ad in to get one call?

Award-winning poet, 27 yrs., seeks short-term, intense, doomed relationship for inspiration. Must be attractive, sensual, articulate, ruthless, 21-30 yrs., under 5'6". Break my heart, please.

Desperate lonely loser, SWM, 32, tired of watching TV and my roommate's hair fall out. Seeks depressed, unattractive SWF, 25-32, no sense of humor, for long talks about the macabre.

Eureka! Your brain produces enough electricity to power a lightbulb.

NEWS CORRECSHIONS

Each year a media watchdog site called Regret the Error releases its Crunks awards, which highlight the funniest news flubs. Here are some of our favorites.

"The 'Greek Special' is a huge 18-inch pizza, and not a huge 18-inch penis, as described in an ad. Blondie's Pizza would like to apologize for any confusion Friday's ad may have caused."

—*The Daily Californian*

"In last week's *Democrat*, some words were transposed through a typesetting error. The paragraph that began 'Occasionally circus elephants spent 95% of their lives chained by two legs…' should have read 'A majority of circus elephants…' while the paragraph that began 'A majority of circus elephants go mad…' should have read 'Occasionally circus elephants…'"

—*Coös County Democrat*

"In our story on London Hosts, it was stated that the 'Pub 80' concept probably appealed more to the younger drinker or those looking for bad food. This should, of course, be 'bar food'. We apologize for any embarrassment caused."

—*Morning Advertiser*

"A book review…quoted a passage from the book incorrectly. It says, 'Your goal should be to help your daughter become a sexually healthy adult'—not 'a sexually active, healthy adult.'"

—*The New York Times*

"The following corrects errors in the July 17 geographical agent and broker listing. International: Aberdeen is in Scotland, not Saudi Arabia; Antwerp is in Belgium, not Barbados; Belfast is in Northern Ireland, not Nigeria; Cardiff is in Wales, not Vietnam; Helsinki is in Finland, not Fiji; Moscow is in Russia, not Qatar."

—*Business Insurance*

"Due to a typo in last week's issue, the words 'Con-Men' appeared on the border of an Ashley & Nephews advertisement. 'Con-Men' was the headline of a story that wasn't used due to lack of space and has absolutely nothing to do and is in no way connected with Ashley & Nephews."

—*The Enfield Independent*

When General George S. Patton's troops reached the Rhine River in WWII, he peed in it.

"Just to keep the record straight, it was the famous *Whistler's Mother*, not Hitler's, that was exhibited at the recent meeting of the Pleasantville Methodists. There is nothing to be gained in trying to explain how the error occurred."

—*Titusville (PA) Herald*

"Tuesday's edition called a charge residents pay for 911 service a 'surge' charge. It is, of course, a sir charge."

—**Carlsbad *Current-Argus***

"An article about Ivana Trump and her spending habits misstated the number of bras she buys. It is two dozen black, two dozen beige, and two dozen white, not two thousand of each."

—*The New York Times*

"In our issue of November 30 we reported that the Lubavitch Foundation in Glasgow held a 'dinner and ball' to celebrate its tenth anniversary. This was incorrect. A spokesman explained: 'The Lubavitch movement does not have balls.'"

—*Jewish Chronicle*

"Sunday's Lifestyle story about Buddhism should have stated that Siddartha Gautama grew up in Northern India, not Indiana."

—*Bloomington Herald-Times*

"The following typo appeared in our last bulletin: 'Lunch will be gin at 12:15 p.m.' Please correct to read '12 noon.'"

—**California Bar Association newsletter**

"I would like to point out that what I did in fact write was that the council forced piped TV 'on us' not 'up us' as printed in the *County Times* on October 25. T. A. Wilkinson"

—*County Times & Express*

"November is a heavy publishing month for newspapers and with large issues misprints inevitably increase. Note, however, that there are 5000 characters in every full column of type. Even if there are five misprints a column that is only an error of 0,1 percent. We are working constantly on the problem, aiming to keep problem, aiming to keep—Editor"

—*The Johannesburg Star*

* * *

"Editor: one who separates the wheat from the chaff and prints the chaff."

—**Adlai Stevenson**

IF THEY MARRIED

This may be the stupidest wordplay game ever invented.

• If Paula Abdul married Kareem Abdul-Jabbar, she'd be **Paula Abdul-Abdul-Jabbar**.

• If America Ferrera married Billy Idol, she'd be **America Idol**.

• If Philip Seymour Hoffman married Ebeneezer Scrooge, then divorced him and married Minnie Driver, he'd be **Philip Scrooge-Driver**.

• If Ellen Page married Sebastian Bach, then divorced him and married Clay Aiken, she'd be **Ellen Bach-Aiken**.

• If Isla Fisher married David Vernon (Aussie writer), then divorced him and married JT Money (rapper), she'd be **Isla Vernon-Money**.

• If Naomi Watts married Sir Thomas Moore, then divorced him and married Eddie Money, she'd be **Naomi Moore-Money**.

• If Portia de Rossi married Bob Costas, then divorced him and married Giorgio Armani, then divorced him and married Adrian Legg (English guitarist), she'd be **Portia Costas-Armani-Legg**.

• If Beyoncé Knowles married Daniel Ball (actor), she'd be **Beyoncé Ball**.

• If Amanda Seyfried married Bob Huggins (basketball coach), then divorced him and married Zoltán Kiss (Hungarian athlete), she'd be **Amanda Huggins-Kiss**.

• If Scarlett Johansson married Dr. Johnny Fever (character on *WKRP in Cincinnati*), she'd be **Scarlett Fever**.

• If Lika Roman (Ukrainian beauty queen) married Thomas Røll (Danish athlete), then divorced him and married David Ling (hockey player), then divorced him and married Matt Stone (*South Park* cocreator), she'd be **Lika Røll-Ling-Stone**.

• If Rita Hayworth married Derrial Book (character on *Firefly*), she'd be **Rita Book**.

• If Han Ji-min (South Korean actress) married Adrian Solo (Swiss singer), and Sue Grafton (American author) married Carlos Bacca (Colombian soccer player), they'd be **Han Solo** and **Sue Bacca**.

• If Liv Tyler married Colin Ng (Singaporean yachtsman), then divorced him and married Eddie Large (British comic), she'd be **Liv Ng-Large**.

• If Kim Jong Un married Gary Cole, then divorced him and married Elton John, he'd be **Kim Jong Un-Cole-John**.

*   *   *

THE GREAT GEORGE CARLIN SPEAKS HIS MIND

"The other night I ate at a real nice family restaurant. Every table had an argument going."

"If the shoe fits, get another one just like it."

"McDonald's 'breakfast for under a dollar' actually costs much more than that. You have to factor in the cost of coronary bypass surgery."

"Recently, in a public bathroom, I used the handicapped stall. As I emerged, a man in a wheelchair asked me indignantly, 'Are you handicapped?' Gathering all my aplomb, I looked him in the eye and said, 'Not now. But I was before I went in there.'"

"There is something refreshingly ironic about people lying on the beach contracting skin cancer in an attempt to acquire a purely illusory appearance of good health, while germ-laden medical waste washes up on the sand all around them."

"Honesty may be the best policy, but it's important to remember that apparently, by elimination, dishonesty is the second-best policy."

"Some people see things that are and ask, Why? Some people dream of things that never were and ask, Why not? Some people have to go to work and don't have time for all that s**t."

"HEALTH" "FOOD"

*We put quotes around both words because these
actual products barely qualify as either.*

SIZE MATTERS. In 2007 a Japanese company introduced a line of snack food to help women become "more feminine," which is ad-speak for "grow bigger boobs." The bust-enhancing treats include F-Cup Cookies, F-Cup Cakes, and F-Cup Pudding cups. The snacks all contain *Pueraria mirifica*—a plant containing phytoestrogens, which are sometimes marketed as natural breast enhancers. Hopeful women will have to decide for themselves if a larger cup size is worth the reported side effects: giddiness, vomiting, diarrhea, and, as one user reported, "the uncomfortable feeling of going through puberty again."

A BEACH-READY BOD. Rodial, maker of Brazilian Tan products, has introduced a new way to get ready for the beach: Skinny Beach Sticks—a diet drink that's high in beta carotene, which, Rodial claims, somehow offers protection against UV rays, and "a slim, toned, ready-to-tan body." (Word of warning: Beta carotene is what makes carrots orange, peppers red, and flamingos pink.)

GIVE ME S'MORE. Considering collagen injections? Marshmallows could become the new skin-plumpers of choice. Every packet of Eiwa Grapefruit Collagen Marshmallows contains 3,500 mg of collagen, which, the manufacturer claims, offers the same benefits as injections but without the pain. Dermatologists at the British Skin Foundation find no scientific evidence that consuming collagen orally works the way injecting it does, but marshmallows do have one advantage: They can be squished between two graham crackers and topped with chocolate.

A ROSE BY ANY OTHER NAME. Another Japanese innovation: a deodorant in the form of chewing gum. Fuwarinka Scented Gum reportedly freshens the breath *and* causes the body to secrete the scent of roses from the pores. According to the manufacturer, gum chewers smell "as fresh and clean as a spring garden" for up to six hours.

The 1st handheld cell phone ('73) was as big as a brick and weighed 2.5 lbs.

ALL CREATURES GREAT & FUNNY

The funniest "Animals in the News" entries from our archives. Ribbit!

TOAD AWAY

Australian cane toads are nearly as big as dinner plates…and poisonous. Their venom has been known to kill large dogs within minutes. That's why Jackson Crews was worried when he saw his dog Bella mistake a cane toad for a pie he was feeding her in his backyard in Bakewell, Australia. "She swallowed it whole," said Crews. He rushed Bella to the vet, where they gave her "an injection to help her vomit." Finally, 40 minutes later, she threw up and out came the toad. And it started hopping around. Amazingly, both animals survived. Vet workers then caught the toad and kept it at their office. They named it Spew.

A BIG DAM PROBLEM

In 2008 environmental activists inspecting a nature reserve in northern Poland were shocked to find evidence of illegal logging. They reported that at least 20 trees had been removed, and more were marked for later felling. The investigators followed a trail through the woods where it was evident that trees had been dragged away. The trail led them all the way out of the reserve…right to a beaver dam in a nearby river.

WABBIT SEASON

Thirty-one inmates were working in a garden outside a Ugandan prison in 2002 when a rabbit jumped out of the bushes. All five guards took off after it…and all 31 of the inmates, including one murderer, took the opportunity to escape. None of them were captured. And neither was the rabbit.

WHAT A FABULOUS DOG!

A man, a woman, and a dog walked into the Thai Spice restaurant in Adelaide, Australia, in 2009, only to be told by a waiter: "We don't allow dogs in here!" The woman responded (in her native Australian accent), "But he's a guide dog!" Offended, the waiter—who was from Thailand—

Foul fowl: When presented with the opportunity, pigeons will eat human vomit.

told them to leave immediately. A few days later the restaurant's owner, Hong Hoa Thi To, received a call from South Australia's Equal Opportunity Tribunal asking him why service was refused to a blind man who came in with a friend and his guide dog. "*Guide* dog?" asked Hong? He thought the woman had said "*gay* dog." The restaurant was ordered to apologize to the man and pay him $1,500. "My staff genuinely believed that it was an ordinary pet dog which had been desexed to become a gay dog," said Hong.

WEAR A SUIT TO WORK

In a nature reserve in China's Sichuan province, biologists wear full-body panda suits whenever they interact with a group of orphaned baby pandas. Their goal: to raise the young bears free of human influence before they're released into the wild. The suits are bulky, and the scientists aren't nearly as graceful as real giant pandas. (It looks like a scene from a cheesy movie.) The scientists admit that they have no way of knowing whether the young pandas are fooled.

POLLY WANNA %@#$*&!

Shortly after the Warwickshire Animal Sanctuary in Nuneaton, England, took in a parrot named Barney in 2005, they discovered—the hard way—that the bird had learned a few choice phrases from its original owner. When the town's mayor and a female vicar visited, Barney told the mayor to "f*** off!" When the vicar asked if she had heard what she *thought* she'd heard, Barney squawked, "You can f*** off, too!" They thought it was funny, but sanctuary owner Geoff Grewcock didn't. He decided it was time to put the rude bird in a private cage…but not before Barney had taught two other parrots at the sanctuary how to curse. "It sounds like a construction site, with all the verbal abuse flying about," said Grewcock.

INSERT YOUR OWN "BIRDIE" JOKE HERE

In 1987 the small African nation of Benin had no golf courses. This didn't stop Mathieu Boya from practicing his game. One day he was hitting golf balls in an open field adjacent to the Benin Air Base. He hit a high drive that struck a bird in flight. The stunned bird fell into the open cockpit of a fighter plane preparing for takeoff. The startled pilot lost control of the jet and crashed into four other planes parked on the runway. All five planes— the entire Benin Air Force—were destroyed.

Vocabulary booster: A person with great energy and vitality is a *spizerinctum*.

FIND A STRANGER IN THE ALPS

When movies air on TV, the bad words are overdubbed with not-so-bad words that still kind of sound like the bad words but aren't bad at all—just silly.

THE EXORCIST (1973)

Big Screen: The possessed Regan (Linda Blair) informs Father Karras (Jason Miller) that his mother "sucks [expletives] in hell!"
Small Screen: "Your mother sews socks that smell!"

REPO MAN (1984)

Big Screen: Car repossessor Bud (Harry Dean Stanton) uses a certain epithet, also involving a mother, a lot.
Small Screen: Bud says "melon farmer" a lot.

DIE HARD 2 (1990)

Big Screen: Lieutenant John McClane (Bruce Willis) says, "Yippee kai-yay, mother [expletive]!"
Small Screen: "Yippee kai-yay, Mr. Falcon!"

THE BIG LEBOWSKI (1998)

Big Screen: As he's smashing a Corvette with a tire iron, Walter (John Goodman) yells to the presumed owner, "See what happens when you [expletive] a stranger in the [buttocks]?"
Small Screen: "See what happens when you find a stranger in the Alps?"

SNAKES ON A PLANE (2006)

Big Screen: The most famous line from this over-the-top action movie is FBI agent Neville Flynn (Samuel L. Jackson) screaming, "I've had it with these mother [expletiving] snakes on this mother [expletiving] plane!"
Small Screen: "I've had it with these monkey-fighting snakes on this Monday to Friday plane!"

A Brazilian company created a Doggie Love sex doll for "lonely" pets.

NATIONAL LAMPOON'S VACATION (1983)

Big Screen: After getting his family lost late at night in a dangerous neighborhood, Clark (Chevy Chase) asks a stranger for directions. The man rudely responds, "[Expletive] your mama!"

Small Screen: The man says, "Who do I look like, Christopher Columbo?"

KILL BILL, VOL. 1 (2003)

Big Screen: The Bride (Uma Thurman) wakes up from a coma just in time—she is about to be assaulted by a guy who announces, "My name is Buck, and I like to [expletive that rhymes with Buck]."

Small Screen: "My name is Buck, and I like to party."

NOVOCAINE (2001)

Big Screen: A criminal named Duane (Scott Caan) threatens a dentist (Steve Martin) to stay away from Duane's sister (Helena Bonham Carter). In a moment of anger and frustration, Duane screams, "Jesus Christ!"

Small Screen: "Cheese and spice!"

THE USUAL SUSPECTS (1995)

Big Screen: In a police lineup, Kevin Spacey, Gabriel Byrne, Stephen Baldwin, Kevin Pollak, and Benicio del Toro are each made to read a line heard by a witness, "Hand me the keys, you [expletiving expletive] sucker!"

Small Screen: "Hand me the keys, you fairy godmother!"

*　　　*　　　*

A LOVE STORY

A tree toad loved a she-toad who lived up in a tree.

He was a two-toed tree toad, but a three-toed toad was she.

The two-toed tree toad tried to win the three-toed she-toad's heart,

For the two-toed tree toad loved the ground the three-toed tree toad trod.

The two-toed tree toad tried in vain to sate her every whim.

From her tree toad bower with her three-toed power,

The she-toad vetoed him.

"The tough coughed as he ploughed through the dough." —Dr. Seuss

WIKIALITY CHECK

We live in an age when you can alter "reality" with the click of a button.

THE ELEPHANT IN THE CHAT ROOM

On a 2006 episode of his Comedy Central show *The Colbert Report*, Stephen Colbert made fun of mainstream news outlets for using the website Wikipedia as a research source. Colbert's issue: The website allows anyone—expert or not—to edit any of its 22 million articles. "If everyone agrees that what's in Wikipedia is true," he said, "then anyone can change reality simply by editing Wikipedia."

He called this new reality "wikiality" and suggested his viewers edit the Wikipedia article on elephants to read: "Elephant population in Africa has tripled over the past six months." A fan complied. A Wikipedia staffer removed the line; another fan put it back. After this happened a few more times, Wikipedia "locked" the elephants article so no more edits could be made. Here are more instances of people creating their own wikialities.

SARAH PALIN

In 2012 the former VP candidate was touring historic sites in Boston when she mentioned that on Paul Revere's famous ride in 1775, he was "ringin' those bells." Palin's history was off: Revere didn't ring any bells. The press mocked her, but she stood by her version of the events. Meanwhile, one of her supporters edited the Wikipedia entry on Paul Revere to reflect Palin's version. Wikipedia fixed the article and locked out any further changes. (Colbert later tried to "help" Palin by asking his viewers to change the entry on bells to include Palin's account of Revere's ride.)

JUSTIN BIEBER

In 2011, after jazz singer and bassist Esperanza Spalding won the Best New Artist Grammy over Bieber, his fans were upset. In the hours that followed, Spalding's Wikipedia entry was edited more than 90 times with such new "facts" as: "JUSTIN BIEBER DESERVED IT GO DIE IN A HOLE!" Another disgruntled fan logged on and changed Spalding's middle name to Quesadilla.

Ronald Reagan's nickname for his son Michael: "Little Schmuck."

HALLE BERRY

An anonymous Wikipedia user named "Ciii" added this quotation to Berry's biography in 2006: "I've always loved to sing and this album will show people that I can do more than act." Based on that, several news outlets, including the *Washington Post*, *Rock & Roll Daily*, and *Rolling Stone* magazine, reported that the Oscar winner was about to record a pop album. That prompted an official denial from Berry, who has no plans to become a singer.

BATMAN

In 2007 some joker deleted all of the text from the article on the Caped Crusader and replaced it with this:

Batman
From Wikipedia, the free encyclopedia

DUH NUH NUH NUH NUH NUH DUH NUH NUH NUH NUH NUH BATMAN! DUH NUH NUH NUH NUH NUH DUH NUH NUH NUH NUH NUH BATMAN! DUH NUH NUH NUH NUH NUH DUH NUH NUH NUH NUH NUH BATMAN! BATMAN! BATMAN! DUH NUH NUH NUH NUH NUH DUH NUH NUH NUH NUH NUH BATMAN! DUH NUH NUH NUH NUH NUH DUH NUH NUH NUH NUH NUH **BATMAN!!!!!!!!!!!!!!!!!!!!!!!**

(If you're not familiar, those are the "lyrics" to the theme song of the campy 1960s *Batman* TV show.)

TITIAN

In the British House of Commons in 2009, Labour Party head Gordon Brown said during a speech that 16th-century Italian painter Titian died when he was 90. Conservative leader David Cameron later claimed that Titian died when he was 86...and then mocked Brown for his "lack of education." Later that day, one of Cameron's staffers called the BBC News and told them to go to Titian's Wikipedia page...which proved that Cameron—not Brown—was correct. Suspicious, a BBC reporter discovered that Titian's Wikipedia entry had recently been changed to reflect Cameron's version of the truth. When pressed, Cameron admitted that one of his staffers was responsible. (Titian's actual birth date is unknown.)

THE HALLS OF CONGRESS

• **Rep. Joe Donnelly (D-IN)** deleted the fact that he broke with Democratic leadership on several budget issues to maintain his reputation as a more conservative "Blue Dog" Democrat.

• **Vice President Joe Biden**'s staffers removed references to alleged plagiarism in his speeches.

• **Rep. John Mica (R-FL)** quashed reports that he wore a toupee—rumors started by Stephen Colbert.

THE SEIGENTHALER INCIDENT

In 2005 an anonymous Wikipedia user created a fake page about NBC News journalist John Seigenthaler, claiming that he was a suspect in the assassinations of both John F. and Robert Kennedy and that he had lived in the Soviet Union from 1971 to 1984.

None of it is remotely true, but somehow the hoax went unnoticed for more than four months. Wikipedia eventually tracked down the saboteur: Brian Chase, 38, a delivery service manager in Nashville. "It was just a joke," Chase claimed, adding that he thought the site was "some sort of gag encyclopedia." He was forced to resign from his job. Chase later called Seigenthaler to apologize, saying he didn't think anyone would take it seriously.

The incident prompted Wikipedia to add more editorial oversight to its articles, which is why suspect entries have disclaimers at the top. The rules were changed so that a person must register on the site before they can make any changes (but they don't have to use their real name). In 2012 the company added new software that alerts a core group of trusted editors of article changes so that, if necessary, they can be fixed immediately. However, errant "facts" can still slip through the cracks. Seigenthaler summed up his experience in an editorial in *USA Today*: "We live in a universe of new media with phenomenal opportunities for worldwide communications and research—but populated by volunteer vandals with poison-pen intellects."

* * *

FROM AN ACTUAL NEWS REPORT

"An Oak Hill couple discovered a thief in their home Saturday after the homeowner told a joke and heard someone laugh upstairs."

The *Mystery Science Theater 3000* spaceship set cost $200, built out of parts from Goodwill.

FUNNY LADIES

Jerry Lewis once admitted, "I don't like any female comedians…As a viewer,
I have trouble with it. I think of her as a producing machine that brings babies
into the world." Well, these baby-producing machines would beg to differ.

"Studies reveal that rectal thermometers are the best way to take a baby's temperature. Plus, it really shows them who's boss."
—**Tina Fey**

"I'm a godmother, that's a great thing to be, a godmother. She calls me 'God' for short. That's cute. I taught her that."
—**Ellen Degeneres**

"It's one of life's most memorable moments: the marriage proposal. I fantasize about it. Will he hire a plane to write, 'Will you marry me?' in the sky? And if I don't want to marry him, do I have to hire a plane to write, 'No'?"
—**Rita Rudner**

"My husband thinks I'm crazy, but I'm not the one who married me."
—**Wendy Liebman**

"I saw a truck today with a sign that said 'Driver has no cash.' I'm broke, too. But I don't plaster it all over the side of my car."
—**Margaret Smith**

"If you were to send a werewolf to the moon, would he be a werewolf permanently?"
—**Kristen Schaal**

"I hope cell phones aren't bad for us, but I would like the excuse: 'I can't talk right now. You're giving me cancer.'"
—**Whitney Cummings**

"Florida has so many strip clubs, they need to change the state flag to a brass pole."
—**Wanda Sykes**

"My son is into that nosepicking thing. The least he can do is act like an adult—buy a car and sit in traffic."
—**Roseanne Barr**

"I feel pretty lucky. Thousands of people die every single day, and it's not me."
—**Sarah Silverman**

"There will be sex after death; we just won't be able to feel it."
—**Lily Tomlin**

ROCK 'N' ROLL DIARY

Gossip and trivia from pop music.

RADIOHEAD. Bucking the tradition of rock groups trashing hotel rooms, Radiohead actually does the opposite. Not only do they clean up their own rooms, but they once snuck back into a hotel after checking out to clean up a room that their opening band had trashed.

THE WHITE STRIPES. Before he was a rock star, Jack White repaired furniture. At 21 years old, he even started his own business, called Third Man Upholstery. (His slogan: "Your furniture's not dead.") Although White enjoyed the work, he wasn't into the business aspect of it, which began to suffer when his clients stopped taking him seriously. Why? According to White, he'd write poetry inside their furniture and write his invoices in crayon.

HAWKWIND. The 1970s progressive-rock band was playing an outdoor concert during a rainstorm. As part of their theatrical act, singer Nik Turner dressed up in a frog costume and ran onto the stage. On this particular day, however, the stage was muddy and Turner slid all the way across, over the edge, and into a muddy puddle on the ground (just like a real frog).

JOHN & YOKO. In 1969 Lennon and Ono released the avant-garde *Wedding Album*. Side 1 featured 22 minutes of the couple yelling each others' names. Side 2 featured recordings of the couple on their honeymoon. According to the book *Rock Bottom*, "The album caused great hilarity when it was reviewed by a London journalist who was sent an advance copy, in the form of two single-sided discs. Sadly, he didn't realize that some record companies distribute test pressings in this form, and commented that he preferred the two sides which contained an electronic hum."

THE COMMODORES. How did they get their name? In 1968 keyboardist William King put on a blindfold, opened up a dictionary, and placed his finger on a random word. "We lucked out," King recalled. "We almost became the Commodes!"

UNCLE JOHN'S PAGE OF FUNNY LISTS

This page is dedicated to classical music composer Franz Liszt.

7 Names for a Mullet
1. Ape drape
2. Business in front, party in back
3. Camaro hair
4. Beaver paddle
5. Mud flap
6. Kentucky waterfall
7. Achy-breaky-bad-mistakey

6 Nicknames of Elvis Presley's Girlfriends and Mistresses
1. Ann-Margret: "Bunny," "Thumper," "Scoobie"
2. Malessa Blackwood: "Brown Eyes"
3. Margrit Buergin: "Little Puppy"
4. Dolores Hart: "Whistle Britches"
5. Ursula Andress: "Alan"
6. Ginger Alden: "Gingerbread," "Chicken Neck"

10 Actual Canadian Town Names
1. Goobies
2. Blow Me Down
3. Jerry's Nose
4. Witless Bay
5. Malignant Cove
6. Meat Cove
7. Swastika
8. Spuzzum
9. Stoner
10. Mayo

4 Tony Danza Roles
1. Tony, *Taxi*
2. Tony, *Who's the Boss?*
3. Tony, *Hudson Street*
4. Joe, *Family Law*

6 Baseball Players' Weird Nicknames
1. Putsy Caballero
2. Togie Pittinger
3. Bots Nekola
4. Pid Purdy
5. Twink Twining
6. Waddy MacPhee

3 Roman Delicacies, circa 200 A.D.
1. Parrot tongue
2. Thrush tongue
3. Nightingale tongue

Jerry Seinfeld's 4 Levels of Comedy
1. Make your friends laugh
2. Make strangers laugh
3. Get paid to make strangers laugh
4. Make people talk like you because it's so much fun

4 Unintentionally Dirty Business Websites
1. Pen Island (*penisland.com*)
2. Celebrity agent directory Who Represents (*whorepresents.com*)
3. Electric company Italian Power Generator (*powergenitalia.com*)
4. Design firm Speed of Art (*speedofart.com*)

THE SOCIETY FOR THE COALITION OF ORGANIZATIONS AND ASSOCIATIONS

Since 1988, the Bathroom Readers' Institute has stood up for those who like to sit down and read in the bathroom. In the spirit of camaraderie, we thought we'd showcase a few other societies of people who band together for a specific cause. Because if they didn't, who would?

Society for Barefoot Living. "We are a group of people who **love** going barefoot pretty much **everywhere**." (They also love bolding certain **words** on their website.) Founded in 1994, the SBL's mission is to remind the shoe-wearing public that it's a lot healthier and more fun to let your soles touch the ground than to keep them covered up. They also dispel the myths about going barefooted, such as the likelihood of catching athlete's foot (it's less than with shoes); that it's illegal to walk into a restaurant without shoes (it isn't); and that it's gross to go into a public restroom in bare feet ("Urine is **not** a toxic waste product and this has been scientifically **proven**!").

National Coalition for the Advancement of Baton Twirling. Don't think spinning around a metal stick is a sport? The NCABT says, "Try it." Not only is baton twirling a sport, but a very difficult one to master, and therefore should get the respect it deserves. The NCABT, formed by a group of coaches, is lobbying the NCAA to make it an officially sanctioned college sport. Meanwhile, another organization, the U.S. Twirling Association, is working tirelessly to make baton twirling an Olympic event.

Society for Creative Anachronism. If you don't feel at all weird referring to your friends as "Milord" and "Milady," then you just might be

---

stout-hearted enough to join the SCA. Formed in 1966 by a group of history buffs in Berkeley, California, members dress up as medieval knights, damsels, royalty, and villains. The SCA has 30,000 members all over the world, which they've broken up into 19 "kingdoms," such as "Calontir" (the U.S. Midwest) and "Drachenwald" (Europe, Africa, the Middle East). SCA members hold local events and attend renaissance fairs, where they compete in tournaments of jousting, archery, and axe-throwing. After the last foe has been waylaid, they feast merrily and pay tribute to the guy who's dressed up as the king.

The Skeptics Society: Do you believe in ghosts, aliens, Bigfoot, or ESP? Then this isn't the organization for you. "Some people think we are a bunch of grumpy curmudgeons unwilling to accept any claim that challenges the status quo, but this is not so," says scientist Michael Shermer, who founded the society in 1992. Its 55,000 members simply maintain that "seeing is believing." And for the kids, they offer the Junior Skeptic Club. Their hero: Scooby-Doo. Why? Because at the end of every cartoon, the dog (and those meddling kids) prove that the ghost isn't real.

National Coalition for Men. Is today's man still supposed to open a door for a woman? Is it okay for guys to talk about their feelings? What specifically is the role of the male in this increasingly complex society? The NCFM—born in 1977 at the height of the women's liberation movement—aims to help "emotionally adrift" men. They hold workshops and conduct support groups in an effort to help guys gain their freedom from male stereotyping, conditioned competitiveness, fear of sharing their feelings, getting their sense of identity from their jobs, thinking that violence is manly, having distant emotional relationships with their children, and a host of other issues. (And it's still okay to open the door for a woman.)

The Society for the Scientific Study of Sexuality. Founded in 1957, this nonprofit organization consists of more than 1,000 educators, doctors, psychologists, anthropologists, sociologists, and biologists who share theories and findings with each other. They operate under the assumption that science illuminates sexuality, and sexuality enhances the quality of our lives. The 2009 SSSS Annual Congress was held at a spa in Puerto Vallarta, Mexico.

In a 1988 poll, Batman comic book readers voted to have Robin killed by the Joker.

JIM ROCKFORD'S ANSWERING MACHINE

Every episode of the classic 1970s TV show The Rockford Files *opened with the same signature audio gag. You'd hear James Garner's voice say, "This is Jim Rockford. At the tone, leave your name and message. I'll get back to you," followed by the beep of his answering machine, and then a joke message. Over the show's seven-year run, coming up with funny lines became a challenge for the writers, but like Rockford, they always came through. Here are some of our favorites.*

BEEEP! "Jim, It's Norma at the market. It bounced. You want us to tear it up, send it back, or put it with the others?"

BEEEP! "It's Laurie at the trailer park. A space opened up. Do you want me to save it, or are the cops going to let you stay where you are?"

BEEEP! "Really want Shimbu in the seventh? C'mon, that nag couldn't go a mile in the back of a pickup truck. Call me."

BEEEP! "I staked out that guy, only it didn't work out like you said. Please call me. Room 234, County Hospital."

BEEEP! "That #4 you just picked up from Angelo's Pizza? Some scouring powder fell in there. Don't eat it. Hey, I hope you try your phone machine before dinner."

BEEEP! "Hello? You the guy who lost a wallet in the Park Theater? Well, I'm kinda like into leather. So, I'll be returning the money, but I'm going to keep the wallet."

BEEEP! "Mr. Rockford? You don't know me, but I'd like to hire you. Could you call me at…my name is, uh, never mind. Forget it."

BEEEP! "Jimmy, old buddy, buddy. It's Angel! You know how they allow you one phone call? Well, this is it."

BEEEP! "It's Pete. Hope you enjoyed using the cabin last week. Only next time, leave the trout in the refrigerator, huh? Not in the cupboard."

BEEEP! "Hey, Jimbo, Dennis. Really appreciate the help on the income tax. Wanna help on the audit now?"

BEEEP! "This is Globe Publications. Our records show you did not return your free volume of the *Encyclopedia*

In 1968 Steven Spielberg and George Lucas took a directing class taught by Jerry Lewis.

of Weather. So, we'll be sending you the remaining 29 volumes. You'll be billed accordingly."

BEEEP! "Good morning, this is the telephone company. Due to repairs, we're giving you advance notice that your service will be cut off indefinitely at ten o'clock. That's two minutes from now."

BEEEP! "Jim, thanks for taking little Billy fishing, he had a great time. Turns out he wasn't even really seasick. Um, have you ever had chicken pox?"

BEEEP! "Sonny, this is Dad. Never mind giving that talk on your occupation to the Grey Power Club. Hap Dudley's son is a doctor, and everybody'd sorta…well, rather hear from him, but thanks."

BEEEP! "Say, I'm the one who hit your car at Fork City. I've got no insurance. I'm broke. But I really wanted you to know how sorry I am. If it makes you feel any better, I hurt my arm."

BEEEP! "Uncle Jim? It's Ralph. I got your letter, but I moved out here anyway. I really want those detective lessons."

BEEEP! "Rockford? Alice, Phil's Plumbing. We're still jammed up on a job, so we won't be able to make your place. Use the bathroom at the restaurant one more night."

BEEEP! "Jim, Coop. I'm at the address you wrote down for the poker game tonight. This is a gas station, it's closed, there's no one around, and now my car is stalled. Now, you got to call me at 4-6-6-3-*click*."

BEEEP! "Jim, Joel Myers at Crowell, Finch, and Merriwether. We're going to court tomorrow with that Penrose fraud case, but steno misplaced your 200-page deposition. Could you come down tonight and give it again?"

BEEEP! "This is Betty Frenell. I don't know who to call, but I can't reach my Foodaholics partner. I'm at Vito's on my second pizza with sausage and mushrooms. Jim, come and get me."

BEEEP! "This is the Baron. Angel Martin tells me you buy information. Okay, meet me at 1:00 a.m. behind the bus depot, bring $500, and come alone. I'm serious."

BEEEP! "Hey, Rockford, very funny. I ain't laughing. You're gonna' get yours."

The password signaling the start of the WWII invasion at Normandy was "Mickey Mouse."

NATURE'S SINGLES BAR

You think human mating rituals are weird? You're right. But so are animals'.

Doo-Doo You Love Me? The male hippo uses an odd form of foreplay to make him irresistible to females. When the mood strikes, he urinates and defecates simultaneously. Then he uses his tail to stir up the mess and throw it about. Once he's caught a female's attention, the pair proceeds to mate in water (where, presumably, they will wash off).

Explosive Love. Mating is dangerous work for the male honeybee—when he's done, he literally explodes. His body separates from his genitals, which remain inside the female, preventing her from mating with any other male.

Just Call Him Mommy. Sea horses have reversed gender roles: the male sea horse gets "pregnant" and nurtures the unborn young. Females use an organ called an ovipositor to deliver her eggs into a male's body and impregnate him. Even better, sea horses mate for life and never cheat.

Cardinal Sins. Male Japanese cardinal fish nurture their immature young by incubating them in their mouths. But if a male encounters a female who is more desirable than his offspring's mother, the male fish quickly eats up all the babies and tries to woo the newcomer.

Won't You Come Up to My Place? To attract a mate, the male bowerbird of Australia and New Zealand builds an elaborate bachelor pad out of sticks and twigs, called a *bower*. He decorates it with colorful leaves, feathers, dead insects, and even candy wrappers. Female bowerbirds make the rounds of the various bowers before settling on a favorite. When she chooses one, the male launches into an energetic song-and-dance routine—cawing loudly, hopping about, and throwing feathers. If he struts his stuff successfully, she'll return to his bower every year for the rest of her life.

Chompto-pus. If an amorous male octopus approaches a female octopus who is not in the mood, she simply bites off his sex organ. Fortunately, he has seven more.

Yes, there's a National Leprechaun Museum. It's in Dublin, Ireland—where else?

NOT A SCHOLAR

This real-life exchange actually took place in a court of law.

Clerk: "Please repeat after me: 'I swear by Almighty God…'"

Witness: "I swear by Almighty God."

Clerk: "That the evidence that I give…"

Witness: "That's right."

Clerk: "Repeat it."

Witness: "Repeat it."

Clerk: "No! Repeat what I said."

Witness: "What you said when?"

Clerk: "That the evidence that I give…"

Witness: "That the evidence that I give."

Clerk: "Shall be the truth and…"

Witness: "It will, and nothing *but* the truth!"

Clerk: "Please, just repeat after me: 'Shall be the truth and…'"

Witness: "I'm not a scholar, you know."

Clerk: "We can appreciate that. Just repeat after me: 'Shall be the truth and…'"

Witness: "Shall be the truth and."

Clerk: "Say: 'Nothing…'"

Witness: "Okay." (Witness remains silent.)

Clerk: "No! Don't say nothing. Say: 'Nothing but the truth…'"

Witness: "Yes."

Clerk: "Can't you say: 'Nothing but the truth'?"

Witness: "Yes."

Clerk: "Well? Do so."

Witness: "You're confusing me."

Clerk: "Just say: 'Nothing but the truth.'"

Witness: "Is that all?"

Clerk: "Yes."

Witness: "Okay. I understand."

Clerk: "Then say it."

Witness: "What?"

Clerk: "Nothing but the truth…"

Witness: "But I do! That's just it."

Clerk: "You must say: 'Nothing but the truth.'"

Witness: "I WILL say nothing but the truth!"

Clerk: "Please, just say the words: 'Nothing.' 'But.' 'The.' 'Truth.'"

Witness: "You mean, like, now?"

Clerk: "Yes! Now. Please!"

Witness: "Nothing. But. The. Truth."

Clerk: "Thank you."

Witness: "I'm just not a scholar."

Are they hungover? Honeybees have hair on their eyes.

PAGING MR. STENCH

Celebrities divulge their innermost secrets!

"I ate a bug once. It was flying around me. I was trying to get it away. It went right in my mouth. It was so gross!"

—**Hilary Duff**

"I used to think I actually *was* Batman."

—**Justin Timberlake**

"I'd kiss a frog even if there was no promise of a Prince Charming popping out of it. I love frogs."

—**Cameron Diaz**

"I always cry when I watch myself on-screen."

—**Clint Eastwood**

"I like cars and basketball. But you know what I like more? Bananas."

—**Frankie Muniz**

"What kills me is that everybody thinks I like jazz."

—**Samuel L. Jackson**

"I'm horrible to live with. I forget to flush the toilet."

—**Megan Fox**

"The kindest word to describe my performance in school was 'sloth.'"

—**Harrison Ford**

"I cheated a lot at school. I just couldn't sit and do homework. I usually sat next to someone extremely smart."

—**Leonardo DiCaprio**

"All reporters ask exactly the same questions, and I say exactly the same answers. I don't have to think; I can just stand there like a broken record going LALALA…"

—**Emma Watson**

"I don't keep track of paper that well. My desk is a mess."

—**Barack Obama**

"I've never seen a phone bill of mine in my life."

—**Paris Hilton**

"I used to use the name 'Mr. Stench.' It was funny to be in a posh hotel and hear a very proper concierge call out, 'Mr. Stench, please.'"

—**Johnny Depp**

Geordi's eye visor on *Star Trek: The Next Generation* was a spruced-up engine air filter.

WORLD-CLASS LOSERS

Everyone makes mistakes. Some are just better at it than others.

PAPER WEIGHT

In 1965 an aspiring English publisher named Lionel Burleigh announced he was starting a newspaper called the *Commonwealth Sentinel,* which he promised would be "Britain's most fearless newspaper." Burleigh did everything it took to make the paper a success—he promoted it on billboards, sold advertising space, wrote articles, and printed up 50,000 copies of the first issue so that there would be plenty to go around. Burleigh remembered every detail, except for one very important thing: distribution.

In fact, he had forgotten it completely until he received a phone call from the police informing him that all 50,000 copies had been deposited on the sidewalk in front of the hotel where he was staying. They were blocking the entrance. Could he please come and remove them?

Britain's "most fearless paper" folded after just one day. "To my knowledge, we only sold one copy," Burleigh remembered years later. "I still have the shilling in my drawer."

A LOAD OF BULL

In 1958 the town of Lindsay, Ontario, organized the country's first-ever bullfight. There aren't many bullfighting bulls in Canada, and even fewer matadors, so they had to bring in both from Mexico. But the bulls brought ticks with them, and ticks from other parts of the world aren't allowed into Canada. The bulls had to be quarantined for a week. By the time they got out, the matadors had returned to Mexico. Result: no bullfight.

HORSE SENSE

Horatio Bottomley (great name) was a convicted fraud artist and former member of the English Parliament. In 1914 he figured out what he thought was a foolproof way to rig a horse race: He bought all six horses in the race, hired his own jockeys to race them, and told them in which order he wanted them to cross the finish line.

Then he bet a fortune on the horses he'd picked to win, and also placed bets on the order of finish. Everything went according to plan...until a thick fog rolled in over the track in the middle of the race. It was so thick that the jockeys couldn't see each other well enough to cross the finish line in the proper order. Bottomley lost every bet he placed.

MORE LOSERS

Not to be outdone by civilians, the "military intelligence" personnel of past war machines have had their day in the doghouse as well.

Brits in the Pits. In the early 1940s, the English military came up with what they thought would be a simple but powerful antitank weapon: a four-and-a-half-pound hand grenade covered with sticky adhesive that would help it stick to the sides of tanks. The grenade was withdrawn from service a short time later. Reason: It stuck a little too well...to the soldier who was trying to throw it. It was so sticky, in fact, that the only practical way to put it to use was to run up to the tank and stick the grenade on manually—which was practically a suicide mission because the bomb's short fuse gave its user less than five seconds to get away.

Peru's Blues. As part of its Air Force Week celebrations in 1975, the Peruvian military decided to show off the might of its newest fighter planes. Fourteen derelict fishing boats were towed a short distance out to sea to serve as targets. After the crowds had gathered along the coast, a squadron of 30 fighters swooped down and attacked the boats with bombs and machine-gun fire for 15 minutes.

They didn't sink a single boat.

France's Chance. In 1870 the French military made preparations to use its own new machine gun, called the *mitrailleuse*, in the imminent war against Prussia. Machine guns were new at the time and the government wanted to keep the technology a secret. So it distributed the guns to military units... without instructions for how to use them; the instructions weren't sent until *after* the war had begun. But by then it was too late—France lost.

*   *   *

"Whoever said, 'It's not whether you win or lose that counts,' probably lost."
—**Martina Navratilova**

One Alaska Airlines plane is painted like a fish. Nickname: the "Salmon-Thirty-Salmon."

SINE OF THE TIMES

Do these math puns add up? We're divided.

"Help me, Doc," said the math book. "I've got problems."

A nice view out the window is a weapon of math disruption.

That mathematician ate the bunch of fruit so fast that it was gone in a bananasecond.

Trigonometry for farmers: swines and coswines.

Algebra is the loneliest of the maths because it always wants you to find its X.

"My life is pointless," said the retired geometry teacher. (At least he's not going in circles.)

Don't worry about running out of math teachers. They're always multiplying.

For a good prime, call 555.793.7319.

The math teacher's pet parrot refused to eat, so he called it Polynomial. Then it died, so he called it Polygon.

There are 10 kinds of people, those who understand binary, and those who don't.

I didn't say you were average, just mean.

"Three!" said one math prof. "No, five!" said the other. They were at odds.

I'll do trigonometry, I'll do algebra, I'll even do statistics, but graphing is where I draw the line!

I personally found Newton's *Principia Mathematica* to be quite derivative.

I didn't understand addition, so the teacher summed it up for me.

Who's the fattest knight at the Round Table? Sir Cumference. Why so big? Too much pi.

Pickup line: Don't think me obtuse, but you're acute girl.

The geometry student was denied a loan because he couldn't get a cosine.

I'm partial to fractions.

Atheists can't solve exponential equations because they don't believe in higher powers.

I failed math so many times I've lost count.

Uncle John's favorite three-digit number? Too farty.

Jerry Springer producers bleep out non-curse words to make guests seem more interesting.

TATTOOS IN THE NEWS

Some stories that will make you ask: What were they inking?

PREMATURE ILLUSTRATION

In March 2014, a Kentucky Wildcats college basketball fan named Tyler Black got a tattoo that read "2014 Nati9nal Champions." Only problem: the NCAA tournament hadn't even started yet. At the time of the inking, Kentucky was favored 30 to 1 to win the national title. And they did go pretty deep into the tournament—they made it to the title game...but then lost to the University of Connecticut. (Black claims he'll keep the not-quite-accurate tattoo.)

FACING HIS FEAR

Some psychologists say that to overcome one's fears, one must directly face them. A Florida man named Eric Ortiz was weary of his crippling fear of spiders, which he encountered daily during his job as a landscaper. So he decided to do something about it. Did he adopt a pet tarantula? Did he visit the zoo's spider-and-insect house? Nope. He decided to diminish his fear's power by getting a tattoo of a black widow spider...that now occupies the entire right side of his face.

A PET CAUSE

In 2014 "Mistah Metro" (real name: Alexander Avgerakis) posted a picture of his dog on Instagram. The dog, looking very uncomfortable, was sporting a heart tattoo. It's real. "One of the many reasons my dog is cooler than yours! She had her spleen removed today, and the vet let me tattoo her while she was under." At the time, Avgerakis worked at Red Legged Devil, a tattoo parlor featured on the reality TV show *NY Ink*. Accusations of animal cruelty over the tatoo have since led Avgerakis to resign.

NOT HAPPY TO SEE THEM

One morning in March 2014, Michael Smith of Norridgewock, Maine, awoke to find several tree-removal workers in his yard. Smith went outside—shirtless—and yelled at the men to leave his property. They did. A short time later Smith was awakened for a second time. A policeman with a megaphone

---

Q: Did you hear about the dyslexic devil worshipper? A: He sold his soul to Santa.

was ordering Smith to come out of the house and surrender, adding that several armed state troopers were in the driveway. Smith came out with his hands up, and he and the police quickly realized that there had been a misunderstanding. The tree removers thought Smith had a handgun tucked into the waistband of his pants. He didn't—but he does have a tattoo of a handgun on his waist.

WHAT A TWIT

British rapper Dappy loves Twitter. He has more than 839,000 followers and posts messages and photos throughout the day, every day. The "hashtag"—an unspaced phrase that starts with "#"—is a tool Twitter users employ to search the site for people discussing a certain subject—click on a hashtag to find all mentions of that phrase. The most-used hashtagged subjects are listed each day as "trending topics." In 2014 Dappy got a pea-sized tattoo of the hashtag # on his right cheek so he could "stay trending forever."

MESSAGE TO MICHAEL

A Sudanese woman was discovered to have a tattoo of the name "Michael" on her right thigh. Why is that newsworthy? Because the woman is a 1,300-year-old mummy, making her tattoo one of the oldest ever discovered. The mummy, who died around the year 700, has the ancient Greek characters "MIXAHA" on her leg, which translates to the modern name of Michael. Archaeologists at the British Museum doubt the woman was declaring her devotion to a boyfriend, though. It more likely refers to the Archangel Michael, biblical leader of God's armies and patron saint of medieval Sudan.

EXHIBIT M

In 2014 Jeffrey Chapman of Kansas was put on trial for the 2011 murder of Damon Galyardt. Chapman has many tattoos, but his lawyer filed a motion with the court to allow one specific tattoo to be removed from his neck. The motion was denied, as state law requires tattoo removal to be performed only at licensed tattoo parlors, and the judge would not let Chapman be transported to one. Chapman had to stand trial with a neck tattoo that his lawyer said would be "extremely prejudicial" if seen by jurors—a large tattoo below his chin that spells out the word "MURDER."

JACK PAAR'S NEARLY FATAL BATHROOM JOKE

Did you know that bathroom humor almost killed
The Tonight Show in 1960? Here's the tale.

POTTY TALK

It began like any other night. Host Jack Paar walked out onstage and greeted the audience. This night, however, Paar did something different: He said that he wanted to tell a joke he'd heard from a friend, who had learned it from his daughter, who learned it when her junior high school teacher told it to the class. The joke was slightly risqué by 1960s TV standards, but Paar figured that if it was appropriate for schoolkids, it was appropriate for his television audience. "There's a slight question of taste involved here," he said. "I do this only with full knowledge that we're an adult group gathered at this hour, and we're not here to do anyone any harm." And then he told the joke.

THE JOKE

"An English lady, while visiting Switzerland, was looking for a room, and she asked the schoolmaster if he could recommend any to her. He took her to see several rooms, and when everything was settled, the lady returned home to make the final preparations to move. When she arrived home, she realized that she had not seen a W.C. That's a water closet to the British. We would call it a bathroom. So she wrote a note to the schoolmaster asking him if there were a W.C. around. The schoolmaster's English was very poor, so he asked the parish priest if he could help in the matter. Together they tried to discover the meaning of the letters W.C. and the only solution they could find for the letters was a 'wayside chapel.' The schoolmaster then wrote to the English lady the following note:

'DEAR MADAM: I take great pleasure in informing you that the W.C. is situated nine miles from the house you occupy, in the center of a beautiful grove of pine trees surrounded by lovely grounds. It is capable of holding 229 people and is open on Sunday and Thursday only. As there is a great number of people and they are expected during the summer months, I would suggest that you come early, although there is plenty of standing room as a rule.

'You will no doubt be glad to hear that a good number of people bring their lunch and make a day of it, while others who can afford to go by car and arrive just in time. I especially recommend that your ladyship go on Thursday when there is musical accompaniment.

'It may interest you to know that my daughter was married in the W.C. and it was there that she met her husband. I can remember the rush there was for seats. There were ten people to a seat usually occupied by one. It was wonderful to see the expressions on their faces.

'The newest attraction is a bell donated by a wealthy resident of the district. It rings every time a person enters. A bazaar is to be held to provide plush seats for all the people, since they feel it is a long-felt need. My wife is rather delicate, so she can't attend regularly.

'I shall be delighted to reserve the best seat for you if you wish, where you will be seen by all. For the children, there is a special time and place so that they will not disturb the elders. Hoping to have been some service to you, I remain

'Sincerely,
The Schoolmaster'

NOT LAUGHING

The joke got a hearty laugh from the audience. Paar thanked them and said, "You're my kind of people." But apparently they weren't NBC's kind of people. Then, as now, *The Tonight Show* was taped in the afternoon, and broadcast at 11:30 p.m. after NBC censors had a chance to look it over. They had never made any substantive changes before…but that night they excised the entire joke without telling Paar in advance. "Some idiot got concerned about the words 'water closet,'" he later explained.

Paar was angry when he found out what had happened, but he thought the controversy would make for an interesting discussion on his show. He proposed airing the censored joke the following evening, to "let the viewers decide for themselves" whether it was appropriate. NBC refused. Paar was furious—he felt the censorship was damaging to his reputation, since it implied that he had told a smutty joke on TV.

In Yukon, Oklahoma, it's illegal for patients to pull their dentist's teeth.

TAKE THIS JOB AND SHOVE IT

The following evening, Paar walked out onto the stage as usual, but rather than deliver his monologue, he vented his rage at NBC. Calling the censorship "a question of free speech," Paar announced that he was quitting *The Tonight Show*. "There must be a better way to make a living than this," he said. "I love NBC…but they let me down." Then he bade farewell to the audience, telling them, "You've always been peachy to me, always."

Paar walked off the stage and went home, leaving his shocked sidekick, Hugh Downs, to finish the show alone. "Is he gone?" Downs asked in amazement, telling the audience, "Jack frequently does things he regrets."

HIDING OUT

The incident made headlines all over the country. But Paar was nowhere to be found—he and his wife, Miriam, had escaped to Florida, where they hid out in a half-finished luxury hotel that a friend was building.

The Paars didn't have a phone at the hotel, but NBC somehow learned of their hiding place, and network president Robert Kintner flew down to talk things out. He eventually talked Paar into coming back…but only after he and Robert Samoff, the chairman of NBC, both publicly apologized for censoring the joke. Paar returned on March 7 after being absent nearly a month. "As I was saying before I was interrupted…" he joked to the audience. "There must be a better way of making a living than this. Well, I've looked. And there isn't!" (Applause.)

PAAR'S NO. 1 PROBLEM

Paar's protest increased his celebrity status and made him a hero of sorts with the public. Ironically, however, the bathroom joke that nearly ended his career was now making it almost impossible for him to use public restrooms, because wherever he went—even to the bathroom—admirers would approach him and congratulate him on his victory.

"Finally you reach the porcelain," he lamented, "and find that—with all eyes on your performance—you cannot! What to do? They are all watching! You panic because now they might think you are some kind of weirdo or voyeur looking around. You press the handle of the urinal, you whistle, and you wish you could get the battery jump-starter from the trunk of your auto. I tell you, it's very hard being a star in a men's room!"

LOOSE SMUT & F-HOLES

*Although they might look like it, none of the words or expressions
listed below are in any way dirty, and to prove it we're giving
you the correct definitions. (But use them at your own risk.)*

Bed Load: Solid particles, like the pebbles in a stream, that are carried along by flowing water.

Titbits: The British spelling for the word "tidbits." *Tit-Bits* was the name of a British weekly magazine published from 1881 to 1984.

Loose Smut: A fungus that attacks wheat crops.

Oxpecker: A small bird native to sub-Saharan Africa. (Also known as tickbirds, they eat parasites that infest the hides of livestock.)

Dick Test: If your doctor suspects you have scarlet fever, you may be given this diagnostic test invented by Dr. George Dick and his wife Gladys in 1924.

Vaginicola: A single-celled organism found in pond water.

Crack Spread: The difference in value between unrefined crude oil and the products that can be made by refining, or "cracking," the oil.

F-holes: The f-shaped sound holes cut into the front of violins, cellos, and other stringed instruments.

Rump Party: In British politics, when one faction of a political party breaks away to merge with or form a new party, the faction left behind is known as the "rump party."

Urinator: A person who dives underwater in search of pearls, sunken treasure, or other riches.

Spermophile: A genus, or grouping, of more than 40 species of ground squirrel.

Crap Mats: The name of a mountain in the Swiss Alps.

Fucoid: An adjective that means "having to do with seaweed."

Fucose: A type of sugar found in human breast milk and in seaweed.

Titubate: To stumble, either in step or in speech.

Dickcissel: A species of finch native to the central U.S.

In 2004 the Russian Orthodox Church officially ruled that playing chess is not a sin.

IT SEEMED LIKE A GOOD IDEA AT THE TIME

Life is constantly presenting us with interesting challenges. These challenges have many possible solutions...some good, some not so good, and some just plain bad. These belong in the third category.

THE KEYS TO SUCCESS

Challenge: A tourist at Montana's Glacier National Park wanted to take a picture of a squirrel that had scurried away into its rocky den.

Bad Idea: Trying to coax the animal out of its lair, the man dangled his only set of car keys in front of the opening.

Outcome: The squirrel darted out, snatched the keys right out of the man's hand, and disappeared back into the ground. Rangers tried to assist the frantic tourist, but the squirrel (and the keys) were nowhere to be found. The man had to call a locksmith out to the park and pay a hefty sum to get his car back on the road.

BACKFIRING BOOBY TRAP

Challenge: A 66-year-old Dutchman had some very important "stuff" in his garden shed and was afraid someone would steal it.

Bad Idea: Using some ropes, he devised a booby trap that hung a shotgun inside the door and set it to go off when the door was opened. Then he proudly opened the door to give his friends a demonstration.

Outcome: The man was shot in the stomach by his own gun and needed emergency surgery. After he recovered, he went to jail. (Police discovered the "stuff" he was guarding: 15 full-grown marijuana plants.)

LIGHT ONE CANDLE

Challenge: A 29-year-old man from St. Paul, Minnesota, identified only as Robert, wanted to clean the grit out of his bathtub.

Bad Idea: He used gasoline to clean the tub, which left the bathroom smelling really bad. To mask the odor, Robert lit aromatic candles.

Cats have been known to try to seduce dogs. (Few succeed.)

Outcome: Robert blew up his apartment. He sustained severe burns, but survived. (The apartment did not.)

DROVE MY CHEVY TO THE LEVEE

Challenge: In 1993, 24-year-old James Scott lived on the Illinois side of the Mississippi River. His wife worked on the Missouri side. All Scott wanted to do was "party," but his wife wouldn't let him.

Bad Idea: Scott removed some sandbags from a nearby levee, hoping the river would wash out the road that his wife used to take home.

Outcome: Not only did Scott wash out the road…he also flooded 14,000 acres, destroying crops as well as dozens of homes and businesses, and causing a local bridge to be closed for more than three months. After bragging about his "success" to his friends, Scott was arrested and sentenced to life in prison (the maximum penalty for "causing a catastrophe").

IN NEED OF A LIFT

Challenge: Somjet Korkeaw, a 42-year-old office worker from Bangkok, Thailand, was leaving work on a Saturday afternoon when he suddenly realized he'd forgotten something and had to return to his office on the 99th floor to get it. Unfortunately, the passenger elevators had already been turned off for the weekend and the stair doors were locked.

Bad Idea: He decided to take a small cargo elevator (designed to carry food and documents). It was small, so he had to crouch into a ball to fit, but it was the only way back to the office.

Outcome: Korkeaw weighed 150 pounds, far too heavy for the lift to carry. Result: It got stuck between floors. He had to wait, bent over and crammed inside the little box, for more than 40 hours until the building reopened on Monday morning.

SHELL SHOCK

Challenge: A 19-year-old man from Spokane, Washington, wanted to make a necklace out of bullets. The only way to string the necklace together was to punch holes in the live ammunition.

Bad Idea: He punched a hole in the live ammunition.

Outcome: He survived the explosion, but will never play piano again.

Baseball axiom: The guy in the stands with the biggest gut will be the first to take off his shirt.

BIN LADEN IS A WOMAN!

…and other great (and real) tabloid newspaper headlines.

MAN REINCARNATED AS HIMSELF

Cubs Boost World Series Hopes With Holy Water

Man Takes Out Restraining Order Against Imaginary Friend

Gnomes of Death Lure Divers to Drowning Horror

Prune Juice Makes You Stupid

God's Autograph Sells for $500 Million

NEBRASKA DOESN'T EXIST, SAYS AUTHOR

Blood-Sucking Dracula Squirrels Invade U.S.

New Study Says "Stitch in Time" Saves Only 8

GRIM REAPER TO RETIRE—PEOPLE WILL LIVE FOREVER!

World's Oldest Woman Thrives on Lard and Booze

Jungle Tribe Worships Jay Leno's Chin

Massive Loch Ness Monster Fart Swamps Tourist Boat

Earwax DNA Doesn't Lie—Osama Bin Laden Is a Woman!

Mr. Rogers' Ghost Terrorizing Children!

Beer Cans & Old Mattress Found on Mars

ALIENS TRAVEL TO EARTH FOR CHINESE TAKEOUT

VIKINGS WERE WIMPS!

Hair Space Alien Lives on Donald Trump's Head!

Art Collector Buys Forged Art With Counterfeit Money

Scientists Clone Jerry Springer

Pope Has Super Powers!

CREDIT CARD EXPLODES WHEN GAL GOES OVER LIMIT

"He who laughs, lasts." —Mary Pettibone Poole

MR. POTTY MOUTH

*On June 20, 2004, Vice President Dick Cheney made an off-color remark
to Senator Patrick Leahy of Vermont…and made history. We can't
print exactly what he said, but neither could the news media.
Here are a few of the creative ways they reported the story.*

• **Washington Post:** "Cheney exploded in colorful profanity."

• **CBS News:** "Cheney Gives Leahy An 'F'."

• **Capital Times:** "Dick Cheney to Pat Leahy: Go f*$@! yourself."

• **Spokesmanreview.com:** "Cheney delivered a popular epithet (see *The Sopranos*)."

• **Boston Herald:** "Bleep the veep: Angry Cheney tells senator to **** OFF!"

• **Christian Science Monitor:** "The Vice President allegedly used a four-letter word to suggest Leahy engage in a procreative anatomical impossibility."

• **L.A. Times:** "Go…yourself."

• **Charleston Post Courier:** "Go [expletive deleted] yourself."

• **The Calgary Sun:** "Go (bleep) yourself."

• **Weekly World News:** "Cheney On F-Word Rampage!"

• **Herald Sun:** "Cheney swears an oath."

• **Springfield News Leader:** "Cheney dismissed Leahy with the offensive language."

• **CNN:** "Cheney replied 'f— off' or 'go f— yourself.'"

• **Japan Today:** "Cheney used a naughty word…"

• **USA TODAY:** "Tells Sen. Leahy to "go f*** yourself."

• **DNCNews:** "Cheney uses 'Big-time' swear word."

• **Canada Free Press:** "Oh, fudge!"

• **MSNBC:** "Cheney then used the 'f' word."

• **Houston Chronicle:** "Cheney… vulgarly proposed that Leahy do something impossible to himself."

• **FOXNEWS:** "…one of George Carlin's seven deadly words."

• **Vice President Cheney:** "I felt better after I'd done it."

The Brown Comet: Americans use enough toilet paper each year to stretch to the sun and back.

MRS. ORPHEUS?

These are actual answers to questions on students' tests
submitted to education websites by frazzled teachers.

Q: What type of bond holds the sodium ions and chloride ions together in a crystal?
A: James Bond

Q: What is hard water?
A: Ice

Q: What happens during puberty to a boy?
A: He says goodbye to his childhood and enters adultery.

Q: Name six animals which specifically live in the Arctic.
A: 2 polar bears and 3 4 seals

Q: What was Sir Walter Raleigh famous for?
A: He invented cigarettes and started a craze for bicycles.

Q: Briefly explain why breathing is important.
A: When you breathe, you inspire. When you do not breathe, you expire.

Q: What is a fossil?
A: A fossil is an extinct animal. The older it is, the more extinct it is.

Q: Explain why phosphorous trichloride (PCl_3) is polar.
A: God made it that way.

Q: Name the wife of Orpheus, whom he attempted to save from the underworld.
A: Mrs. Orpheus.

Q: Name one measure to avoid river flooding in times of extensive rainfall.
A: Flooding may be avoided by placing a number of dames into the river.

Q: Why do mushrooms have their distinctive shapes?
A: Mushrooms always grow in damp places and so they look like umbrellas.

Q: Name one of the Romans' greatest achievements.
A: Learning to speak Latin.

Q: Expand (a+b)n
A: (a + b) n

Q: Where was the Declaration of Independence signed?
A: At the bottom.

Evel Knievel was fired from a mining job for making an earth-moving machine do a wheelie.

"I WANT A BEER AS COLD AS MY EX-WIFE'S HEART"

You don't have to be a fan of country music to appreciate the toe-tappin' wit of these real-life country song titles.

"I Gave Her My Heart and a Diamond and She Clubbed Me with a Spade"

"You're a Hard Dog to Keep Under the Porch"

"Four on the Floor and a Fifth Under the Seat"

"You Done Stomped on My Heart (and You Mashed That Sucker Flat)"

"I Went Back to My Fourth Wife for the Third Time and Gave Her a Second Chance to Make a First Class Fool Out of Me"

"You Can't Have Your Kate and Edith Too"

"I'd Rather Pass a Kidney Stone than Another Night with You"

"Feelin' Single and Drinkin' Doubles"

"If My Nose Was Full of Nickels, I'd Blow It All on You"

"I Bought the Shoes That Just Walked Out on Me"

"Jesus Loves Me but He Can't Stand You"

"I Fell in a Pile of You and Got Love All Over"

"One Day When You Swing That Skillet (My Face Ain't Gonna Be There)"

"I Gave Her the Ring, and She Gave Me the Finger"

"Thanks to the Cathouse, I'm in the Doghouse with You"

"You're the Ring Around My Bathtub, You're the Hangnail of My Life"

"I Want a Beer as Cold as My Ex-Wife's Heart"

"Did I Shave My Legs for This?"

"If You Can't Live without Me, Why Aren't You Dead?"

"I Wouldn't Take Her to a Dawg Fight, 'Cause I'm Afraid She'd Win"

"He's Got a Way with Women…and He Just Got Away with Mine"

TRUTH IS FUNNIER THAN FICTION

More tales that are more funny because they really happened.

WITH FRIENDS LIKE THESE...

In 2008 a health spa in Zneleznovodsk, Russia, dedicated a statue to an important member of its team: the enema. "We administer enemas nearly every day," said spa administrator Alexander Kharchenko. "So I thought, why not give it a monument?" They commissioned local artist Svetlana Avakina to create the work. She drew inspiration from 15th-century Renaissance painter Sandro Botticelli's *Venus and Mars*, which depicts three cherubs stealing a sword from the god of war. Avakina replaced the sword with an enema syringe. The bronze statue stands five feet tall and cost $42,000. "An enema is an unpleasant procedure, as many of us may know," said Avakina. "But when cherubs do it, it's all right."

WHATEVER

In September 2008, Framingham State College in Massachusetts sent a fund-raising letter to alumni. Here's an excerpt:

> With the recent economic downturn and loan crisis, it has become even more important for Framingham State College to receive your support. Blah, blah.

Was it a goof? Did an incomplete draft get sent by mistake? No. The 312-word letter—which had 137 "blah"s—was supposed to be funny. However, many of the 6,000 recipients contacted the school and said they were insulted. Framingham's vice president of admissions, Christopher Hendry, admitted that it was a "misguided and embarrassing attempt to connect with alumni in a different way." Or as one graduate commented: "The fund-raising letter was impudent and childish. Blah, blah, blah, blah, blah."

TOXIC AVENGER

Legal aide Erin Brockovich made history in 1996 by winning a class-action lawsuit against a giant utility company, Pacific Gas & Electric, for toxic contamination of groundwater in a small California town. The $333 million settlement was the largest to date and made Brockovich famous—especially after Julia Roberts played her in a movie about the lawsuit. She got a $2 million bonus for winning the case and bought her dream house in Agoura Hills, California, for $600,000. Shortly after moving in, Brockovich discovered that it was contaminated with toxic mold. (She sued.)

CAP'N CRUNCHED

Concerned drivers in Needham, Massachusetts, called to notify police that a vehicle was driving erratically, crossing double yellow lines, and tailgating other cars. When police pulled over the driver they found him eating a bowl of cereal…with milk. His excuse: "I was hungry."

SUX-OPHONE

A street musician from the Dutch town of Leiden was so inept at playing his saxophone that local shop owners called the police. After hearing the man play, the cops confiscated his instrument.

NIGHT OF THE DRIVING DEAD

Rescue crews in Portland, Oregon, were called to the scene of a single-car accident one summer evening in 2010. When they arrived, they were alarmed by the extent of the injuries. The victims' faces were all bleeding; their skin was white, as if they were dead; and blood and guts were smeared all over their clothes. It was quite gruesome. Or was it? It turned out that, when the accident happened, the five people were on their way to a costume party, all dressed and made up like zombies. Said police sergeant Greg Stewart, "We're glad that everyone is alive, despite being undead."

NIGHT OF THE LIVING EDS

In a baseball game in the early 1950s, Philadelphia Phillies right fielder Bill Nicholson hit a high pop-up that was destined to come down somewhere near the mound. Pittsburgh Pirates pitcher Bill Werle didn't want to catch it, so he called for one of his fielders to step in. "Eddie's got it! Eddie's got it!" he shouted. Then everyone in the Pirates' infield stood and watched as the ball landed on the grass…including catcher Eddie Fitzgerald, first baseman Eddie Stevens, and third baseman Eddie Bockman.

Real book title: *Stray Shopping Carts of Eastern North America: A Guide to Field Identification*

YOU'RE CLEARED FOR TAKEOFF...IDIOT

What do these actual recordings of air-traffic controllers talking to airline pilots tell us? That air traffic controllers are grumpy...and pilots are smart-asses.

Tower: TWA 2341, for noise abatement, turn right, 45 degrees.
Pilot: Center, we're at 35,000 feet. How much noise can we make up here?
Tower: Sir, have you ever heard the noise a 747 makes when it hits a 727?

Tower: Delta 351, you have traffic at ten o'clock, six miles.
Pilot: Give us another hint. We have digital watches.

(After waiting for a long time in a takeoff line)
Pilot: I'm f***ing bored!
Tower: Last aircraft transmitting, identify yourself immediately!
Pilot: I said I was f***ing bored, not f***ing stupid!

(After a DC-10 came in fast, with a very long roll-out)
Tower: American 751, make a hard right turn at the end of the runway, if you are able. If you are not able, take the Guadalupe exit off Highway 101, make a right at the lights, and return to the airport.

Tower: Eastern 702, cleared for takeoff, contact Departure on frequency 124.7.
Pilot: Tower, Eastern 702 switching to Departure. By the way, after we lifted off we saw some kind of dead animal on the far end of the runway.
Tower: Continental 635, cleared for takeoff behind Eastern 702, contact Departure on frequency 124.7. Did you copy that report from Eastern 702?
Pilot: Continental 635, cleared for takeoff, roger; and yes, we copied Eastern. We've already notified our caterers.

In 1992, 30,000 people signed a petition requesting Maui be renamed "Gilligan's Island."

(At Munich International Airport, Germany)

Pilot (in German): Ground, what is our start clearance time?

Tower (in English): If you want an answer you must speak in English.

Pilot (in English): I am a German, flying a German airplane, in Germany. Why must I speak English?

Pilot from another plane (with a British accent): Because you lost the bloody war.

Tower: United 329 heavy, your traffic is a Fokker, one o'clock, three miles, eastbound.

Pilot: Approach, I've always wanted to say this...I've got the little Fokker in sight.

(While taxiing at London Gatwick Airport, US Air 2771, departing for Fort Lauderdale, made a wrong turn and came nose-to-nose with a United 727.)

Tower (irate female): US Air 2771, where the hell are you going? I told you to turn right onto Charlie taxiway! You turned right on Delta! Stop right there. I know it's difficult for you to tell the difference between C and D, but get it right! God! Now you've screwed everything up! It'll take forever to sort this out! You stay right there and don't move till I tell you to! You can expect progressive taxi instructions in about half an hour and I want you to go exactly where I tell you, when I tell you, and how I tell you! You got that, US Air 2771?

Pilot, US Air 2771: Yes, ma'am.

Voice from another plane: Wasn't I married to you once?

*   *   *

WHY ISN'T OUR KIDS MORE INTELLIGENTER?

The North Carolina State Board of Education asked a research firm to study how schools could combat illiteracy. Here was the research firm's response: "The conceptual framework for this evaluation posits a set of determinants of implementation which explains variations in the level of implementation of the comprehensive project."

In Turkey, turkeys are called "the American bird."

U.K. COMICS

Some people prefer the humour with an extra 'u'.

"A lady with a clipboard stopped me in the street the other day. She said, 'Can you spare a few minutes for cancer research?' I said, 'All right, but we're not going to get much done.'"

—**Jimmy Carr**

"I enjoy using the comedy technique of self-deprecation, but I'm not very good at it."

—**Arnold Brown**

"Piracy doesn't kill music. Boy bands do."

— **Ricky Gervais**

"I realized I was dyslexic when I went to a toga party dressed as a goat."

—**Marcus Brigstocke**

"Before birds get sucked into jet engines, do they ever think, 'Is that Rod Stewart in first class?'"

—**Eddie Izzard**

"Last night me and my girlfriend watched three DVDs back-to-back. Luckily I was the one facing the telly."

—**Tim Vine**

"My first job was selling doors, door to door. That was tough. Ding-dong. 'Can I interest you in a…oh, you've got one already. Never mind.'"

—**Bill Bailey**

"When you say, 'Bedtime!' that's not what the child hears. What he hears is, 'Lie down in the dark…for hours…and don't move. I'm locking the door now.'"

—**Dylan Moran**

"I watched a documentary on how ships are kept together. Riveting!"

—**Stewart Francis**

"I'm friends with 25 letters of the alphabet. I don't know why."

—**Chris Turner**

"My mum's so pessimistic, if there was an Olympics for pessimism, she wouldn't fancy her chances."

—**Nish Kumar**

"I was decorating, so I got out my stepladder. I don't get along with my real ladder."

—**Peter Kay**

Use both ears: It's possible to hear corn grow.

"You know you're working class when your TV is bigger than your bookcase."

—**Rob Beckett**

"I was raised as an only child, which really annoyed my sister."

—**Will Marsh**

"It's strange, isn't it. You stand in the middle of a library and yell '*aaaaagghhhh*' and everyone just stares at you. But you do the same thing on an airplane, and everyone joins in."

—**Tommy Cooper**

"Before you judge a man, walk a mile in his shoes. After that, who cares? He's a mile away and you've got his shoes."

—**Billy Connolly**

*   *   *

PROFESSOR 911

Here's an actual exchange between a little boy and a 911 operator:

911: 911 Emergency.

Johnny: Yeah, I need some help.

911: What's the matter?

Johnny: I need help with my math.

911: With your mouth?

Johnny: No, with my math. I have to do it. Will you help me?

911: Sure. (pause) What kind of math do you need help with?

Johnny: I have take-aways.

911: Oh, you gotta do the take-aways?

Johnny: Yeah.

911: All right, what's the problem?

Johnny: Okay. 16…

911: Yeah.

Johnny: …take away 8. Is what?

911: You tell me. How much do you think it is?

Johnny: I dunno. 1?

911: How old are you?

Johnny: I'm only four.

911: Four?

Mom (yells in the background): Johnny, what are you doing?

Johnny (to mom): This policeman's helping me with my math!

Mom: What did I tell you about playing on the phone?

911: Listen to your mother.

Johnny: You said when I need help to call somebody!

Mom: I didn't mean *the police*!

Cosmic question: What's another word for synonym?

DINER LINGO

*Diner waitresses and short-order cooks have a language all their own—
a sort of restaurant jazz, with clever variations on standard menu
themes. Here's a collection of some of our favorites.*

Shingle with a shimmy and a shake: Toast with butter and jam or jelly

Baled hay: Shredded Wheat

Cackle fruit: Eggs

Cats' heads and easy diggins: Biscuits and gravy

Warts: Olives

Why bother, high and dry: A cup of decaf coffee, no sugar and no cream

Bronx vanilla: Garlic

Drag one through Wisconsin, don't cry over it: One cheeseburger, hold the onions

Slab of moo, let 'em chew it: A rare steak

Cops and robbers: Doughnuts and coffee

Mousetrap, give it wings: A grilled-cheese sandwich, and the customer is in a hurry

Irish turkey, give it shoes: An order of corned beef and cabbage to go

Drown the kids: Two hard-boiled eggs

Bucket of cold mud: A bowl of chocolate ice cream

Guess water: Soup

Soup jockey: A waitress

Campers: A party that hogs a booth for too long a time

Looseners: Prunes

Whistleberries: Baked beans

Dog soup/One on the city: A glass of water

Roach cake: Huckleberry pie

Machine oil: Pancake syrup

Pair of drawers: Two cups of coffee

Honeymoon salad: Lettuce, alone (Get it?)

Indiana Jones: Customer who arrives "in the nick of time"— just as the diner's about to close

C-board: A to-go order (in a cardboard container)

Lumber: A toothpick

Whiskey, cremate it: Rye toast

Bloodhounds in the hay: Hot dogs and sauerkraut

In 1992 St. Augustine, FL, passed a law requiring horses in the downtown area to wear diapers.

KANYE THE NUCLEUS

There's having self-confidence…and then there's hip-hop artist Kanye West.

"I am God's vessel. But my greatest pain in life is that I will never be able to see myself perform live."

"I think what Kanye West is going to mean is something similar to what Steve Jobs means. I am undoubtedly, you know, Steve of Internet, downtown, fashion, culture. Period. By a long jump."

"You know, if Michael Jordan can scream at the refs, me as Kanye West, as the Michael Jordan of music, can go and say, 'This is wrong.'"
—*after not winning an award*

"I'm a pop enigma."

"Anyone who doesn't give my album a perfect score is lowering the integrity of their magazine."

"Love your haters—they're your biggest fans."

"Sometimes people write novels and they are so wordy and so self-absorbed. I am not a fan of books. I would never want a book's autograph."

"The Bible had 20, 30, 40, 50 characters in it. You don't think that I would be one of the characters of today's modern Bible?"

"I will go down as the voice of this generation."

"I put a life-sized poster of me on the wall because I was the only person that had me on the wall at that time. And now that a lot of people have me on their wall, I don't really need to do that anymore."

"How could you be me and want to be someone else?"

"When I think of competition I try to create against the past. I think about Michelangelo, Picasso, you know, the pyramids."

"I will be the leader of a company that ends up being worth billions of dollars, because I got the answers. I understand culture. I am the nucleus."

Ignorance *is* bliss: Scientists say that stupid people laugh more than smart people.

YOU CALL THAT ART?

*Ever been in a gallery or museum and seen something that
made you wonder, "Is this really art?" So have we. Is it
art just because someone says it is? You be the judge.*

ARTIST: Mark McGowan

THIS IS ART? This London-based artist has a reputation for odd endeavors, such as pushing a nut with his nose to Prime Minister Tony Blair's office as a protest against the high cost of school tuition, and rolling on the ground for seven kilometers while singing "We Wish You a Merry Christmas" to highlight the work of office cleaners. McGowan caused quite a stir in 2005 when he announced his latest "performance art" piece: He went to Scotland and "keyed" (scratch with a key) 47 cars in the greater Glasgow area, then he took photos of his handiwork.

ARTIST'S STATEMENT: "I do feel guilty, but if I don't do it, someone else will. They should feel glad that they've been involved in the creative process."

UPDATE: It was a hoax, and the press (and we at the BRI) fell for it. McGowan later admitted that he didn't key the cars he photographed, but rather found already keyed cars and pretended like he'd keyed them. You fooled us all, Mark! Good for you!

THE ARTIST: Lee Mingwei

THIS IS ART? The Taiwanese artist cooked a meal and then picked a stranger at random to eat it with.

ARTIST'S STATEMENT: "When people ask me, is it art? I ask them, What is an apple? Usually they give a descriptive answer—it's a fruit, it's red, etc. Then I ask, when do you really know it's an apple? And most people say, when I eat it. That's when you know it's art, when you experience it with your senses, with your memory. That would be a better way to decide it's art—or maybe you don't have to decide at all."

ARTIST: Jessica May, the Rembrandt of Roadkill

THIS IS ART? May, a 24-year-old graduate art student at Southern

Professional clowns register their makeup designs to prevent other clowns from copying them.

Illinois University–Edwardsville, decided that the roadkill lying on the roadsides in and around her Midwestern town needed a little sprucing up. So she dressed dead raccoons in baby clothes, put nail polish on the claws of dead possums, and gave a deer carcass a coat of gold spray paint. May wears gloves when she works on her art, because when she finds the animals, they're "pretty far gone."

ARTIST STATEMENT: "I think of this as my way of paying homage to these animals."

ARTIST: James Robert Ford

THIS IS ART? Ford's piece, entitled *Bogey Ball*, was two years in the making. He displayed it in four London galleries, but was unable to attract a buyer. It now rests on a shelf in his apartment, waiting for someone willing to shell out the asking price of £10,000 (about $18,000). What is it? A golf ball–sized ball of Ford's dried snot. (He's been collecting it since 2003.)

ARTIST'S STATEMENT: "It's a physical record of all the different places I have been and people I've met. And it will be hard to let go, but at the same time, it's hard not to have any money."

ARTIST: Damien Hirst

THIS IS ART? Critics call Hirst, a conceptual artist from Leeds, England, "Mr. Death." Why? He sliced two dead cows in half and placed the pieces in four large clear plastic vats filled with formaldehyde. The "artwork"— *Mother and Child, Divided*—earned him the 1995 Turner Prize, one of the art world's most prestigious awards.

ARTIST'S STATEMENT: "I chose a cow because it's banal. Nothing. Doesn't mean anything. What is the difference between a cow and a burger? Not a lot. I want people to look at cows and feel 'Oh my God,' so then in turn, it makes them feel like burgers."

THE ARTIST: Carlos Capelán

THIS IS ART? This Uruguayan artist attempted to re-create fractal patterns…using his toenail clippings. The pieces were displayed at a London gallery in 2004.

ARTIST STATEMENT: My work "playfully explores issues of self, ego and identity."

The movie *Titanic* takes 40 minutes longer to watch than the actual *Titanic* took to sink.

TWINKIE SUSHI

Take packaged junk food…and turn it into something "gourmet" with one of these weird recipes. (Warning to healthy eaters: DON'T LOOK!)

• **Chicken McBigMac.** Not getting enough meat in your diet? Try this: Buy a McDonald's Big Mac and three McChicken sandwiches. Remove the three bun slices on the Big Mac and replace them with the fried McChicken chicken patties.

• **Coke Seafood Au Gratin.** Combine two tablespoons of butter and two of flour. On low heat, add in a cup of milk and a half cup of grated Parmesan. As it thickens, add a half cup of Coca-Cola. Pour the sauce over a half pound each of cooked shrimp, crab, lobster, and sole. Top with bread crumbs and bake for 20 minutes.

• **Twinkie Sushi.** Cut Twinkies into inch-long pieces and wrap them in strips of green Fruit Roll-Ups. The result looks like sushi. Serve with dried mango strips (which look like pickled ginger).

• **Pringles Candy.** Mix three cups of crushed Pringles potato chips into a melted package of almond bark. Stir in a cup of Spanish peanuts. Pour onto wax paper; cool, dry, and break into pieces.

• **Kool-Aid Pickles.** Soak some dill pickles in a pitcher filled with equal parts vinegar and cherry or tropical punch–flavored Kool-Aid. The result is a pickle that's sweet, sour…and bright red.

• **Peppers with Creamy Sauce.** Remove the seeds from six green (or red) bell peppers that have been cut in half. Melt a package of marshmallows. Fill the peppers with the creamy marshmallow sauce and bake until brown.

• **Funyun Onion Rings.** Grind a bag of Funyuns in a blender. (Funyuns are made from cornmeal that's formed into rings and heavily seasoned with onion powder.) Dip slices of real onions in the Funyun crumbs, then dip in egg whites and cook in a deep-fryer.

• **Maple Bacon Doughnut.** If you like bacon, waffles, doughnuts, and maple syrup, you'll love this simple treat: Take a maple bar (a doughnut with maple frosting, also called a maple long john) and place two strips of crispy bacon on top…and hope you have good health insurance.

I was on the toilet for so long, I finally said, 'I'm getting too old for this sh*t.'" —Doug Benson

DR. DOCTOR

We're not doctors; we just quote fake ones from TV.

"Treating illnesses is why we became doctors. Treating patients is what makes most doctors miserable."

—**Dr. House,** *House, M.D.*

Patient: "You're a kid."

Doogie: "True, but I'm also a genius. If you have a problem with that, I can get you someone who's older but not as smart as me."

—*Doogie Howser, M.D.*

Dr. Fishman: "It looks like he's dead."

Michael: "Just to be clear: *looks* like he's dead, or he *is* dead?"

Dr. Fishman: "It just looks like he's dead. But he's going to be fine."

—*Arrested Development*

"Don't worry, you won't feel a thing....till I jam this down your throat."

—**Dr. Nick,** *The Simpsons*

"My dear girl, I'm a doctor. When I peek, it is in the line of duty."

—**Dr. McCoy,** *Star Trek*

Hurley: "How is it called again, when docs appease their patients?"

Jack: "You mean 'doctor-patient relationship'?"

Hurley: "Yeah, that. You suck at that."

—**LOST**

Dr. Fiscus: "I have a hunch."

Dr. Craig: "So did Quasimodo."

—*St. Elsewhere*

Henry: "I was never very good with my hands."

Radar: "Guess that's why you became a surgeon, huh, sir?"

—**M*A*S*H**

"Each and every one of you residents is going to kill a patient.... Cross your fingers and hope that the guy that you murder is a jackass with no family. Great to see you, kids. All the best!"

—**Dr. Cox,** *Scrubs*

Nurse Piggy: "May I remind you that this is a hospital?"

Dr. Bob: "I'm glad you did. The way these jokes are dying, I thought it was a morgue!"

—*The Muppet Show*

The iVoodoo application lets you use your iPhone as a voodoo doll.

LET'S DO A STUDY!

If you're worried that the really important things in life aren't being researched by our scientists, keep worrying.

• Researchers at Georgetown University found that caterpillars can "shoot" their feces a distance of 40 times their body length.

• A 2002 study in Saudi Arabia concluded that women were responsible for 50% of the car accidents in the country. (Women aren't allowed to drive in Saudi Arabia.)

• In 2002 food industry researchers reported that when children were told they couldn't have junk food, they wanted it even more. Industry spokespeople said that the study showed that children should decide for themselves how much junk food they should eat.

• Researchers at Northwestern University in Illinois used their federal grant money to study female sexuality…by paying female students to watch pornographic films ($75 per film).

• A 2001 study found that 60% of men in the Czech Republic do not buy their own underwear.

• According to a *British Medical Journal* report in 2003, Korean researchers have proven that karaoke is bad for your health.

• Scientists at Birkbeck College in England discovered that, like humans, dogs can "catch" yawns from people. A 29-dog study found that after they made eye contact with a yawning person, 21 of the dogs yawned as well.

• University of London doctoral students Sarah Carter and Kristina Aström discovered that as male college professors ascend the academic ladder—from lecturer to senior lecturer to tenured professor— they are more likely to grow beards.

• In 2005 linguists from the University of Barcelona discovered that rats have difficulty telling the difference between Japanese spoken backward and Dutch spoken backward.

• A joint study conducted by the Gloucestershire Royal Foundation Trust

---

"Arnold Schwarzenegger looks like a condom full of walnuts." —Clive James

and the Sword Swallowers Association International (really) concluded that sword swallowers were at high risk for sore throats, cuts in the esophagus, and internal bleeding, especially if they were distracted while swallowing swords.

• In the 2004 study "Fragmentation of Rods by Cascading Cracks," French physicists Basile Audoly and Sebastien Neukirch looked into why when dry spaghetti is bent, it breaks into lots of smaller pieces, instead of cleanly in half.

• After studying overweight children playing with weighted and unweighted blocks, researchers at Indiana State University concluded that lifting weights burns more calories than *not* lifting weights. (They had to do a study to figure that out?) The scientists plan to use the findings to help fight obesity by manufacturing teddy bears with three-pound weights inside.

• In 2005 John Mainstone and Thomas Parnell of the University of Queensland (Australia) determined that congealed tar flows through a funnel at a rate of about one drop per nine years. How did they know? They'd been monitoring the tar for 78 years.

• In 1999 Harvard University conducted a study called "Gorillas in our Midst." Test subjects were instructed to watch people pass a basketball back and forth. Meanwhile, the subjects failed to notice a person in a gorilla suit walking around the room. Researchers' conclusion: When we're paying too close attention to one thing, we tend to overlook what's going on right around us. (Even a person in a gorilla costume.)

• Cognitive psychologist Daniel Oppenheimer of Princeton wrote a study arguing that short, simple words make writers seem more intelligent than long words do. The name of Oppenheimer's study: "Consequences of Erudite Vernacular Utilized Irrespective of Necessity."

*   *   *

COMIC STRIP WISDOM

Calvin: "People think it must be fun to be a super genius, but they don't realize how hard it is to put up with all the idiots in the world."

Hobbes: "Isn't your zipper supposed to be in the *front* of your pants?"

Tom Cruise's daughter's Suri's name means "horse mackerels" in Italian.

BENNIFER'S ILL GIG

Most really bad movies die a quick death in the theaters and then gather dust on video store shelves. But not this one.

RECIPE FOR DISASTER

- Take two A-list movie stars: Ben Affleck and Jennifer Lopez.
- Add a torrid off-screen love affair that doesn't translate into onscreen chemistry.
- Add a dollop of media hype about how great the movie's going to be.
- Mix in a vulgar, inane script.

Stir it all together and you have 2003's *Gigli* (pronounced *zheelie*), a movie that rivals *Ishtar* and *Battlefield Earth* for the title of Hollywood's biggest flop. Good news: You don't have to see the picture—you can be entertained just by reading the scathing reviews. Here are some samples.

"Looking for something to praise in *Gigli* is like digging for rhinestones in a dung heap."
    —**Northwest Herald**

"There is not one iota of dramatic weight to it, and so we just sit, slack-jawed, as *Gigli* unfolds, a cinematic train wreck of distinguished proportions."
    —*Entertainment Today*

"Larry and Ricki eventually climb between the sheets in a scene that is insulting to the sexuality of all living creatures, from plankton on up."
    —*Boston Globe*

"If you're going to skip one film this year—make it *Gigli*."
    —*Talking Pictures*

"*Gigli* looks like a project that was intended for appreciation by precisely two people in the entire universe: Ben Affleck and Jennifer Lopez. For their sake, I hope they buy a lot of tickets."
    —**EFilmCritic.com**

"*Gigli* is a rigli, rigli bad movie."
    —**Mercurynews.com**

"*Gigli* is so unrelentingly bad that people may want to see it just as a bonding experience; viewers (read: victims) will want to comfort each other afterwards."
    —*San Francisco Examiner*

"This is a film that inspires hatred."
    —**FilmThreat.com**

The children's song "La Cucaracha" is about a cockroach who ruins his life by smoking pot.

"Fifty minutes into this bomb, one character yells, 'I'm getting tired of this!' One audience member yelled back, 'Me too!'"

—**CrankyCritic.com**

"For two hours, not a single hair moved on Ben's head—not even when every hair in the audience was growing in the direction of the exit's welcoming glow."

—**Movie Juice**

"Lopez even gives a long, carefully detailed speech about how to not only gouge out someone's eye, but to remove the memory of everything they've ever seen. Which, by the end of the movie, wasn't starting to seem so bad."

—*The Star-Ledger*

"Test audiences reportedly balked at the film's happy ending and wanted Gigli and Ricki to die bloody deaths. And they say critics are harsh."

—*Rolling Stone*

"Not helping things is Lopez's Betsy-Wetsy lisp that transforms a line like 'brutal street thug' into 'bruel threet fug.'"

—**Film Freak Central**

"As awkward as the word itself. I suggest you spell *Gigli* backwards so it sounds like 'ill gig.'"

—**Critic Doctor**

"If miscasting was a crime, *Gigli* would be proof of a felony."

—**CNN**

"How on Earth did director Martin Brest envision this film? As *Chasing Amy* meets *Rain Man* meets *Pulp Fiction*? Did anyone think that sounded like a winning combination?"

—*Chicago Tribune*

"The rare movie that never seems to take off, but also never seems to end."

—*USA Today*

"Mr. Affleck and Ms. Lopez's combined fees reportedly ran close to $25 million, and they earn their money by hogging as much screen time as possible and uttering some of the lamest dialogue ever committed to film."

—*The New York Times*

"It wasn't good, and we got buried."

—**Ben Affleck**

Double relief: Experts say that a belly laugh can help relieve constipation.

THE DUMBEST CROOKS

A rogue's gallery of our all-time funniest stupid criminals.

HI HITLER, HOW YA DOIN'! White supremacist Donald Leroy Evans of Fort Lauderdale, Florida, filed a motion in court (he was facing murder charges) to be allowed to wear his Ku Klux Klan robe during his trial. He also wanted to be referred to as "the honorable and respected Hi Hitler." Why? Evans thought Hitler's subjects were chanting "Hi, Hitler" instead of "Heil, Hitler."

NOT ALL THAT SPARKLES IS DIAMONDS. In 2009 a would-be jewel thief entered the Black Diamond Company in Salt Lake City, Utah. Armed with an ice pick, he ordered two employees: "Give me your precious gems!" The employees explained that Black Diamond doesn't sell diamonds or any other precious gems—they sell rock-climbing gear. The robber stole several computers instead.

EAU DE STUPID. In 2008 Michael Kaminski of Akron, Ohio, attempted to rob two men in the parking lot using a gun shaped cologne dispenser. Bad move: One of the "victims" was a martial arts expert who easily pinned Kaminski to the ground. Adding insult to injury, the cologne bottle broke and spilled all over Kaminski, who spent a fragrant night in jail.

SHOULDA SAW IT COMING. In 1996 Karen Lee Joachimi of Lake City, Florida, tried to rob a Howard Johnson's with an electric chain saw. Her chances would have been better had she plugged in the chain saw first.

THE TWO STOOGES. Regan Reti was facing jail time. Tiranara White was facing sentencing. The two men—handcuffed together after their respective hearings—were awaiting transport back to the Hastings, New Zealand, jail when they decided to make a break for it. The connected convicts darted across the street and encountered a lamppost. One man went to the right, the other to the left...and they slammed into each other on the other side. Each blamed the other for going the wrong way. Both were returned to the jail.

It is illegal to die in the U.K.'s Houses of Parliament, or to enter wearing a suit of armor.

DUMMIES. Thieves broke into a cell phone store in Moriela, Mexico, in 2009 and made off with some hollow plastic cell phone replicas that were on display. Employees told police that the burglars passed up dozens of real cell phones just a few feet away and stole the fake ones.

AT LEAST HE MADE A CLEAN GETAWAY. Dennis Sullivan, 23, of Manassas, Virginia, ran up to the driver of what he must have thought was an armored car, pulled out a sawed-off shotgun, and told the driver, "Give it up!" Confused, the driver replied, "What?" Sullivan grabbed what he thought was a bag of money and ran off. The armored car turned out to be a linen truck. And Sullivan, who was later arrested for armed robbery, had made off with a bag of mop heads.

NOT VERY SHARPIE. In Carroll, Iowa, two friends—Matthew McNelly, 23, and Joey Miller, 20—decided to break into the apartment of a man who was allegedly involved with Miller's girlfriend. Instead of wearing masks, they used a permanent marker to scribble black ink all over each other's faces. After failing to break into the apartment, they drove away. When police (who were called by a neighbor) pulled them over, McNelly and Miller were arrested for attempted robbery. Quipped police chief Jeff Cayler: "We're very skilled investigators and the black faces gave them right away."

DON'T BE SO HASTY. In August 1992, Donald Murray was on trial in Gastonia, North Carolina. When the jury retired to the deliberation room to decide his fate, he got so scared they would return with a guilty verdict that he jumped up and ran out of the courtroom, successfully escaping. A few moments later, the jury returned with its decision: not guilty. An arrest warrant was issued for Murray.

MMM...PIZZA. In 2009 police responded to a robbery call at an Italian restaurant in Croatia. The cops entered and asked the employees which way the suspect went. A worker pointed to a man named Ante Baranovic, who was sitting in a booth gobbling up a slice of pizza. "I know I should have run," he said as the officers were arresting him, "but this pizza is good!"

JOE UNCOOL. "This has got to rank as one of the worst attempted jailbreaks ever," said a prison official in Albany, Isle of Wight, England.

No joke: Studies show that 80% of adult laughter is unconnected to any joke or funny situation.

The first problem: The perpetrator tried to break into the wrong prison; his cousin—whom he was trying to free—was incarcerated at a prison in a neighboring town. Second, the man's weapon was a squirt gun. Third, the man—who tried to no avail to kick down a door—was wearing a Snoopy costume. "He wasn't too inconspicuous," said the official.

I SAID TO BRING THE CLOWN CAR! A man walked into a Chase Bank in Chicago wearing a clown mask with a big red nose and red hair. Brandishing a toy machine gun, he handed a demand note to a teller, who filled up a bag with money. The clown ran out of the bank and tried to climb onto his getaway vehicle: a bicycle. It took him a minute or so to get going (the mask, toy gun, and bag of money made it difficult). That was all the time a police officer needed to chase down the clown and tackle him.

THIS PLACE IS LIKE A PRISON! Carly Houston, 29, was hauled into the Naperville, Illinois, police station in 2010 after she threatened a taxi driver and refused to calm down when police attempted to reason with her. She was arrested for disorderly conduct. At the station, officers informed Houston that she could make a phone call to someone who could come in and post her bail. So who did Houston call? 911. "I'm trapped! You gotta get someone in here to get me out of here!" One more charge was added: making a false emergency call.

*   *   *

COP TALK

Car Fisher: A criminal who steals things from parked, unlocked cars

Boozer Cruiser: A bicycle or other non-car vehicle used by someone who's lost their driver's license due to a D.U.I.

Loser Cruiser: An ex-police car, still painted in police colors but lacking lights and other police gear, driven by a civilian wannabe cop

Mirror Meeting: When two patrol cars park driver's side to driver's side so that the officers can exchange information

NBSS: A crime with witnesses but no one willing to testify ("Nobody Saw Sh*t")

Harpo Marx and George Burns enjoyed golfing together in their underwear.

TOWN NAME MISHAPS

Our favorite goofs are the ones that stick around for hundreds of years.

BANGOR, MAINE. When settlers in the area decided to incorporate and become a town in 1791, the Reverend Seth Noble talked them into calling the town Sunbury, then went to Boston to deliver the petition himself (Maine was then part of Massachusetts). He happened to be whistling a hymn titled "Bangor" when the court official asked him what he wanted to name the town. Thinking the official was asking about the hymn, he replied, "Bangor."

PEKIN, ILLINOIS. Named in 1830 by one Mrs. Nathaniel Cromwell, who 1) wasn't much of a speller, and 2) was apparently convinced that Pekin was exactly on the opposite side of the globe from Peking, China. (She wasn't much of a geographer, either.)

SELMER, TENNESSEE. Named by one P. H. Thrasher, who wanted to name his town in honor of Selma, Alabama. (Apparently he was just as bad a speller as Mrs. Cromwell.)

CLEVELAND, OHIO. The town was surveyed in 1796 by a man named Moses Cleaveland and named in his honor by his employees. So why not Cleaveland? In 1831 the editor of the fledgling *Cleveland Advertiser* newspaper realized the town's name was too long to fit on the paper's masthead, so he dropped the "a," and it's been spelled Cleveland ever since.

CALISTOGA, CALIFORNIA. In the early 1850s, Sam Brannan, publisher of San Francisco's *California Star* newspaper, learned of a natural hot spring in the Napa Valley north of San Francisco. He bought up more than 2,000 acres of the surrounding land and drew up plans for a resort town and a health spa fed by the spring. He wanted to model the town after Saratoga Springs, New York, and one night over dinner with friends (and after a few too many drinks), he gushed that the town would one day be "the Calistoga of Sarafornia!"

AUTHOR VS. AUTHOR

The pen truly is mightier than the sword.

Mary McCarthy on Lillian Hellman: "Every word she writes is a lie, including 'and' and 'the.'"

Robert Louis Stevenson on Walt Whitman: "A large, shaggy dog just unchained scouring the beaches of the world and baying at the moon."

Stephen King on Stephenie Meyer: "They both write for young people, but the real difference is that Jo Rowling is a terrific writer and Meyer can't write worth a darn."

Harold Bloom on J. K. Rowling: "If you cannot be persuaded to read anything better, Rowling will have to do."

D. H. Lawrence on Herman Melville: "Nobody is more clown-ish, more clumsy and sententiously in bad taste."

Truman Capote on Jack Kerouac: "That's not writing, that's typing."

Dorothy Parker on Ayn Rand: "*Atlas Shrugged* is not a novel to be tossed aside lightly. It should be thrown with great force."

Virginia Woolf on James Joyce: "*Ulysses* is the work of a queasy undergraduate scratching his pimples."

Salman Rushdie on Dan Brown: "Do not start me on *The Da Vinci Code*, a novel so bad that it gives bad novels a bad name."

Ralph Waldo Emerson on Jane Austen: "Vulgar in tone, sterile in artistic invention, imprisoned in the wretched conventions of English society, without genius, wit, or knowledge of the world. Never was life so pinched and narrow."

Mark Twain on Jane Austen: "Every time I read *Pride and Prejudice*, I want to dig her up and hit her over the skull with her own shin-bone."

William Faulkner on Mark Twain: "A hack writer who would not have been considered fourth rate in Europe, who tricked out a few of the old proven sure-fire literary skeletons with sufficient local color to intrigue the superficial and the lazy."

Most impossible band name to pronounce: an American dance-rock band called !!!.

OOPS!

*Everyone loves tales of outrageous blunders, especially
when they happen to someone else. So go ahead
and feel superior for a few minutes.*

HERE COMES TRUFFLE

One Sunday in 2014, a restaurant patron (unnamed in press reports) was having brunch at the Equinox in Washington, DC, when she saw a complimentary snack on a display plate under a glass dome. She picked it up and took a bite, then put the rest of it on her bread plate and took it to her table. Just then, the restaurant's owner, Ellen Kassoff Gray, walked up and explained to the woman that this was no ordinary snack, nor was it complimentary—it was in fact a rare White Alba truffle. And Gray was charging customers $20 for a single shaving. Estimated cost of the woman's bite: $300. Adding insult to injury, "she didn't like the taste," said Gray, "and suggested the chef salvage the unbitten part." That didn't happen. The woman wasn't charged, but the pricey truffle was a total loss.

NEXT THEY'LL MOVE TO THE TOWN OF HIGHWATER

Several families on the coast of Washington lost their homes to rising tides, battering winds, and a storm surge in late 2014. But they can't say they weren't warned—nearly 200 homes there have washed away into the ocean in the last century. "I knew it was going to happen sooner or later," said unlucky homeowner Ray Miller, "but I had hoped it wasn't this soon." One thing that might have tipped him off: the area's nickname. It's known as Washaway Beach.

PLANTED

Ronald Podlaski is a Portland, Maine, artist who calls himself "RookSye." One night in 2014, he drank a few beers and decided to prank a friend by entering her third-story apartment through the window. The inebriated man went up the fire escape and then climbed into what he thought was his friend's window, but it wasn't even her apartment. Turns out it wasn't even her building. (She was in El Salvador with her fiancé at the time.) The window belonged to a florist shop, and just as Podlaski realized that he was in the wrong place, the burglar alarm went off. He tried to escape but tripped over a "vine-like material" and then toppled out of the third-story window, taking a candelabra with him. When he came to on the ground, he had a sprained wrist... and there were two police officers standing over him. At first, Podlaski refused to give his real name, only saying, "I am RookSye." The cops arrested him, believing he'd tried to burgle the shop, but let him go the next day when they realized he wasn't a criminal, but merely—as Podlaski himself described it—"foolish."

ACCIDENTAL TEETOTALERS

The town of Hanover, Manitoba, had been "dry" since the 1800s; the sale of alcohol was illegal there. Then, in 2014, a proposal was submitted to let the townspeople vote to end the prohibition. The first step: town leaders needed to track down the original law…but they couldn't locate it. So they hired a law firm to sift through the town records. They couldn't find it, either. Reason: it turned out that there never was an official alcohol ban in Hanover—everyone had just assumed there was for more than a century.

KEYLESS EXIT

It was Guy Fawkes Night in November 2014, and the people of Alexandra, New Zealand, were celebrating loudly. That's why no one heard Brian and Mollieanne Smith honking their car horn. They were stuck inside their new Mazda3 hatchback, which was parked in their garage. The couple, both in their sixties, didn't have the key fob with them. And the doors were locked. They tried using a car jack to break the window, but that didn't work. So the Smiths sat trapped in their car for 13 hours. When a neighbor discovered and freed them the next morning, they were near death. That's when Brian discovered the manual locking mechanism on the door. "Once I found out how simple it was," he sheepishly admitted, "I kicked myself that I did not find the way out sooner."

KOOKY KAMPAIGN

In 2015 the Krispy Kreme doughnut chain posted an announcement on its U.K. Facebook page for upcoming events at a Krispy Kreme in Hull, England. Shortly after the post went up, hundreds of the page's 200,000 fans commented that it probably wasn't a good idea to abbreviate the "Krispy Kreme Klub." Here's what was posted:

> Why not come and join us in our Hull store during the holiday with the children for our fun activities…Funday Monday, Colouring Tuesday, KKK Wednesday, and Face Painting Thursday!

Once company officials realized that "KKK" is the name of the American white supremacist organization, they deleted the post, apologized profusely, and promised to never do it again.

For each word you speak, you spray 2.5 microscopic droplets of saliva.

FUNNY TWEETS

*If you spend time on Twitter, you know how difficult it is to be clever
in the original format of 140 characters or less. Yet plenty of writers manage to do it.
Here are a few examples of how to be funny and brief.*

"I always get confused by the phrase 'stop, drop, and roll.' The 'stop' part doesn't belong. That's just extra time for being on fire."
—**Jon Friedman**

"I hope you all like the haircut I gave Miley Cyrus."
—**Helen Keller**

"Some people assume that I think I'm something special. Look, I'm just a regular guy telling people what I think. Like Jesus, I guess."
—**Ricky Gervais**

"Something that's been bugging me for years: the sequel to *Scooby Doo* should have been called *Scooby Doo Deux*."
—**Michael Ian Black**

"My mechanic just told me I could pick my car up at 5 p.m. and that they 'might be having a few beers there after work.' OMG is this a date?!"
—**KatyDidSays**

"At what age does Ryan Gosling have to change his name to Ryan Goose?"
—**Megan Amran**

"I love NY and its inhabitants. I could wander the street licking people's faeces just to convey my affection. Sorry, I meant faces. Either."
—**Russell Brand**

"Obama sobs as he signs Theres No More Ice Cream Act. 'Its really all gone?!' he cries. Biden winks to crowd as he sneaks up w/ giant sundae."
—**Horton Atonto**

"The girl kept her eyes on the ground as the cashier rang up her cat litter & tampons. 'I have a lot of internet friends,' she whispered."
—**Mary Charlene**

"I love that moment when you make eye contact with a dog and he slyly smiles and nods to let you know he's secretly a tiny man in a dog suit."
—**Mike Henry**

"Let me get this straight—we can put a man on the moon but we can't replace the sound of my toilet flushing with a rimshot?"
—**Conan O'Brien**

THE MAN UPSTAIRS

*In death, as in real estate, sometimes the only thing
that matters is location, location, location.*

DECEASED: Richard Poncher, a businessman and social acquaintance of baseball legend Joe DiMaggio

DETAILS: DiMaggio married actress Marilyn Monroe in January 1954, but the marriage lasted only nine months. That fall, while DiMaggio was in New York, he ran into Poncher. "You want to buy two crypts?" the slugger asked. Now that DiMaggio was splitting from Monroe, he wanted to sell the two aboveground burial spaces he'd bought for Monroe and himself in the wall of a mausoleum at Westwood Memorial Park, a cemetery in Los Angeles.

GOING MY WAY: Poncher agreed to buy the crypts, but he did it only as a favor to his friend, nothing more. Then when Monroe died in 1962, DiMaggio had her interred in another crypt in the same wall, which turned out to be directly beneath one of the crypts he'd sold to Poncher eight years before.

Suddenly realizing he'd be spending eternity next to Hollywood's biggest sex symbol, Poncher decided to make the most of it. He took the crypt above Marilyn's for himself and gave the other one to his wife, Elsie. Before he died in 1986, he made one last request. "He said, 'If I croak, if you don't put me upside down over Marilyn, I'll haunt you the rest of my life,'" Elsie told the *Los Angeles Times* in 2009. She passed the request on to the funeral director, perhaps thinking he'd laugh it off. He didn't: "I was standing right there, and he turned him over," Elsie told the *Times*. Poncher has been lying facedown over Marilyn ever since.

UPDATE: How long he'll stay there is anyone's guess. The plaque on his crypt reads, "To the man who gave us everything and more," and he may not be done giving. In 2009 Elsie listed his crypt on eBay, hoping to sell it for enough money to pay off the $1.6-million mortgage on her Beverly Hills home. An anonymous bidder in Japan made the winning bid of $4.6 million, only to back out later. A second auction attracted no bids at all. (If the crypt ever does sell, Elsie plans to move Poncher over to her crypt, so he'll still be in the neighborhood.)

A "Motown" is a poker term for 2 jacks and 2 fives—or jacks on fives. (Get it? Jackson Fives!)

A'S HOLE GETTING DEEPER

Some of our all-time favorite real newspaper headlines.

JUDGES APPEAR MORE LENIENT ON CRACK COCAINE

GARBAGE TRUCK LANDS ON SATURN

Rangers' Hamilton to Get Shot for Sore Knee

11 HIGH STUDENTS SCORE PERFECT GRADE

MOUSTACHIOED HORSE EVADES BARBERS

Material in Diapers Could Help Make the Deserts Bloom

ACADEMICS TO DISSECT BOB DYLAN AT NY CONFERENCE

Something Went Wrong in Jet Crash, Expert Says

Texans Support Death Penalty, But Only for the Guilty

Homeless Man Under House Arrest

SEVEN TESTIFY TODDLER LOOKED HOT

Climber Who Cut Off Arm to Escape Speaking at MSU

Arson Suspect is Held in Fire

DEATH IS NATION'S TOP KILLER

LEBANON WILL TRY BOMBING SUSPECTS

Hooker Named Lay Person of the Year

Nuns Forgive Break-In, Assault Suspect

A's Hole Keeps Getting Deeper

OLD SCHOOL PILLARS ARE REPLACED BY ALUMNI

19 FEET BROKEN IN POLE VAULT

Kicking Baby Considered to Be Healthy

Dealers Will Hear Car Talk At Noon

PEDESTRIAN DEATHS LARGELY FLAT IN U.S., MARYLAND

Ancient Blonde Corpses Raise Questions

STUDY REVEALS THOSE WITHOUT INSURANCE DIE MORE OFTEN

Officials Warn Clams, Oysters Can Carry Virus

In Japan, the TV show *Jersey Shore* was called *The New Jersey Life of the Macaroni Rascals*.

TERRIBLE TYPOS

The devil's in the detales…er, details.

• In 2012 a group called Citizens Opposed to the Library Project was fighting a tax referendum to build a new library in Franklin, Indiana. In submitting their financial disclosure documents, they made one little mistake: They listed their name as "Citizens Apposed to the Library Project." Said a pro-library spokesman, "That proves our point right there."

• In a *Reader's Digest* headline, the "R" in "Rights" was replaced by a "T," so readers saw "Movers & Shakers in Women's Tights."

• In 2010 a clerk at the Chicago Board of Elections entered Illinois Green Party gubernatorial candidate Rich Whitney into electronic voting machines, but accidentally left out the "n." Result: Headlines across the country read "Rich Whitey Running for Illinois Governor!" (He lost.)

• A graphic designer at the *Pittsburgh Tribune-Review* attempted to create a reflection effect on the words "Suit Yourself" to accompany an article about summer swimsuits. Because of the reflection, the "u" in *suit* ended up looking more like an "h." Before the mistake was caught, more than 40,000 copies were printed that featured a bikini-clad supermodel standing next to a headline that appeared to say "Sh*t Yourself."

• In 2012 Mitt Romney's presidential campaign released an iPhone app called "With Mitt." At the top of every page it said "A Better Amercia."

• Realtor Shirley Hunsperger submitted an ad for a new home in Mount Shasta, California, with a "huge deck for entertaining," but when it appeared in the newspaper, the "e" in *deck* had been replaced with an "i."

• In 2003 Sunrise Elementary School in Fort Worth, Texas, changed its name to Sunrise-McMillian Elementary in honor of its first-ever teacher, Mary McMillan. In 2012 one of McMillan's relatives alerted the school that an extra "i" had been added to her name. (It's *McMillan*, not *McMillian*.) Embarrassed school officials fixed the sign out front, but admitted that it would take a few years to replace the rest of the signage— along with all the stationery, business cards, library cards, visitor's passes, spelling bee award certificates…

What were *buckets*, *crates*, *flivvers*, and *heaps*? 1920s slang terms for cars.

WHEN AUDIENCES ATTACK

It's not really funny when comedians and audiences
turn on each other. (Well, sometimes it is.)

THE PHILADELPHIA EXPERIMENT. In 2006 comedian Bill
Burr was part of a stand-up show organized by morning radio
shock jocks Opie and Anthony, whose rowdy fans filled Philadelphia's Susquehanna Bank Center amphitheater. By the time it was Burr's
turn to go on, the crowd had already booed two comedians off the stage.
And these comics, Irish-American tough guy Robert Kelly and Philadelphia native Dom Irrera, were no pushovers. Knowing it was pointless to
try to do his usual act, Burr opened with, "F*** all you people! I hope
you all f***ing die and I hope those f***ing Eagles never win the Super
Bowl!" For the next 12 minutes, Burr dropped an atomic f-bomb on
everything holy to Philadelphians: their beloved sports teams, the Liberty
Bell, the statue of Rocky. He even called their town so irrelevant that
"terrorists will never bomb you." By the end of his set, Burr had laid waste
to the City of Brotherly Love…and won them over. Someone in the
audience made a cell phone video of the set and uploaded it to YouTube,
where it became a viral hit, jumpstarting his career.

KRAMER'S DARK SIDE. Michael Richards isn't a seasoned stand-up
comedian—he's the comic actor who starred as Kramer on *Seinfeld*. But in
2006 he decided to give stand-up a try, and his inexperience in handling
crowds became national news. During a set at the Laugh Factory in
Hollywood, a few people in the audience told Richards they didn't think
he was funny. Instead of making fun of their clothes or their need for
attention—typical comic responses to heckling—Richards went on an
unhinged, racist rant, calling his hecklers the N-word several times. Once
cell phone video of the incident spread, Richards had to go into full-on
damage control and apologize for his actions. Richards has never done
stand-up again.

CHAPELLE'S NO-SHOW. When Funny or Die announced its inaugural Oddball Festival tour in 2013, it created shock waves by landing Dave
Chappelle as the headliner. Since abruptly quitting his sketch comedy

TV show, *Chappelle's Show*, in 2005, Chappelle popped into a comedy club from time to time but was essentially retired. When the Oddball Festival played Hartford, Connecticut, members of the audience started shouting catchphrases from *Chappelle's Show* as he took the stage, before he could even begin his set. When the crowd ignored his requests to stop yelling, Chappelle took out a pack of cigarettes, stopped doing his set, and told the crowd that when his contractually obligated time was up, he was leaving the stage. Chappelle then proceeded to kill time by reading a book and making fun of the audience until his set was over. While many fans fretted about how audiences would treat Chappelle on the rest of the tour, his other shows went off without a hitch. He said he would never go back to Hartford ("Not even for f***ing gas"). But he did. He made a surprise return to Hartford for the 2014 edition of the festival. This time, he got a standing ovation.

GIRL TALK. Joe Rogan was performing in a Las Vegas theater in 2006. A table of drunken women began to reply personally to all of his jokes, but the tipping point came after Rogan made fun of the movie *March of the Penguins*. One of the women yelled out, "Aww, I love penguins!" Rogan responded by making fun of her voice, angering the woman enough to yell, "You don't have a girlfriend!" After some more insults back and forth, the woman once again accused Rogan of not having a girlfriend. And that's when Rogan began a minute-long rant. "Don't get confused on your place in the big picture. I'm not saying I'm anything special, but guess what, you're not either. We're all humans. You're pretty now, but you're only, like, what, 24? Talk to me when you're 44, and you're desperate and drunk." The crowd went wild, the heckler backed off, and the woman piped down.

MAKING HIS MARK. One night in the early 2000s comedian Jeff Garlin was performing at Caroline's in New York. His *Curb Your Enthusiasm* co-star Cheryl Hines, and a friend, came in to watch his set. A heckler started talking back to Garlin, derailing his routine. That's when another heckler with a thick Irish accent started yelling at the first heckler to quiet down. The first heckler apologized and quieted himself. "You are no match for this man," Garlin told the initial heckler, revealing that the second heckler was Hines's friend...Robin Williams.

"Power corrupts. Absolute power is kind of neat." —John Lehman, U.S. Secretary of the Navy

PASTEUR CURED RABBIS

…and other real answers given on real tests by real students, collected by their poor, poor teachers and passed along to us.

"Sir Francis Drake circumcised the world with a 100-foot clipper."

"Ancient Egypt was inhabited by mummies and they all wrote in hydraulics."

"The Magna Carta provided that no man should be hanged twice for the same offense."

"The Civil War was between China and Pakistan."

"A myth is a female moth."

"Miguel de Cervantes wrote *Donkey Hote*."

"The colonists won the War and no longer had to pay for taxis."

"Ben Franklin discovered electricity by rubbing two cats backward and declared, 'A horse divided against itself cannot stand.'"

"To change centimeters to meters you take out centi."

"Lincoln's mother died in infancy, and he was born in a log cabin which he built with his own hands."

"In the Olympic games, Greeks ran races, jumped, hurled the biscuits, and threw the java."

"The sun never set on the British Empire because the British Empire is in the East and the sun sets in the West."

"Louis Pasteur discovered a cure for rabbis."

"Lincoln went to the theater and got shot in his seat by one of the actors in a moving picture show."

"The French Revolution was accomplished before it happened and catapulted into Napoleon."

"Homer was not written by Homer but by another man of that name."

"Nero was a cruel tyranny who would torture his subjects by playing the fiddle to them."

"Gravity was invented by Isaac Walton. It is chiefly noticeable in the autumn when the apples are falling off the trees."

Pot head: Kevin Shelley cracked a world-record 46 toilet seats over his head in one minute.

ECCENTRIC ARTISTS

*True story: While compiling articles for the original book, Uncle John's faithful minion
Jay could only use nine of his fingers. That's because Jay has the strange habit
of compulsively chewing gum while he writes, and he was so into his work
while replacing a piece of Trident that he bit his right ring finger…hard.
How hard? The finger became infected and Jay lost the fingernail,
so he had to wear a big bandage on his finger. Now that we have
that embarrassing confession out of the way, here are some
other creative geniuses with some odd working habits.*

• American painter **James Whistler** believed that art should concentrate
on the proper arrangement of colors, not on realism. Putting that theory to
work, he once dyed a dish of rice pudding green so it would better match
the green walls of his dining room.

• Nineteenth-century French poet **Gerard de Nerval** kept a pet lobster.
He liked to take it on walks around Paris on a leash made out of ribbon.
Nerval defended his choice of pet, saying, "He was quiet and serious, knew
the secrets of the sea, and did not bark."

• German composer **Gustav Mahler** was obsessed with death from a
young age, and wrote his first funeral dirge at the age of six. Decades later
and well into his career, he noticed that Schubert, Beethoven, and many
other composers had only lived long enough to compose nine symphonies.
Mahler concluded it was unlucky to write more than eight, so he called his
ninth symphony "A Song Cycle" instead of a symphony. It didn't work.
Just after completing the "cycle," Mahler died of strep throat at age 50.

• Another German composer, **Robert Schumann**, claimed he got all his
musical ideas from two imaginary musicians named Eusebius and Florestan.

• When she was a child, *Little Women* author **Louisa May Alcott** developed an intense crush on her neighbor, author Ralph Waldo Emerson. She
wrote dozens of love letters to him, but never sent them. Instead, she sat in
a tall walnut tree outside of his house in the middle of the night, singing.

• Animal instincts: **Robert Louis Stevenson** had a hobby of reading the

Bible out loud to sheep. Irish poet **William Butler Yeats** liked to try to hypnotize hens.

• **Charles Dickens** is said to have walked 20 miles every day. He also always arranged his bed so it faced north-south, and he liked to touch objects three times for good luck.

• Many artists have a series of rituals they go through to get inspired. Eighteenth-century German poet **Friedrich von Schiller** could write only with his feet resting on a block of ice. He also needed to inhale the fumes given off by rotting apples.

• Poet **Gertrude Stein** could write only while seated in the driver's seat of her Ford, which she nicknamed "Godiva." And she wrote only on random scraps of paper she'd found.

• To relax after he finished *Gulliver's Travels* in 1724, **Jonathan Swift** wrote a book called *Human Ordure*. The book, a thorough exploration and appreciation of poop, was published under the pen name "Dr. Sh*t."

• French author **Alexandre Dumas** (*The Count of Monte Cristo*) started every day the same way: He ate an apple at 7 a.m. under the Arc de Triomphe.

• When American novelist **Anne Rivers Siddons** (*Peachtree Road*) is ready to start writing a new novel, she reportedly gets in the mood by surrounding herself with a nest made of papers. Then she walks into walls, as if in a trance.

• **Henry David Thoreau** claimed that he could communicate with animals: "I once talked to the woodchuck in quasi forest lingo, baby talk, at any rate in a conciliatory tone, and thought that I had some influence on him."

*　　*　　*

HUH?

From a letter to the editor in the *Arkansas Democrat* (2007): "As you know, Daylight Saving Time started a month earlier this year. You would think that members of Congress would have considered the warming effect that an extra hour of daylight would have on our climate. Or did they?"

Yum! Pork-stuffed crickets are a popular snack in Burma.

CURTAINS!

*When you go to the theater, you expect to see a well-rehearsed play,
but that's not always what you get. Sometimes actors forget
lines or the scenery falls and the cast has to find a way to
keep the show going...sometimes with hilarious results.*

A KNOCKOUT PERFORMANCE

During a performance of *Rumpelstiltskin* at the Afternoon Players of Salt Lake City, the actor playing Rumpelstiltskin made an unscripted leaping exit—and knocked himself out on a door frame. The actress playing the Princess had no idea that he'd been hurt. According to the plot, the Princess has to guess Rumpelstiltskin's name by midnight or he'll take away her baby. The actress sat onstage and waited for the Rumpelstiltskin character to reappear. When he didn't, she began to improvise.

"I wonder where that funny little man is?" she asked, loudly. "That funny little man was supposed to come back here and I was supposed to guess his name." Still no Rumpelstiltskin. While she improvised, the actors backstage were frantically trying to think of what to do. Finally two of them put on silly hats and ran onstage. "You know that funny little man?" one of them said, in a very meaningful way. "Well, he's *never* coming back."

The Princess's eyes widened in horror. "You mean, he's *never* coming back?"

"No. He's *never* coming back." The three stood there in dead silence. Finally the other actor spoke. "But he told us to tell you that he knew you had guessed his name. It's Rumpelstiltskin. And now you can keep your baby! Hooray!" Curtain down. End of play.

"IT'S A MIRACLE!"

The Miracle Worker tells the story of Helen Keller, who was deaf, mute, and blind. In one production in the Midwest, the actor playing the Doctor was discovered to have a drinking problem. But as his character was only in the first scene, the director took pity on him and cast him anyway.

At the start of the play, the Doctor is supposed to inform the Keller family that a fever has left their infant without the use of her eyes, ears, or

---

vocal cords. Unfortunately, on opening night, the actor drunkenly blurted, "Mr. and Mrs. Keller, I've got bad news. Your daughter is…dead."

The other actors were stunned. If little Helen was dead, the play couldn't go on. Thinking quickly, the actress playing Mrs. Keller ad-libbed, "I think we need a second opinion."

The curtain came down, and the drunken actor was yanked off the stage. The stage manager put on the Doctor's white coat and took his place on stage. When the curtain went up again, the new Doctor declared, "Your baby is alive, but she'll be deaf, dumb, and blind for the rest of her life."

The actor playing Mr. Keller was so relieved to hear the correct lines that he clasped his hands together and cried, "Thank God!"

A CROSS TO BEAR

Every summer, Passion plays are performed throughout the South. These spectacles tell the story of Jesus using huge casts, massive sets, and lots of special effects. In one production in Texas, an actor playing a Roman guard was supposed to stab the actor playing Jesus with a spear that had a special retractable blade. Oops—the guard grabbed the wrong prop backstage and poked a *real* spear into Jesus' rib cage. Jesus cried out in agony, "Jesus Christ! I've been stabbed!"

The stage manager quickly brought down the curtain and called an ambulance. As sirens wailed in the distance, the curtain rose to reveal a new Jesus—a 260-pound stagehand in a loincloth.

When the time came for him to be lifted to heaven on special ropes, the new actor said, "And now I shall ascend!" The ropes were attached to a special counterweight system—that had been rigged for a man who weighed 100 fewer pounds. The stagehand pulling the rope couldn't lift him. He added more weights to the system as the actor repeated, "And now I shall ascend." This time Jesus was lifted a few feet above the cross, but quickly dropped back down again. The desperate stagehand quickly put all the weights he could find onto the system and pulled the rope as the actor playing Jesus said, "And now I shall…AAAAIIIIEEEEE!"

Jesus' scream could be heard across town as he was catapulted straight up into the metal grid at the top of the theater and knocked senseless.

Another ambulance was called, and the show was canceled.

Q: Why did Tigger put his head in the toilet? A: He was looking for Pooh.

FOR SALE BUY OWNER

We're back with one of our favorite features. Be they on a wall or a roadside, these actual signs are proof that some of the funniest things in life aren't necessarily meant to be funny.

In an office: "Would the person who took the step ladder yesterday please bring it back or further steps will be taken."

On the door of a photographer's studio: "Out to lunch: If not back by five, out for dinner also."

Outside a new town hall: "The town hall is closed until opening. It will remain closed after being opened. Open tomorrow."

Outside a London disco: "Smarts is the most exclusive disco in town. Everyone welcome."

In a safari park: "Elephants Please stay in your car"

Outside a photographer's studio: "Have the kids shot for Dad from $24.95."

At a railroad station: "Beware! To touch these wires is instant death. Anyone found doing so will be prosecuted."

In a department store: "Bargain Basement Upstairs"

In an office building: "Toilet out of order. Please use floor below."

Outside a Burger King: "Now Hiring Losers"

In Cape Cod: "Caution Water on Road During Rain"

In Pennsylvania: "Auction Sunday—New and Used Food"

Next to a red traffic light: "This light never turns green"

Outside a house: "For Sale Buy Owner"

At a McDonald's: "Parking for Drive-Thru Service Only"

In Massachusetts: "Entrance Only Do Not Enter"

Also in Massachusetts: "Lake Chargoggagoggmanchauggagogg-chaubunagungamaugg"

The funniest running foot in this book is on page 98.

MEMBERS ONLY

*Emergency-room workers have all sorts of disgusting
stories having to do with…well, people's private parts.
(Warning: These stories are cringe-inducing.)*

A TREE GROWS IN GRANNY

An elderly North Carolina woman arrived at the ER saying she had green vines growing in her "virginny," as she quaintly called it. An exam and a few X-rays confirmed her story: It was a vine, and it had sprouted…out of a potato. The woman explained that her uterus had prolapsed, or fallen out (a condition not uncommon in elderly women), so she'd popped in a potato to hold it up—and had forgotten about it.

BAD KITTY!

A woman brought her unconscious boyfriend into the ER in a panic and explained that she'd found him lying in the bathtub. Doctors noted a large lump on the man's head…as well as some curious scratches on his scrotum. As they were trying to determine what happened, the man woke up and told his story: He'd been cleaning his tub in the nude, and while kneeling to scrub the drain, he didn't realize that his swaying testicles had drawn the attention of his cat. The cat pounced, and the man jumped in pain…then hit his head on the tiles and knocked himself out.

WIENER DOG

In a fit of depression and self-loathing, a middle-aged man did the unthinkable—he cut off his own penis. The urologist at the ER believed he could reattach it if it was found, but time was running out. So a police officer rushed to the man's house to look for it. There, he heard a choking sound coming from the man's poodle. After a brief struggle, the officer was able to wrench the man's missing member from the dog's mouth. Sadly, it was too damaged to reattach, but the cop was given a citation for service "above and beyond the call of duty."

Aerosmith has made more money from Guitar Hero than from the sales of any of their albums.

WHY ASK WHY?

Sometimes, the answer is irrelevant—it's the question that counts.

If the doctor always says to take two aspirins, why don't we just double their size?

Why doesn't "Buick" rhyme with "quick"?

Is there ever a day when mattresses are *not* on sale?

Doesn't "expecting the unexpected" make the unexpected expected?

Do bees get wax in their ears?

Why do mirrors reflect backward, but not upside down?

If Walmart keeps lowering its prices every day, how come nothing in the store is free?

Why is it that no matter what color of bubble bath you use, the bubbles are always white?

Why does it take so little time for a child who is afraid of the dark to become a teenager who wants to stay out all night?

How can traffic come to a standstill? Shouldn't it be a sitstill?

Why do you start slowing down immediately when the sign says "Speed Zone Ahead"?

How much faster would lightning travel if it didn't zigzag?

How do you write zero in Roman numerals?

Why do drugstores make sick people walk to the back to get their prescriptions, while healthy people can buy cigarettes at the front?

Why isn't *palindrome* spelled "palindromeemordnilap"?

How come you have to go to the "Start" menu to shut down your computer?

When the stars are out, you can see them; when the lights are out, you can't. Why?

Can you be a closet claustrophobic?

Why is it that one match can start a forest fire, but it takes a whole box to light a barbecue?

If swimming is such great exercise, how come whales are fat?

Why "milkshake"? Shouldn't it be called a "milkshook"?

Why is it that most nudists are people you would never want to see naked?

"If a word in the dictionary were misspelled, how would we know?" —Steven Wright

SPACED-OUT SPORTS

These people are paid to play, coach, and announce sports.
They should get paid extra for making us laugh.

"Our similarities are different."

  —Dale Berra, on his father

"Sutton lost 13 games in a row without winning a ball game."

—Ralph Kiner, MLB announcer

"It's not so much maturity as it is growing up."

  —Jay Miller, hockey player,
  on whether his improved
  play was due to maturity

"I've got a great repertoire with my players."

  —Danny Ozark, MLB coach

"Three things are bad for you. I can't remember the first two, but doughnuts are the third."

  —Bill Petersen, NFL coach

"There comes a time in every man's life, and I've had plenty of them."

  —Casey Stengel, MLB player

"Noah."

  —Barry Bonnel, former Seattle
  Mariner, asked to name his
  all-time favorite Mariner

"Tony Gwynn was named player of the year for April."

  —Ralph Kiner, MLB announcer

"I just talked to the doctor. He told me her contraptions were an hour apart."

  —Mackey Sasser, MLB player,
  on his wife's pregnancy

"He slides into second with a stand-up double."

—Jerry Coleman, MLB announcer

"Not true at all. Vaseline is manufactured right here in the USA."

  —Don Sutton, on accusations
  that he doctored baseballs
  with a foreign substance

"What would I do that for? It only gets Spanish stations."

  —Jeff Stone, MLB player, on
  why he would not bring his
  TV back to the U.S. after
  playing in Venezuela

"No comment."

  —Michael Jordan, on being
  named one of the NBA's most
  reporter-friendly players

World record for the most people in one place dressed up like Smurfs: 2,510.

IVAR THE BONELESS

Throughout history, many leaders were given lofty nicknames—
Catherine the Great or Richard the Lionhearted, for example.
But not everyone could be Great or Magnificent. Some
rulers got strange, and strangely specific, nicknames.

ALFONSO THE SLOBBERER: King Alfonso IX ruled León
(now part of France) from 1188 to 1230. He was prone to fits of
rage, and any time he got especially angry, especially while in
battle, he drooled uncontrollably, sometimes to the point of foaming at
the mouth.

PIERO THE GOUTY: Heir to the powerful Medici family, which ruled
Florence, Italy, in the 1500s, Piero suffered from gout, a form of arthritis
commonly characterized by a large, painful sac of uric acid that forms
somewhere inside the body. In Piero's case, it was in his big toe.

HARALD THE LOUSY: At the age of 12, Harald vowed to found a
kingdom for the Norwegian people. He also vowed not to cut his hair until
he achieved that goal. By 872, he'd founded the kingdom, but in the 10
years since he'd made his vow, Harald's hair had grown extremely dirty and
was riddled with lice. This earned him the nickname "the Lousy," meaning
"full of lice," not "inadequate." (Oh, that's better.)

IVAR THE BONELESS: Historians believe that the ninth-century
Danish Viking chieftain suffered from *osteogenesis imperfecta*, or extremely
brittle bones. That, however, didn't stop him from becoming a Viking
warlord and leading successful invasions into northern England.

IVAN I DANILOVICH, MONEYBAGS: In the 14th century, Ivan was
the grand prince of Muscovy, now part of Russia. He earned his nickname
not only from his wealth but also because he was a tax collector for the
Tatar Empire, which required him to haul around big bags of money.

Bug Bomb: When threatened, a bombardier beetle can release a blast of 212°F air from its rear.

CONSTANTINE THE DUNG-NAMED: Eighth-century Byzantine emperor Constantine V got his nickname from political opponents who started a rumor that as a baby, he had pooped in a baptismal font. (He might have—he *was* a baby, after all.)

PTOLEMY VI THE MOTHER-LOVER: Ptolemy was the king of Egypt in the second century B.C. He ascended to the throne at age six and ruled jointly with his mother, the queen—Cleopatra I. Due to the fact that kings and queens are generally married to each other, Ptolemy became known as "the Mother-Lover." But he didn't really *love* his mother. (He did, however, marry his sister.)

ETHELRED THE UNREADY: Although Ethelred was just 10 years old when he became king of England in 978, that's not where the nickname originates. "Unready" comes from an Anglo-Saxon word that meant "ill-advised," which reflects the unpopular decisions made by his advisors.

ERIC THE PRIESTHATER: King Eric II of Norway (1280–99) earned his nickname from his (successful) efforts to keep the Catholic Church from garnering special favors and obtaining land from the Norwegian government.

LONGSHANKS: Edward I of England (reigned from 1272 to 1307) had very long "shanks," or legs. Standing at more than six feet, he was extremely tall for that era.

BOLESLAW THE WRY-MOUTHED: A duke of Poland in the 12th century, Boleslaw III was a scheming dictator who assumed power after forcing out his brother. "Wry" means "cleverly humorous" as well as "physically crooked," and by historical accounts, Boleslaw possessed both kinds of wry mouth.

IVAILO THE CABBAGE: A rebel leader and briefly the emperor of Bulgaria in the 1270s, Ivailo probably got the name because, before becoming a politician, he was a peasant farmer. According to some translations, Ivailo was also known as "Radish" and "Lettuce."

In a recent poll, 1% of Americans named Jesus "the greatest American of all time."

FUNNY BUSINESS

*Uncle John once decided to promote the series by hiring a fleet of airplanes
to drop several cases of Bathroom Readers over crowded school yards.
As the news outlets were all reporting the carnage, and Uncle John
was being led away in handcuffs, he said, "As God as my
witness, I really thought Bathroom Readers could fly."
Here are a few more boneheaded business blunders.*

ALPHABET SOUP. In the 1980s, the Pfeiffer Brewing Company decided to use its successful print ad campaign on the radio. They realized it was a mistake when they heard the announcer say their written slogan aloud: "Pfeiffer's...the beer with the silent P."

OFF WITH HIS... In 1999 Court TV scheduled a series of specials on Super Bowl Sunday, hoping to attract women uninterested in the game. But the network began receiving complaints after viewers noticed that all of the specials were about women who attacked their husbands—starting with the trial of Lorena Bobbitt, accused of cutting off her husband's genitals. Court TV called the promotion "Wives with Knives," and even ran a commercial showing a disgruntled wife reaching for a knife to get revenge on her football-obsessed husband. The network issued an apology.

BREATHLESS. In 2003 the Hong Kong Tourism Board put their new slogan—"Hong Kong Will Take Your Breath Away"—in ads in several major publications in England. But the entire campaign was soon scrapped after Hong Kong was hit by an outbreak of SARS (Severe Acute Respiratory Syndrome). One of the condition's main symptoms is shortness of breath.

DIG IT. In 2006 Dr Pepper announced that it had buried a rare coin worth "as much as $1 million" in Boston's 350-year-old Granary Burying Ground, the final resting place of Paul Revere, Samuel Adams, and John Hancock. Dr Pepper encouraged the public to ransack the cemetery to find the coin. Thankfully, city officials got wind of the promotion and closed off Granary before the desecration could begin. Dr Pepper executives apologized and took back the coin (actual value: $10,000).

Q: Did you hear about the constipated accountant? A: He couldn't budget.

JUICED. In 1994 Starburst fruit candy unveiled a new campaign featuring the slogan "The juice is loose." Later that year, millions of people watched a two-hour low-speed car chase on live TV as police apprehended O. J. Simpson, also known as "the Juice," for the alleged murder of his ex-wife. Within days, Starburst replaced "The juice is loose" with "Turn up the juice."

AY CARAMBA. In the early 1980s, Coors introduced its beer to Latin America using a translation of its slogan, "Turn it Loose." What they didn't know was that in Spanish "turn it loose" translates to "suffer from diarrhea."

WHAT A DRAG. The Powys County Council forced the manufacturers Black Mountains Smokery to change the name of "Welsh Dragon Sausages" to "Welsh Dragon Pork Sausages." Why? They were afraid some people might be confused. "I don't think any of our customers believe that we use dragon meat in our sausages," complained company owner Jon Carthew.

ONE MORE FOR THE "DO NOT PLACE IN MICROWAVE" LIST. The staff of Argentina's *Claudia* magazine shared this beauty tip: "To make your old, dried-out nail-polish good as new, simply heat it up in the microwave for three minutes." Apparently, no one at the magazine's offices actually field-tested this tip. Then they would have discovered that nail polish plus microwave radiation usually leads to an exploding microwave. More than 100 angry readers of *Claudia* learned that lesson the hard way.

HOT CUP OF WHAT? The advertising company Saatchi & Saatchi came up with a clever idea to help sell Folgers coffee: Paint New York City manhole covers so they look like full cups of coffee viewed from above. As the manhole covers emit steam, they look like steaming cups of Folgers coffee. One problem: The steam that rises from the manholes doesn't smell like coffee, but rather like something much worse and much less appetizing.

THE SEXIER SIDE OF NEWS. In 2002 CNN ran a commercial for news anchor Paula Zahn's new show, *American Morning*: "Where can you find a morning news anchor who's provocative, super-smart, and oh, yeah, just a little sexy? CNN…Yeah, CNN." And as he says "sexy," the word appears on the screen—followed by the sound of a zipper opening. CNN was immediately slammed by rival networks for using sex to sell a news broadcast. The spot was pulled after being shown only twice.

The German language has words to describe 30 different types of kisses.

PUN FOR THE MONEY

This page is dedicated to one of our heroes, George Takei—
Star Trek's Mr. Sulu—a lover of puns.

TWO ESKIMOS were sitting in a kayak. They got chilly, so they decided to light a fire in the craft. Unfortunately, it sank—proving once and for all that you can't have your kayak and heat it, too.

TWO BOLL WEEVILS grew up in South Carolina. One went to Hollywood and became a famous actor. The other stayed behind in the cotton fields and never amounted to much. The second one became known as the lesser of two weevils.

THERE WAS A MAN who entered a local paper's pun contest. He sent in ten different puns, hoping that at least one of the puns would win. Unfortunately, no pun in ten did.

A WOMAN HAD TWINS, but gave them up for adoption. One of them went to a family in Egypt and was named Amal. The other went to a family in Spain who named him Juan. Years later, Juan sent a picture of himself to his mom. When she got the picture, she told her husband wistfully that she wished she also had a picture of Amal. Her husband responded: "But they're twins—if you've seen Juan, you've seen Amal."

SOME FRIARS NEEDED TO RAISE MONEY, so they opened up a small florist shop. Because everyone liked to buy flowers from the men of God, the rival florist across town thought the competition was unfair. He asked the good fathers to close down, but they would not. He went back and begged the friars to close. They ignored him.

He asked his mother to plead with them. They ignored her, too. Finally, the rival florist hired Hugh McTaggart, the roughest and most vicious thug in town, to "persuade" them to close. Hugh beat up the friars and trashed their store, saying he'd be back if they didn't close shop. Terrified, they did so—thereby proving (are you ready?) that Hugh, and only Hugh, can prevent florist friars.

"Go to bed in your fireplace. You'll sleep like a log." —Ellen Degeneres

ONLY IN CANADA

Here are a few really weird news stories…that could only have happened in Canada.

SNOWED IN

Nelson Rubia of St. Jude's, Newfoundland, got his snowmobile back from the mechanic in March 2015 and decided to take it for a test ride…only it hadn't been completely repaired. As Rubia attempted to cross a highway, the throttle got stuck and the snowmobile picked up speed. Rubia was thrown from the vehicle, and the snowmobile took off on its own, heading west down the Trans-Canada Highway, bouncing off the snowbanks on either ride of the road. Rubia, uninjured, called the police for help. They were unable to stop the snowmobile, which traveled 15 miles before it hit a snowbank, flipped onto its side, and died.

LIE-BRARY

Lucy Maud Montgomery's 1908 novel *Anne of Green Gables* is about a plucky 11-year-old redheaded orphan named Anne who charms a stuffy town on Prince Edward Island. It's a Canadian classic, and dozens of printings of the book, as well as numerous film and TV adaptations, have depicted Anne exactly the way she's referred to in the original: as an 11-year-old redhead. In 2013 a company called CreateSpace caused a minor uproar when it published a new version of *Anne of Green Gables* with a cover depicting not a redheaded child but a sexy blonde in her 20s.

GRIN AND BEAR IT

In March 2014, cab driver Mohammed Naim had just dropped off a passenger in a Toronto suburb when he spotted a bear. He immediately locked himself in his cab and called police. They quickly arrived on the scene and tracked the bear tracks…to the home of the man Naim had just dropped off. Bear attack in progress? Nope—what Naim thought was a bear was actually a 150-pound very shaggy dog of the Newfoundland breed. The dog's name: Bear.

Wolves make terrible guard dogs—they're more likely to hide from strangers than bark.

LANGUAGE BARRIER

Canada is a bilingual nation, at least legally. Only 22 percent of the general population speaks French, but public signage must be presented in both English and French, a law fiercely enforced by the Office de Langue Francaise (French Language Office). In November 2014, the comedian Sugar Sammy paid for a series of ads in the Montreal Metro subway system that read, "For Christmas, I'd like a Langue Francaise." Because he didn't include the French translation, he got his wish. Sid Lee, the advertising firm responsible for the ads, was required to black out most of the sign's text so that it read, *Pour Noel, j'ai eu une plainte de l'Office de Langue Francaise.* Translation: "For Christmas I got a complaint from the Office de la Langue Francaise."

FOOT IN MOUTH

The signature cocktail of the Downtown Hotel in Dawson City, Yukon, is the Sourtoe. It's a tourist tradition to try the drink—a shot of whiskey with a leathery, black mummified toe in it. It started in 1973; the first toe was the detached frostbitten toe of a 19th-century fur trapper. Customers aren't supposed to consume the toe—only to let it touch their lips (the alcohol reportedly keeps it sterile), but some people have accidentally swallowed the toe. If it happens, the Downtown Hotel charges $500. The hotel has gone through two dozen old toes in the past 40 years and was down to its last toe. In 2013 a man named Josh (from New Orleans) came into the bar, drank a shot with the toe in it, swallowed the toe, slapped $500 on the bar, and left. The hotel is now running this print ad: "Got frostbite? The Downtown Hotel in Dawson City, Yukon, is currently seeking toes for its World Famous Sourtoe Cocktail."

FORT STONEWALLED

When the 2014 winter began, Yann Lefebvre of Beaconsfield, Quebec, promised his four kids that he would build them "the fort of all forts." He did. It was the size of a small house, with two snow couches and a snow coffee table inside. Neighborhood kids loved it, until the city government told Lefebvre in January 2015 that he'd have to remove it. Reason: it was blocking snowplow paths. "We're not against snow forts," Mayor Georges Bourelle told reporters, adding that technically, it was built on city property. Lefebvre had a party, during which he and friends tore it down and rebuilt it farther back from the road. (They invited the mayor, but he didn't show.)

What makes the heavy metal band Hatebeak unusual? Their "frontman" is a parrot.

SMELLING GRAVEYARDS

Now we splatter you with some cheese and wit from the horror movie genre.

"I will not be threatened by a walking meatloaf!"

**—David, to his dead friend,
*An American Werewolf
in London* (1981)**

Charley: "You read way too much *Twilight*."

Ed: "That's fiction! Okay? This is real! He's a real monster, and he's not brooding or lovesick or noble. He's the f***ing shark from *Jaws*! He kills, he feeds, and he doesn't stop until everybody around him is dead!

"And I'm seriously so angry you think I read *Twilight*!"

—*Fright Night* (2011)

"This is nuts! And I have a very high tolerance for nuts."

**—Chucky, *Seed of Chucky*
(2004)**

Katie: "You promised you weren't going to mess with that stuff!"

Micah: "No. I promised you I wasn't going to buy a Ouija board. I didn't *buy* a Ouija board. I borrowed a Ouija board."

—*Paranormal Activity* (2007)

"They will say that I have shed innocent blood. What's blood for, if not for shedding?"

**—Candyman,
Candyman (1992)**

"Your father's one sick mother, you know that? Actually, your mother's one sick mother, too."

**—Fool, *The People Under
The Stairs* (1991)**

Michael: "They're just people f***ing with our heads."

Heather: "But no one knows we're out here."

Michael: "Yeah, but have you ever seen *Deliverance*?"

**—*The Blair Witch Project*
(1999)**

"Ah, I can always smell a graveyard."

—Gabriel, *The Prophecy* (1995)

"Well, let me put it this way. If all the corpses buried around here were to stand up all at once, we'd have one hell of a population problem."

**—Grandpa, *The Lost Boys*
(1987)**

"We don't need a stretcher in there. We need a mop!"
—Paramedic, *A Nightmare on Elm Street* (1984)

"You did it now, boy! You let that bitch-meat get away!"
—Drayton, to Leatherface, *Texas Chainsaw 3D* (2013)

"Hey, dirtbags: You're the disease, and I'm prescribing 50 cc's of kickass!"
—Dr. S, *Dr. S Battles the Sex Crazed Reefer Zombies: The Movie* (2008)

"The girl of my dreams is a vegetable!"
—Chad, *Return of the Killer Tomatoes* (1988)

"Running's not a plan. Running's what you do once a plan fails."
—Earl, *Tremors* (1990)

"No, please don't kill me, Mr. Ghostface, I want to be in the sequel!"
—Tatum, *Scream* (1996)

"You scared, ain't ya? You should be. Christmas Eve is the scariest damn night of the year!"
—Grandpa, *Silent Night, Deadly Night* (1984)

"Okay, well, you're dead. Which is unusual, because we don't normally see this much activity in a dead person."
—Dr. Bronson, *My Boyfriend's Back* (1993)

"Well, hello, Mister Fancypants. I've got news for you, pal: You ain't leadin' but two things right now—Jack and sh*t. And Jack left town."
—Ash, *Army Of Darkness* (1992)

Jeff [through the door]: "Who is it?"

The Killer: "Pizza. Delivery."

Jeff: "What's the damage?"

The Killer: "Six…so far."
—*Slumber Party Massacre* (1982)

"Darling. Light of my life. I'm not gonna hurt ya. You didn't let me finish my sentence. I said, I'm not gonna hurt ya. I'm just gonna bash your brains in!"
—Jack, *The Shining* (1980)

"I do wish we could chat longer, Clarice, but I'm having an old friend for dinner. Bye."
—Hannibal Lecter, *Silence of the Lambs* (1991)

In case anyone asks: "filibeg" is another word for kilt.

THE LAST LAUGH: EPITAPHS

*Some unusual epitaphs and tombstone rhymes from around the world,
sent in by our crew of wandering BRI tombstone-ologists.*

In Scotland:
Here lie the bones of
Elizabeth Charlotte
Born a virgin;
died a harlot
She was aye a virgin
at seventeen
A remarkable thing in
Aberdeen

In Wales:
Deep in this grave
lies lazy Dai
Waiting the last great
trump on high.
If he's as fond
of his grave as he's
fond of his bed,
He'll be the last
man up when that
roll call's said.

In Ireland:
Wherever you be
Let your wind go free
For it was
keeping it in
That was the
death of me.

In Texas:
Robert Clay Allison
He never killed a man
that did not need
killing

In New Hampshire:
In memory of Miss
Lucena Wilcox
Death is a debt
By nature due;
I've paid my shot
And so must you.

In England:
In memory of
Robert Philip
Here lie I by the
chancel door
Here I lie because
I'm poor
The farther in, the
more you pay
But here lie I as
warm as they

In Austria:
Here lies Leonhard
Franz Futterknecht
until further notice

In Arizona:
Here lies John Coil,
A son of toil who died
on Arizona soil.
He was a man of
considerable vim
But this here air was
too hot for him.

In England:
John Edwards who
perished in a fire 1904
No one could hold a
candle to him

In England:
Here lies the body of
Martha Dias who was
always uneasy and
not over pious
She liv'd to the age of
three score and ten
And gave that
to the worms
she refus'd to the men

In England:
G. Wild
Not worth
remembering

Sir Isaac Newton invented the cat door. He also died a virgin. Coincidence? Yes.

THE DEPARTMENT OF SILLY MEASUREMENTS

You've heard of a "New York Minute" and a "stone's throw," but how about a "smoot"? Here are a few more strange units of measurement.

THE ALTUVE (pronounced al-TOO-vay)

Description: A unit of length, meant to be used for baseball statistics, equal to 5.417 feet.

Explanation: In 2012 Houston Astros fan Bryan Trostel was watching a game when he heard the announcers joke about how many "altuves" a home run had traveled. They were referring to Astros second baseman Jose Altuve, who, at 5 feet 5 inches (or 5.417 feet) tall, is the shortest active player in Major League Baseball. That inspired Trostel to create a website—www.howmanyaltuves.com —where you can calculate how many altuves something is. (A 450-foot home run? That's 83.07 altuves. A 98-mile-per-hour fastball? A blistering 26.55 altuves per second. And so on.) The website went viral, and the altuve has been jokingly used by Major League Baseball announcers ever since.

THE FRIEDMAN UNIT

Description: A unit of time equal to six months—or, more specifically, the *next* six months—referring primarily to the war in Iraq.

Explanation: In May 2006, the media watchdog group Fairness and Accuracy in Reporting did a study in which they counted the number of times *New York Times* columnist Thomas Friedman predicted that the Iraq War, which Friedman supported, would be resolved "in the next six months." Their finding: over a period of two and a half years, he made the prediction 14 times. That led liberal blogger Duncan Black, an outspoken opponent of the war, to coin the term "Friedman Unit"—or the "F.U."—in honor of Friedman's repeated (and repeatedly wrong) predictions. The F.U. became so well known in press circles that Friedman was asked about it directly a number of times, including by comedian Stephen Colbert on a 2007 episode of *The Colbert Report*. Friedman responded to Colbert's question by saying, "I'm afraid we've run out of six months. It's really time to set a deadline."

Double-0-Heaven: There's a church in Toronto named the St. James Bond United Church.

THE BEARD-SECOND

Description: The distance a beard grows in one second—about five nanometers, or five billionths of a meter.

Explanation: The inventor of the beard-second is unknown, but it's been around since at least the mid-2000s. In *This Book Warps Time and Space*, a 2008 collection of witty essays by scientists, physicist Kemp Bennet Kolb explained that the beard-second came about because scientists wanted a unit similar to a light-year—the enormous distance light travels in a single year—except they wanted it for extremely short distances. "The proposed unit," Kolb explained, "is the *beard-second*: the distance a standard beard grows in one second." He added that "a standard beard is defined as growing on a standard face."

THE SMOOT

Description: A unit of length equal to 67 inches.

Explanation: In October 1958, Oliver Smoot, 18, was pledging to become a member of the Lambda Chi Alpha fraternity at the Massachusetts Institute of Technology (MIT). For a hazing prank, his fraternity brothers had him measure the length of the Harvard Bridge—in *smoots*. (Harvard Bridge spans the Charles River, between Cambridge and Boston.) Smoot—who is 5'7", or 67 inches tall—was used like a yardstick. He laid down at the start of the bridge; his fraternity brothers made a chalk mark at the top of his head. Then Smoot scooted ahead so that he was lying with his feet at the chalk mark, while the top of his head was marked again. And every 10 smoots was marked with paint. (How long is the Harvard Bridge? It's 364.4 smoots "and one ear" long.) The prank became an MIT legend—and it remains so today. When the bridge was renovated in the 1990s, officials had lines scored in the new concrete at 67-inch intervals, in honor of the smoot.

Bonus Fact: In 2011 the *American Heritage Dictionary* added "smoot" to its list of official new words.

ONE MORE SILLY MEASUREMENT

A wheaton is a measurement of followers on the social media site Twitter. One wheaton equals 500,000 followers. The term was coined by English cartoonist John Kovalic in honor of actor Wil Wheaton (best known for playing Wesley Crusher on *Star Trek: The Next Generation*), one of the earliest celebrities to embrace Twitter. As of publication time, Wil Wheaton has more than 3.2 million—or 6.4 wheatons of Twitter followers.

PAUL LYNDE'S GREATEST QUIPS

On the original Hollywood Squares *game show (1966–81), host Peter Marshall would ask one of the star panelists a question, and the star would give a joke response before the real answer. Comedian Paul Lynde, in the center square, usually delivered the best lines. Like these.*

Marshall: "According to the *World Book Encyclopedia*, what is the main reason dogs pant?"

Lynde: "Because they can't talk dirty."

Marshall: "What are 'dual purpose' cattle good for that other cattle aren't?"

Lynde: "They give milk and cookies. I don't recommend the cookies."

Marshall: "True or false: Research says that Columbus liked to wear bloomers and long stockings."

Lynde: "It's not easy to sign a crew up for six months."

Marshall: "Burt Reynolds is quoted as saying, 'Dinah Shore's in top form. I've never known anyone to be so completely able to throw herself into a...' what?"

Lynde: "Headboard."

Marshall: "Do female frogs croak?"

Lynde: "If you hold their little heads under water long enough."

Marshall: "If the right part comes along, will George C. Scott do a nude scene?"

Lynde: "You mean he doesn't have the right part?"

Marshall: "What's the instrument with the light on the end, that the doctor sticks in your ear?"

Lynde: "Oh, a cigarette."

Marshall: "Is it normal for Norwegians to talk to trees?"

Lynde: "As long as that's as far as it goes."

Marshall: "Who's more likely to be romantically responsive: women under 30, or women over 30?"

Lynde: "I don't have a third choice?"

He's no jackass: On a cold, rainy day a horse always stands with its butt to the wind.

Marshall: "Pride, anger, covetousness, lust, gluttony, envy, and sloth are collectively known as what?"

Lynde: "The Bill of Rights."

Marshall: "The great white is one of the most feared animals. What is the great white?

Lynde: "A sheriff in Alabama."

Marshall: "What do you call a man who gives you diamonds and pearls?"

Lynde: "I'd call him 'darling'!"

Marshall: "It is the most abused and neglected part of your body. What is it?"

Lynde: "Mine may be abused, but it certainly isn't neglected!"

Marshall: "Who stays pregnant for a longer period of time, your wife or your elephant?"

Lynde: "Who told you about my elephant?"

Marshall: "Paul, can you get an elephant drunk?"

Lynde: "Yes, but he still won't go up to your apartment."

Marshall: "Nathan Hale, one of the heroes of the American Revolution, was hung. Why?"

Lynde: "Heredity!"

Marshall: "Can chewing gum help prevent a child from catching a cold?"

Lynde: "No, but I know it'll plug a runny nose."

Marshall: "Eddie Fisher recently stated, 'I'm sorry. I'm sorry for them both.' Who or what was he referring to?"

Lynde: "His fans."

Marshall: "If you were pregnant for two years, what would you give birth to?"

Lynde: "Whatever it is, it would never be afraid of the dark."

*   *   *

THE HUMORIST'S BIBLE

On an episode of the sitcom *Third Rock from the Sun*, the alien Dick (John Lithgow) emerges from the bathroom carrying a book. He wonders aloud about the nature of humor. If you look closely you can see that the book he's holding is…*Uncle John's Bathroom Reader*. (We're glad we could help.)

ODD BOOKS

*We like to include a wide variety of topics in our Bathroom Readers.
Here are some real books that have a much more limited focus.*

Reusing Old Graves

*Goblinproofing One's
Chicken Coop*

*Developments in Dairy Cow
Breeding: New Opportunities
to Widen the Use of Straw*

*Managing a Dental Practice:
The Genghis Khan Way*

*Hand Grenade Throwing
as a College Sport*

*The Humanure Handbook:
A Guide to Composting
Human Manure*

The Bright Side of Prison Life

Afterthoughts of a Worm Hunter

*Last Chance at Love:
Terminal Romances*

Teach Your Wife to Be a Widow

Increasing Laundry Output

Where Underpants Come From

*How to Land a Top-Paying
Pierogi Makers Job*

The Radiation Recipe Book

*Castration: The Advantages
and the Disadvantages*

*The Beginner's Guide to
Sex in the Afterlife*

*My Cat's in Love, or How to
Survive Your Feline's Sex Life,
Pregnancy, and Kittening*

*The Madam as Entrepreneur:
Career Management in
House Prostitution*

Collectible Spoons of the 3rd Reich

The Sunny Side of Bereavement

*So Your Wife Came Home Speaking
in Tongues! So Did Mine!*

Old Age: Its Cause and Prevention

*The Golden Fountain: Complete
Guide to Urine Therapy*

*How Tea Cosies
Changed the World*

*Ghosts: Minnesota's
Unnatural Resource*

Eating People Is Wrong

Small world: Walt Disney was a direct descendant of King Edward I.

OTTO-MATIC DRIVE

Uncle John once tried to convince us that clowns are magic. "Otherwise," he said, "how could so many of them fit into one tiny car?" "No way," we countered, "it's just a trick!" We even looked it up to prove Uncle John wrong and discovered that 1) clowns aren't magic, and 2) we're gullible.

ATTACK OF THE CLOWNS

You're enjoying a night under the big top when all of a sudden, a little VW Beetle sputters into to the center of the ring, spewing pink and blue smoke. After much honking, the clown driver gets out, followed by another clown. Then another clown. And another…and another. Eventually as many as 20 clowns emerge. *Where did they all come from?*

Kids of all ages have been applauding the clown car trick for more than 60 years, ever since it was first introduced in 1950 by master clown Otto Griebling at the Cole Brothers Circus. His fellow clowns soon incorporated the bit into their own acts, and it's been a mainstay of big-top mayhem ever since. According to Greg DeSanto, executive director of the International Clown Hall of Fame and Research Center in Baraboo, Wisconsin, the trick remains the most requested of all clown gags.

CLOWNTORTIONISTS

"There's no trick to the clown car gag," DeSanto insists. "No trapdoors, and the cars are real." He should know: He studied at the renowned Barnum and Bailey Clown College in Sarasota, Florida, and went on to perform with "The Greatest Show on Earth."

According to DeSanto, the typical clown car is a fully functional automobile with a stripped-out interior. Everything is removed: seats, door panels, and any barrier to the trunk. Windows are painted over, with only a small space on the windshield left clear for the driver, perched on a milk crate, to see through. Carefully placed handles and ledges allow the other 14 to 20 clowns to cram themselves, and their props and costumes (even those enormous shoes), into about three cubic feet of space each. Once inside, the clown contortionists need only endure a few minutes of discomfort before they're released…to the delight (or horror) of the crowd.

Are you afraid of clowns? If so, you're *coulrophobic*. (Famous coulrophobe: Johnny Depp.)

TRUTH IS FUNNIER THAN FICTION

Our final installment of random hilarity from the BRI archives.

THEY SHOULD HAVE CALLED IT "THE SHOOSHER"

An amusement park ride at the Scandia Family Fun Center in Sacramento, California, lifts customers 160 feet in the air and then spins them around at 60 mph. Nearby residents finally got fed up with the thrill-seekers' bloodcurdling screams and filed a class-action suit against the park. But park manager Steve Baddley is already taking steps to limit the noise on the ride (which he originally purchased because of its relatively quiet motor). Baddley's first step: No screaming allowed. "If we can hear a noise, we're required to take you off the ride," he says. The name of the ride: "The Screamer."

IT COSTS AN ARM AND A LEG

In 2006 India's Medical Association started investigating three doctors who had appeared in television advertisements to promote voluntary amputation surgery to beggars. In India, street beggars can earn more money by eliciting sympathy for missing appendages. The more missing appendages, the more they earn. The doctors charged fees of about $200 for the "investment" of removing a leg below the knee.

MUNCH TIME!

While filming a scene in Baltimore, Maryland, for *Homicide: Life on the Street*, actor Richard Belzer, who played Detective Munch, was standing on a sidewalk in his police costume when a real-life shoplifter turned the corner and happened upon him. The robber dropped his loot and said, "Oh sh*t, it's Munch!" Security officers quickly apprehended the man.

THE OLD REVOLVING-TROOPS TRICK

In September 1864, Civil War general Nathan Forrest was leading his Confederate troops north from Alabama toward Tennessee. He planned to attack the Union post in Athens, Alabama, having heard that Union reinforcements were approaching, and wanted to take the fort before they arrived. The problem: The post was well manned and heavily fortified. Forrest was greatly outnumbered, but he had a plan. He sent a message to Union commander Campbell requesting a personal meeting. Campbell agreed to the meeting. Forrest then escorted him on a tour of the Confederate troops, during which Campbell silently calculated the number of troops and artillery surrounding his fort. What he didn't realize was that Forrest's men—after being inspected and tallied—were quietly packing everything up and quickly moving to a new position, to be counted again. Campbell didn't realize he was seeing the same troops over and over again. Assuming he was vastly outnumbered by the Confederates, he returned to his fort, pulled down the Union flag…and gave up without a fight.

MAY GNEED SURGERY

In 2006 Michael Naylor of North Yorkshire, England, bought a gnome at a yard sale for £10 ($20). An hour after he bought it (he named it "Stan"), Naylor dropped the gnome on his foot and broke a toe. A month later, Naylor moved Stan from his patio to a flower bed because he was creeped out by the gnome staring at him through a window while he was watching TV. During the move Stan fell on Naylor's hand, tearing a ligament. A few weeks later, Naylor was weeding the flower bed around Stan and the gnome's fishing pole stabbed him in the eye. Naylor said he'd like to get rid of Stan, but he's afraid to go near him again.

SPAM A LOT

An anti-spam software company called SpamArrest had to issue this apology to its customers: "Recently we have received some inquiries regarding a mailing we delivered to users of SpamArrest. Because of this, SpamArrest will not send unsolicited bulk e-mail again."

DOMESTIC DISPUTE

In May 2007, drivers in Braunschweig, Germany, noticed a sign in the window of a house that said, "Help! Please call the police!" Next to the sign were a little girl and a little boy. The police were alerted to a possible kidnapping and swarmed the house. The woman who answered the door (the mother of the two children) had no clue what that sign was doing there.

It turned out that the mother had told her daughter to clean her bedroom. The daughter refused, which led to a big fight, after which the disgruntled daughter put up the sign. The cops sided with the mother. "That room looked like a battlefield," said a police spokesman.

STRINGS ATTACHED

In December 2006, Sharon Taylor was rushing into the hospital in West Yorkshire, England—she could feel her baby coming and wasn't sure she could "hold it" until she reached the delivery room. She couldn't. Once inside the doors, the newborn "shot out" of Taylor so fast that her boyfriend tried to catch it. He couldn't. According to reports, baby Ashleigh landed on the floor and skidded a few feet, but then—thanks to the umbilical cord—was retracted right back up into her mommy's arms.

BLUEBIRDS OF SADNESS

The Bluebird is a classic play about two children who go searching for the Bluebird of Happiness. A designer at a Midwestern theater thought it would be a great idea to have real bluebirds fly around the theater at the end of the play. So he sprayed pigeons with blue paint and put them in little cages hanging above the audience. Sadly, he failed to consider what the paint, combined with the heat from the lights, might do to the birds. On opening night, the cages were opened at the end of the show…showering a horrified audience with hundreds of dead "bluebirds."

IT'S A JUNGLE OUT THERE

In April 2010, police in Stevens Point, Wisconsin, received a strange call: A woman said she was walking through town when she felt a sharp pain in her chest. She looked down and saw a tiny dart sticking out of her blouse. A little while later, a similar call came in from another person, and then another, and then another. Then it dawned on police that they were dealing with a serial tiny-dart shooter. Thankfully, the darts weren't poisonous. And the cops had a lead: One of the victims saw a small tube sticking out of the window of a black minivan, which sped away. Police found the minivan; sitting inside was 41-year-old Paula Wolf…and her blow darts. Why did she do it? "I like to hear people say 'ouch.'"

POLITALKS

So what if they're always screwing things up—politicians are hilarious!

"I believe what I said yesterday. I don't know what I said, but I know what I think, and, well, I assume it's what I said."

　　　　—Donald Rumsfeld

"You bet we might have!"

　　—Sen. John Kerry, asked if he would have invaded Iraq

"If I could only go through the ducts and leap out onstage in a cape—that's my dream."

　　—Ralph Nader, on being denied entry to a presidential debate

"Get some devastation in the background."

　　—Sen. Bill Frist, posing for a photo in tsunami-ravaged Sri Lanka

"I'm undaunted in my quest to amuse myself by constantly changing my hair."

　　　　—Hillary Clinton

"'Ever' is a very strong word."

　　—Rep. Tom DeLay, asked if he had ever crossed the line of ethical behavior

"We have people from every planet on Earth in this state."

　　　　—California Gov. Gray Davis

"First they tax our beer, and then they tax cigarettes. Now they are going to increase the tax on gasoline. All that's left are our women."

　　　　—Sen. John East

"Their current lodgings are a bit temporary but they should see it like a weekend of camping."

　　—Silvio Berlusconi, Italian PM, on earthquake refugees

"What a bizarre time we're in, when a judge will say to little children that you can't say the Pledge of Allegiance, but you must learn that homosexuality is normal and you should try it."

　　　　—Rep. Michelle Bachmann

"A showgirl and a bottle of Bombay Sapphire gin."

　　—Oscar Goodman, Las Vegas mayor, to schoolchildren who asked what he'd like on a deserted island

---

Customer: "Why is this coffee so muddy?" Waitress: "It was ground yesterday."

"I believe in natural gas as a clean, cheap alternative to fossil fuels."

—Rep. Nancy Pelosi (unaware that natural gas *is* a fossil fuel)

"To our seniors, I have a message for you: You're going to die sooner if the health-care bill passes."

—Sen. Tom Coburn

"When the stock market crashed, Franklin Roosevelt got on the TV and didn't just talk about the, you know, the princes of greed. He said, 'Look, here's what happened.'"

—VP Joe Biden, forgetting that FDR wasn't president in 1929 (nor was there TV)

"Thanks for the question, you little jerk."

—Sen. John McCain, when asked by a high school student if he was too old to be president

"You'll get a chance to ask questions later and make your stupid statements; now let me make mine."
—Karl Rove, to hecklers

"We're no longer a superpower, we're a super-duper power."

—Rep. Tom DeLay

"We are not going to give up on destroying the health care system for the American people."

—Rep. Paul Ryan

"I'm sure a lot of you have tripped out on alcohol. It's actually a lot safer to do it on marijuana."

—Sen. Mike Gravel, to high school students

"Lemon. Wet. Good."
—Mitt Romney, when asked how a glass of lemonade tasted

"Well, you know, God bless him, bless his heart, the president of the United States, a total failure."
—Rep. Nancy Pelosi, on President George W. Bush

"On behalf of all of you, I want to express my appreciation for this tremendously warm recession."

—Ron Brown, DNC chairman

"What we really expect out of the Democrats is for them to treat us as they would have liked to have been treated."

—Rep. John Boehner

"Come on! I just answered, like, eight questions!"

—Pres. Barack Obama, putting an end to a press conference

Food facts: *Exocannibals* eat their enemies; *indocannibals* eat their friends.

KENTUCKY FRIED PANDA

Since 1989, The Simpsons *has shown hundreds of these blink-and-you-miss-'em sight gags: funny business names. Here are a few favorites.*

Something Wicker
This Way Comes

Donner's Party Supplies

Ah, Fudge
(chocolate factory)

Eastside Ruff-Form School
(dog obedience school)

Tokyo Roe's Sushi Bar

The Three Seasons Motel

All Creatures Great and
Cheap (pet store)

Miscellaneous, Etc.

Wee Monsieur
(kids clothing store)

Restoration Software

Dr. Zitofsky's
Dermatology Clinic

King Toot's Music Store

Louvre: American Style
(museum)

Kentucky Fried Panda

General Chang's
Taco Italiano

I Can't Believe
It's a Law Firm!

Red Rash Inn

Rubber Baby Buggy Bumpers

Hillside Wrangler Steakhouse

Goody New Shoes

The Frying Dutchman
(seafood restaurant)

Texas Cheesecake Depository

Much Ado About Muffins

International House of
Answering Machines

Taj Mah-All-You-Can-Eat

The Sole Provider
(shoe store)

Pudding on the Ritz

The Brushes Are Coming,
The Brushes Are Coming

T.G.I. Fried Eggs

Call Me Delish-Mael
(candy store)

The Buzzing Sign Diner

"The great thing about animation—you don't have to pay the actors squat." —Homer Simpson

THE DOG ATE MY...

More stories of what happens when good dogs eat bad.

Dog: Tucker, a four-year-old Rottweiler mix owned by Lois Matykowski of Stevens Point, Wisconsin
Details: When Matykowski's wedding band went missing in 2008, she suspected that Tucker, her resident "food bandit," might have eaten it. She followed him for more than a week, checking every time he did his business to see if the ring was in it, but it never appeared.

Six years later, on a hot June afternoon, Matykowski and her granddaughter were sitting in her yard eating Popsicles. As Matykowski got up to get some water for Tucker, now 10, the dog wolfed down her granddaughter's Popsicle, stick and all. The veterinarian told her that feeding the dog some Vaseline smeared between slices of bread would bring the stick back up, and a few hours later it did. Two days after that, Tucker barfed again, and as Matykowski cleaned up the mess, she saw that it had brought up something else: "I look in the paper towel and here is my wedding ring. I kid you not, it was in Tucker's puke!" she told a reporter. (The vet suspects the Popsicle stick dislodged the ring from wherever it had been stuck for six years.) "My friends have been telling me, 'I want a dog that throws up diamonds.' Who wouldn't, right?"

Dog: Charlie, a Newfoundland owned by Terry Morgan, a retired pub owner in Cockwood, Devon, in southwest England
Details: When Morgan owned his pub, he used the alarm on his Casio wristwatch to remind him when it was time to announce last call. After he retired, he never turned off the alarm, and one night in July 2014 he heard it go off right on schedule at 10:55 p.m., near where Charlie was laying. But the sound was muffled. "I thought he was lying on it," he told reporters. "Only when I rolled him over did I realize it was inside him." Morgan rushed Charlie to the vet, who informed him that the watch would have to be removed surgically. It probably wasn't the dog's first visit to the doctor, because as soon as he saw the vet's hypodermic needle, he let out a terrified howl and barfed up the watch, saving Morgan the price of the £1,000 surgery (about $1,600).

Dog: Jack, a 13-year-old Jack Russell terrier owned by Tim Kelleher, who lives New York City

Details: In March 2013, Kelleher finished eating a bagel and left the crumpled-up bag on his desk. That's where Jack found it a short time later. As the dog was ripping the bag apart, he knocked it and a jar of pennies onto the floor. Chasing the bag, he licked the last of the crumbs from the floor—and also swallowed some of the pennies, though how many (if any) did not become apparent until after he started vomiting and Kelleher took him to the veterinarian. (Because pennies are made mostly of zinc, which is toxic to dogs, swallowing even one can be fatal if it is not removed in time.) An X-ray revealed that the pennies were still in Jack's stomach and fortunately had not yet made their way to his intestines. That was good news: rather than having to remove the pennies surgically, the vet attached a small net to a medical instrument called an endoscope, inserted it into Jack's throat, and over the next two hours removed five pennies at a time until 111 had been recovered. Jack made a full recovery; Kelleher got to keep the change.

Dog: Liza, an 18-month-old Labrador retriever owned by Mark Meltz and his fiancée, Hillary Feinberg, of Ipswich, Massachusetts

Details: Liza swallowed her owner's wedding ring too, and she couldn't have done it at a worse time: the day before Meltz and Feinberg were to be married in September 2000. The day before the wedding, Liza had a coughing fit when Feinberg took her for a walk. But it wasn't until the following morning, just a few hours before the wedding, when Meltz couldn't find Feinberg's ring that he realized what must have happened. He rushed Liza to the veterinarian to have the dog X-rayed (diagnosis confirmed), then raced to his wedding. When the time came to present the ring to his wife, he gave her the X-ray instead—the ring was still inside the dog. "I explained it and the guests exploded with laughter," Meltz said afterward. Bonus: Liza barfed up the ring, saving the risk and expense of having it surgically removed.

*   *   *

CLASSIFIED AD

FUNNY LAWSUITS

These days, it seems that people will sue each other over practically anything. Here are some real-life examples of unusual legal battles.

THE PLAINTIFF: Wawa, a food store chain
THE DEFENDANTS: Tamilee Haaf and George Haaf Jr., owners of the HAHA market
THE LAWSUIT: In 1996 Wawa, which controlled 500 convenience store outlets in eastern Pennsylvania, filed a suit claiming that HAHA is too similar in sound and could confuse people into believing that HAHA is affiliated with Wawa. The Haafs claim they have a right to use the name since it is simply an abbreviation of their last name.
THE VERDICT: It may sound funny, but HAHA lost. The judge ruled that "HAHA" sounds so close to "Wawa" that it dilutes Wawa's trademark. HAHA boo-hoo, Wawa yee-ha.

PLAINTIFF: Norreasha Gill of Lexington, Kentucky
DEFENDANT: Kentucky radio station WLTO-FM
LAWSUIT: In June 2005, Gill was listening to the station when she heard the host offer to give "one hundred grand" to the tenth caller at a specified time. Gill listened for several hours, called at the right time…and won! The next morning she went down to the station to pick up her $100,000, but the station manager informed her that she had actually won…a Nestle's 100 Grand candy bar. Obviously, Gill was upset. After numerous complaints, the station offered to give her $5,000, but Gill refused and filed suit, demanding the $100,000 (she'd already promised her kids a minivan).
THE VERDICT: What came of the suit wasn't reported, but the station was subsequently investigated and (we hope) fined by the FCC.

THE PLAINTIFF: John Cage Trust
THE DEFENDANT: Mike Batt, a British composer
THE LAWSUIT: In 1952 composer John Cage wrote a piece he called "4'33"." It was four minutes and 33 seconds of silence. In 2002 Batt included a track called "A One Minute Silence" on an album by his rock

---

Elvis Presley owned a pet mynah bird that said, "Elvis! Go to hell!"

band the Planets, crediting it to "Batt/Cage." That's when Cage's estate came in—they accused Batt of copyright infringement. Batt's response: "Has the world gone mad? I'm prepared to do time rather than pay out." Besides, he said, his piece was much better than Cage's: "I have been able to say in one minute what Cage could only say in four minutes and 33 seconds."

THE VERDICT: The suit ended with a six-figure out-of-court settlement. "We feel that honor has been settled," said Nicholas Riddle, Cage's publisher, "because the concept of a silent piece is a very valuable artistic concept."

THE PLAINTIFF: Coca-Cola Co.

THE DEFENDANT: Frederick Coke-Is-It of Brattleboro, Vermont

THE LAWSUIT: Born Frederick Koch, he pronounced his name "kotch," but got fed up with people pronouncing it "Coke." Out of frustration he had his name legally changed to Frederick Coke-Is-It. When the Coca-Cola Company found out about Mr. Coke-Is-It, they sued him on the grounds that he changed his name specifically to "infringe on their rights."

THE VERDICT: They settled out of court…and amazingly, Koch, er, Coke-Is-It, is *still* it—he won the right to keep his new name.

THE PLAINTIFF: Gerald Mayo of Pennsylvania

THE DEFENDANT: "Satan and His Staff"

THE LAWSUIT: Alleging that Satan had made his life miserable, placed obstacles in his path, and plotted his doom, Mayo sued the Prince of Darkness in federal court. "He deprived me of my constitutional rights."

THE VERDICT: Case dismissed. The judge noted that Mayo hadn't included instructions on how to serve Satan with the necessary papers.

THE PLAINTIFF: Tom Morgan, a Portland, Oregon, grocery cashier

THE DEFENDANT: Randy Maresh, a cashier at the same store

THE LAWSUIT: Morgan sued Maresh for $100,000, claiming that his coworker "willfully and maliciously inflicted severe mental stress and humiliation by continually, intentionally, and repeatedly passing gas directed at the plaintiff." Maresh's defense: Farting is a form of free speech and therefore protected by the First Amendment.

THE VERDICT: Case dismissed. The judge said Maresh's behavior was "juvenile and boorish," but conceded that there was no law against farting.

"Seven days without laughter make one weak." —Joel Goodman

BUSTING A GRUMPY

Surprisingly, there are a lot of euphemisms to describe what we all do in the bathroom. Because they're so colorful, they are remarkably disgusting, yet eerily compelling. (Enjoy.)

Bake brownies

Clip a biscuit

Bust a grumpy

See a man about a dog

Release the hostages

Free the chickens from the coop

Let the firetrucks loose

Bust a dookie

Dispatch a Yankee

Squeeze a steamer

Ride the porcelain bus

Stock the lake with brown trout

Pinch a loaf

Lose a farting contest

Mold an action figure

Step into the office

Blow mud

Murder a mud bunny

Build a log cabin

Grease the punchbowl

Free the turtles

Lay hot snakes

Lay wolf bait

Give birth to a food baby

Expel the hamster

Take the Browns to the Super Bowl

Crank an 8-ball

Make a delivery

Hang a root

Empty the manure spreader

Go number 2

Park a custard

Log out

Burn a mule

Send some sailors out to sea

Sink submarines

Pop a squat

Drop a deuce

Sprout a tail

Drop the kids off at the pool

Give birth to sewer bass

Throw a chip

Unhitch a load

Trash the hash

Eat backwards

Visit the chamber of commerce

Duke it out

Lose 10 pounds in one minute

Talk to John

Misfart

Don't get Arkan-sassy: It is against the law to mispronounce "Arkansas" in Arkansas.

FESTIVUS FOR THE REST OF US!

Here's the story of a not-so-hallowed holiday tradition that's way better than any of the actual hallowed holiday traditions because it comes from TV.

CHRISTMAS, SHMISTMAS

The world changed on December 18, 1997. On that cold winter's night, families near and far gathered 'round the warm glow of their television sets to watch the holiday episode of *Seinfeld*. In one fateful scene, the cantankerous Frank Costanza (Jerry Stiller) tells Kramer (Michael Richards) how the Costanza family celebrates the season:

Frank: Many Christmases ago, I went to buy a doll for my son. I reached for the last one they had, but so did another man. As I rained blows upon him, I realized there had to be another way.

Kramer: What happened to the doll?

Frank: It was destroyed. But out of that a new holiday was born... a Festivus for the rest of us!

Kramer: That must've been some kind of doll.

Frank: She was.

Festivus, explained Frank, does not revolve around materialism, but around something much more profound: familial disappointment and feats of strength (both of which were featured prominently in the episode).

TAPE DELAY

But Festivus wasn't invented by a mere TV character; it was invented by a TV writer—or rather, by his father. The story goes back to way before *Seinfeld*—all the way back to 1966 when Daniel O'Keefe, an editor at *Reader's Digest*, celebrated the anniversary of his first date with his wife, Deborah, and named the party "Festivus." Inspired by Samuel Beckett's absurdist play *Krapp's Last Tape* (about an older man who listens to tape recordings of his younger self), O'Keefe started making his own tapes, into

---

In carvings dating to back to 800, the Norse hero Gunther plays a lute with his toes.

which he'd air his grievances about life. These tapings became incorporated into Festivus as the rest of his family joined in and recorded all their complaints, too. But that's not all—the holiday also featured wrestling matches between O'Keefe's three sons.

Many years later, O'Keefe's son, also named Daniel, became a writer for *Seinfeld* and recounted his family's odd holiday tradition to his fellow writers. They agreed it would make for a funny episode. Little did they know they would be creating an actual new holiday.

FIGHT CLUB

Since the show aired, Festivus has taken on a life of its own. Every December 23, friends and family gather to celebrate the holiday. If you want to join in, you're welcome to it, but you have to celebrate properly, or you'll be, as Frank would call you, "weak." So here's how to celebrate Festivus:

1. The Aluminum Pole: Festivus's only decoration, the stark, unadorned pole symbolizes resistance to the commercialization of the holidays. No tinsel is allowed: Frank says it's distracting.

2. The Airing of Grievances: During the Festivus dinner, celebrants go around the table and tell friends and family how much they've disappointed them over the past year.

3. The Feats of Strength: The head of the family must be wrestled to the ground in order for Festivus to end. He or she chooses an opponent (the weaker, the better); and the two wrestle until one is defeated, or they find something better to do, or they get tired, or the police show up.

To make all three of these traditions even more fun, try celebrating the holiday with a wine called Festivus Red, bottled by Oklahoma Winery Grape Ranch. "It's the perfect wine for the un-holiday to end all holidays!"

IT'S A FRICKIN' MIRACLE!

But the most special part of Festivus is the "Festivus miracle." As miracles go, it's only slightly better than no miracle at all, but that's what makes the Festivus miracle so special: It can happen to anyone. All you need is to have something happen to you that doesn't totally suck, and you can declare it a Festivus miracle. Say you find 35 cents in your pocket when you were only expecting to find a quarter. That's a Festivus miracle! Or your shoes stay tied all day. Now *that's* a Festivus miracle!

Real (odd) book title: ***Better Never to Have Been: The Harm of Coming into Existence***

TAKE 2 BUNNY GALLSTONES AND GET SOME REST

We found these actual medieval folk cures in an old book about English medical practices in the Middle Ages. So try them at your own risk.

• **To treat baldness**, rub some horse urine onto your scalp. If horse urine isn't available, dog urine can be substituted.

• **To treat a child's case of whooping cough**, feed some milk to a ferret. Whatever milk the ferret doesn't drink, give to the sick kid.

• **To eliminate jaundice**, drown exactly nine head lice in a pint of beer and drink it. Continue with this treatment every morning for a week.

• **To ease arthritis pain**, wear the skin of a donkey.

• **For deafness**, warm up a mixture of a rabbit's gallstone and fox grease and then pour it into your ear. (Don't make it too hot, though!)

• **Got gout?** Boil a red-haired dog in oil, add some worms and some bone marrow from a pig, and then apply the mixture to the affected area.

• **To stop an asthma attack**, coat some baby frogs and/or live spiders in butter and swallow them.

• **To cure leprosy**, take a bath in the blood of a dog.

• **Venereal disease** can be prevented by rubbing your genitals with vinegar. If that doesn't work and you still get VD, try wrapping your genitals in a freshly killed chicken.

• **Fractures, abscesses, paralysis, epilepsy, nausea, sore throats, and ulcers** can be cured by eating ancient Egyptian mummies. Though not a common practice these days, in medieval England it was quite the fad. Wealthy Europeans acquired the mummies via a trade route from Egypt. However, the fad ended when those wealthy Europeans discovered they weren't actually eating ancient mummies, but recently murdered slaves.

Robin Williams and Tom Cruise were both voted "Least Likely to Succeed" in high school.

GOVERN-MENTAL

More strange-but-true tales from the public sector.

DON'T PICK THIS CLASS

Controversy erupted in Oakland, California, in 2013 when mayor Jean Quan announced in her weekly newsletter that the city was sponsoring a community class entitled "How to Pick Locks." She explained that it was designed to teach people what to do if they got locked out of their residences, but a chorus of critics was quick to point out that the class was being offered at a time when home burglaries in Oakland were up 40 percent from the previous year. "What's next," asked one angry resident, "the Fundamentals of Armed Robbery?"

Quan canceled the class.

LOONY ORANGE LEPRECHAUN?

British prime minister David Cameron was mocked all over the Internet in 2013 when it was revealed that he didn't know what "lol" means. According to Rebekah Brooks, the former head of News International, she and Cameron occasionally exchanged text messages, which he'd conclude with "LOL, DC." He *thought* he was saying "Lots Of Love, David Cameron" until Brooks politely informed him that the abbreviation stands for "Laugh Out Loud."

It turned out that Cameron had been concluding much of his correspondence that way. (He doesn't anymore.)

STRAINER IN A STRANGE LAND

Wearing a large colander on his head, Christopher Schaeffer took his oath of office in the Pomfret (New York) town council in 2014. The colander was not a joke, Schaeffer said, but a symbol of his religion—the Church of the Flying Spaghetti Monster. He is a "Pastafarian Minister." The church was founded in 2005 by a 24-year-old named Bobby Henderson, who defended Schaeffer's odd headwear, saying, "Some people will see it as obnoxious, but I am completely confident that Schaeffer will distinguish himself as a council member of the highest caliber."

SPACED OUT

In 2014, three years into a four-year term, David Waddell decided to leave his seat as city councilman in Indian Trail, North Carolina. And he submitted his resignation letter in Klingon. Weirder still, he botched the translation. Instead of using one of the many websites dedicated to the *Star Trek* characters, Waddell typed the letter into Bing.com, clicked "Klingon" as the language, and copied and pasted the translation. Result:

Teach (the) city (the) constitution.
I will return next time to witness victory.
Resignation occurs in 2014 the 31st of January.
Perhaps today is a good day (to) resign.

Mayor Michael Alvarez couldn't tell whether the letter was bad Klingon or good Klingon, but he still didn't like it, saying it was "childish and unprofessional."

THE TIMES THEY AREN'T A-CHANGIN'

Remember those 3.5-inch floppy disks that PCs used nearly 20 years ago? The U.S. government remembers them…because they're still using them today. The news came to light in a December 2013 *New York Times* article. It explained that the *Federal Register*, "the daily journal of the U.S. government," regularly gathers information from various agencies and then issues a document (online and in print) consisting of proposed rule changes, proclamations, executive orders, etc., so that it can be available for public inspection. However, a few government agencies submit their information on the antiquated floppy disks. Why haven't they upgraded to at least CD-ROMs so modern computers can actually read them? According to the *Times*, "in part because legal and security requirements have yet to be updated, but mostly because the wheels of government grind ever so slowly."

LEAVING HER MARK

Late one night in May 2011, Tennessee state representative Julia Hurley was finishing up her first term as a lawmaker. While sitting in the House chamber, she carved her initials in the desk. Only problem: It wasn't *her* desk; it belongs to the state, and when the carving was discovered, Hurley had to pay to have it repaired. Matters worsened for her when the local news aired a report about the incident. "I don't understand why it's news," she complained, "and I don't want to talk about the desk." But the press wouldn't

---

let up, and Hurley was forced to talk about the desk. "It was like one in the morning on the last day of the session. I wasn't thinking straight."

THE HUNT FOR RED NOVEMBER

The Democratic National Committee wanted to demonstrate that the party is committed to national defense, so on the final night of their 2012 convention, they brought out a four-star general to speak, surrounded by dozens of military veterans. To really push the point home, the video screen behind them displayed an image of four warships. Only problem: The ships are in the Russian Navy. The DNC apologized and blamed the goof on "vendor error."

MINOR MAYOR

In July 2012, Bobby Tufts, age three, was elected mayor of Dorset, Minnesota. His first decree: to make ice cream the top of the food pyramid. When reporters asked what his favorite flavors were, Mayor Tufts replied, "Chocolate. And vanilla. Strawberry. Cotton candy. And rainbow sherbet." Technically, the small town (population: 28) doesn't have a local government, so Bobby's duties are ceremonial, and "elections" consist of drawing someone's name out of a hat…which makes it that much more amazing that at the end of the one-year term, Bobby, then four, was picked for a second time.

*   *   *

AT LEAST WE HAVEN'T COME TO BLOWS

In late 2013, several key members of prime minister Recep Erdogan's ruling party were arrested on corruption charges. Erdogan's supporters in Turkey's National Assembly responded to the arrests by passing a controversial bill that gave Erdogan increased powers over the nation's judiciary branch. That set off a raucous debate on the floor of parliament in February 2014, which quickly turned into a violent scuffle. One MP who threw a punch broke a finger; another took a punch in the face and stumbled away bloodied, with a broken nose. (The bill passed anyway.)

"Win if you can, lose if you must, but always cheat!" —Jesse "The Body" Ventura

TÊTE-À-TÊTE

Sometimes the funniest quotes are exchanges between two people.

Speaker: "I have only 10 minutes and hardly know where to begin."

Voice in back: "Begin at the ninth."

—**Jacob Braude**

Michael Curtiz, director, arranging a scene during *Casablanca*: "Wery nice, but I vant a poodle."

Prop Master: "But you never asked for one. We don't have one!"

Curtiz: "Vell, get one."

Prop Master: "What color?"

Curtiz: "Dark, you idiot, we're shooting in color!"

[A few minutes later, Curtiz is called out to see a large poodle.]

Curtiz: "Vat do I do with this goddamn dog?!"

Prop Master: "You said you wanted a poodle, Mr. Curtiz."

Curtiz: "I vanted a poodle in the street! A poodle. A poodle of water!"

Isadora Duncan, dancer: "You are the greatest brain in the world and I have the most beautiful body, so we ought to produce the most perfect child."

George Bernard Shaw: "What if the child inherits my beauty and your brains?"

Groucho: "You don't mind if I ask you a few personal questions, do you?"

Model: "If they're not too embarrassing."

Groucho: "Don't give it a second thought. I've asked thousands of questions on this show and I've yet to be embarrassed."

—*You Bet Your Life*

Young writer: "I don't know what title to give to my book."

J. M. Barrie: "Are there any trumpets in it?"

Young writer: "No."

J. M. Barrie: "Are there any drums in it?"

Young writer: "No."

J. M. Barrie: "Why not call it *Without Drums or Trumpets?*"

Alison Skipworth: "You seem to forget I've been an actress for forty years."

Mae West: "Don't worry, dearie, your secret's safe with me."

Brazilian soccer star Ramalho once had to spend 3 days in bed after taking a suppository orally.

OOPS!

The final installment of our all-time funniest goofs.

HOG HEAVEN

Australia's *Morning Bulletin* reported a story of seemingly biblical proportions in 2011 after a cyclone caused severe flooding in the northeast part of the country: "There have been 30,000 pigs floating down the Dawson River since last week." At least three other newspapers printed the *Bulletin's* report verbatim. Apparently no one at any of the press offices questioned that incredible figure. Readers, however, had a tough time believing it and challenged the papers. A little digging revealed the truth: When the *Bulletin's* reporter originally interviewed the pig farmer, he didn't say "30,000 pigs" were in the river—but rather "30 sows and pigs." The newspapers all printed corrections.

GONE WITH THE WIND

In 2008 Lefkos Hajji, a 28-year-old contractor from London, bought his girl-friend a $12,000 diamond engagement ring. He took it to a florist and had it placed inside a helium balloon, which was attached by a string to a bouquet of flowers. His plan: She would pop the balloon as he popped the question. But right after Hajji left the florist, the string slipped out of his hand. He watched in horror as the balloon—with his $12,000 ring inside—floated away. He never found it. "I felt like such a plonker," he said.

NOK IT OFF

In 2011 a photographer and his assistants arrived at the Manhattan home of antiquities collector Corice Arman to take pictures of her most prized pieces for *Art+Auction* magazine. Arman's only rule: "Don't move any of the pieces." But for some reason, while Arman was out of the room, an assistant picked up a large terra cotta figurine and moved it across the room…where it fell to the floor and "smashed to smithereens." When Arman returned, she was horrified. The statue, made in Nigeria by the ancient Nok people, was more than 2,600 years old and was valued at $300,000. She is suing the magazine. "I raised two kids around all this artwork," exclaimed Arman, "and they never broke anything!"

Women ingest about 50 percent of the lipstick they apply.

SORRY, HARLEY

In northern California in 2012, a 19-year-old Toyota Prius driver found himself driving behind several Hells Angels riding Harley-Davidsons. The excited teen grabbed his video camera and started filming, but didn't realize how close he was—until he accidentally bumped one of the bikers, who then careened into another biker, sending both of them to the pavement. When paramedics arrived at the scene, they treated the two Hells Angels for minor injuries …and the Prius driver for several punches to the face.

RUSSIAN ROULETTE

In 1980 the mayor of Leningrad held a lavish wedding for his daughter. Using his considerable clout, the mayor was able to convince the Hermitage Museum to lend him one of Mother Russia's most treasured antiques: Catherine the Great's china tea set. During the reception, when the spirits were flowing, one of the inebriated guests dropped his teacup. The other guests thought the man had proposed a toast, so they all followed suit and flung their priceless antiques into the fireplace. No more teacups.

BLACK (HUMOR) FOREST

In 2009 a woman living near a forest in Elmstein, Germany, heard loud screams coming from the woods. Alarmed, she called the police to report that someone was being tortured! Several heavily armed officers—and a rescue helicopter—rushed to the site. They ordered the perpetrator to release his victim and turn himself in. A bit later, a man named Roland Hoffman slowly emerged from the forest. He had gone in there to read a book, and was laughing so loud that the woman mistook it for tormented screams.

WHAT A TANGLED WEB WE WEAVE

A man in Beijing, China, wasn't getting along with his wife, so he started flirting online with a woman who called herself "I Want You." She wasn't getting along with her spouse, either, so after a month of chatting in secret, they decided to meet. But they hadn't shared pictures, so to pick each other out at the restaurant, each agreed to hold a newspaper in their right hand. When the man showed up, the only other person holding a newspaper was…his wife. When she looked up and saw him, they started yelling at each other so ferociously that security guards had to break up the fight.

On February 8, 2000, the meaning of life was auctioned on eBay. Winning bid: $3.26.

THAT'S ENTERTAINMENT?

*Show business wasn't always as highbrow as it is today. Before the dawn
of sophisticated entertainments such as sitcoms, reality shows, and
YouTube, stage performers could do almost any weird act…and
people would pay to see it. Here are some well-known—
and very strange—performers of yesteryear.*

NAME: Orville Stamm

ACT: "Musical Muscleman"

STORY: Stamm was a teenaged singer and fiddle player on the
vaudeville circuit known as "the Strongest Boy in the World." As he
played the violin, a huge bulldog clamped down on and hung from his
bowing arm. For the finale of his act, Stamm laid down on the stage face up
while a small upright piano was lowered onto his stomach. A pianist would
then jump up and down on Stamm's thighs while playing along to Stamm
singing "Ireland Must Be Heaven 'Cause My Mother Came from There."

NAME: Matthew Buchinger

ACT: "The One-Man Variety Show"

STORY: This 17th-century German entertainer had a dazzling array of
talents. He played 10 instruments (some of which he'd invented himself),
sang, danced, read minds, was a trick-shot artist and marksman, bowled,
did magic tricks, drew portraits and landscapes, and did calligraphy. Even
more impressive: Buchinger had no arms or legs. He had finlike appendages
instead of hands, and "stood" only 28 inches tall.

NAME: Datas

ACT: "The Memory Man"

STORY: Born W. J. M. Bottle, this early 20th-century performer's talent
was simply knowing lots of facts. Bottle had left school at the age of 11 to
earn money for his family. But he continued to learn, repeatedly reading
whatever books and newspapers he could find until he had the contents
committed to memory. For his act, he would ask the audience to submit
about 50 questions and then answer them in rapid-fire succession,

---

embellishing answers with extra information or droll humor. For instance, when asked "When was beef the highest?" Datas replied, "When the cow jumped over the moon." After he died, Datas's brain was autopsied. It weighed 69 ounces, the heaviest on record at the time.

NAME: Daniel Wildman

ACT: "The Bee Wrangler"

STORY: Here's his act: He rode a bicycle around a circus ring while a swarm of bees covered his face. Then he'd tell the bees to fly to a specific location…which they did.

NAME: LaRoche

ACT: "The Human Ball"

STORY: LaRoche (born Leon Rauch in Austria in 1857) would stuff himself in a brightly colored, two-foot-wide metal ball and then roll uphill to the top of a 30-foot-high, narrow spiral track. He did it so smoothly that it appeared as if the ball had magically moved upward on its own. In fact, the audience didn't even know anyone was inside until LaRoche popped out of the ball when he'd reached the top.

NAME: Bernard Cavanagh

ACT: "The Starvationist"

STORY: In the 1830s and '40s, Cavanagh amazed large crowds with his claims that he had gone long periods of time—weeks on end—without eating or drinking. He had himself confined without food in a London prison cell for a week in 1841 to prove it. Cavanagh claimed he once even went five years without nourishment. But he was exposed as a fraud when a woman caught him backstage eating sausage, bread, and a quarter pound of ham.

NAME: Tommy Minnock

ACT: "The Singing Martyr"

STORY: Minnock was one of America's most popular vaudevillians in the 1890s. Every night, he'd sing a popular song of the day called "After the Ball Is Over" while he hammered nails into his own hands and feet, attaching himself to a wooden cross.

Don't cry on the electric fence: Tears are made of almost all the same ingredients as urine.

MORE JOKES

Good for any audience!

John stood before the Pearly Gates and St. Peter asked him, "Have you done anything in your life that would qualify you to enter heaven?"

"Well, there's one thing. On a trip to South Dakota, I came upon a gang of bikers who were threatening an old lady. I told them to leave her alone, but they wouldn't listen. So I went right up to the biggest, most heavily tattooed biker. I whacked him on the head, kicked his bike over, ripped out his nose ring and threw it on the ground, and told him 'Leave her alone now, or you'll answer to me!'"

St. Peter was impressed. "When did this happen?"

"Just a couple of minutes ago."

Grandma's 100th birthday party was not a huge success. The family wheeled her onto the lawn for a picnic. When she slowly started to lean to the right, her daughter stuffed a pillow on her right side to prop her up. A bit later, she started leaning to her left. Her son straightened her up and stuffed a pillow on her left side. Soon she started tilting forward. This time her other son caught her and tied a pillow around her waist.

A few minutes later, her nephew arrived. He said, "Hey, Grandma! How's life treating you?"

Grandma, who could no longer speak, took out her notepad and wrote, "Terrible. They won't let me fart."

The mad scientist made a clone of himself, but something went wrong—all the clone wanted to do was stick his head out the third-story window and shout dirty words at passersby. The scientist, seeing no other option, pushed the clone out the window. He was arrested for making an obscene clone fall.

One day an auto mechanic was working under a car and some brake fluid accidentally dripped into his mouth. "Wow," he thought. "That stuff tastes good!" The next day he told a friend about his amazing discovery: "I think I'll have a little more today." His friend was concerned but didn't say anything. The next day the mechanic drank a whole bottle of brake fluid. A few days later he was up to several bottles a day. And now his friend was really worried.

"Don't you know brake fluid is toxic?" said the friend. "You'd better stop drinking it."

"Hey, no problem," he said. "I can stop any time."

An old man wanted to plant a tomato garden, but it was difficult work, and his only son, Vincent, was in prison. The old man described the predicament in a letter: "Dear Vincent, Looks like there will be no tomatoes this year. I'm just too old to be digging. I wish you were here to dig it for me. Love, Dad"

A few days later he received a letter: "Dear Dad, Sorry I'm not there to help, but whatever you do, don't dig up that garden. That's where I buried the bodies! Love, Vincent"

That night, FBI agents arrived and dug up the entire area without finding any bodies. They apologized and left. The next day, the old man received another letter: "Dear Dad, Go ahead and plant the tomatoes now. That's the best I could do under the circumstances. Love, Vinnie"

Two golfers—one old and one young—are playing a round together. On a particularly difficult hole, the young man's tee shot landed about 20 yards short of a large pine tree blocking the green. "You know, sonny," said the old man, "when I was your age, I'd hit that ball right over that tree."

So the young man digs in, swings as hard as he can, and smacks the ball right into the tree. It ricochets back and lands right in front of the two golfers.

"Of course, when I was your age," says the old man, "that tree was only about ten feet tall."

As a man stepped off the curb to cross the street, a car came screaming around the corner and headed straight for him. The alarmed man tried to hurry across the street, but the car changed lanes and maintained its collision course. So the man turned around to run back to the curb, but the car changed lanes again. Panicking, the old man froze in the middle of the road. The car pulled up beside him and the window rolled down. The driver was a squirrel.

"See?" said the squirrel. "It's not as easy as it looks."

Japanese invention: the Choc-U-Lator, a calculator that looks and smells like a chocolate bar.

ON ANIMALS

These comedians just love animals (but not in the gross way).

"A dog goes into a hardware store and says, 'I'd like a job, please.' The hardware store owner says, 'We don't hire dogs, why don't you go join the circus?' The dog replies, 'What would the circus want with a plumber?'"
—**Steven Alan Green**

"Stuffed deer heads on walls are bad enough, but it's worse when they are wearing sunglasses and have streamers in their antlers because then you know they were enjoying themselves at a party when they were shot."
—**Ellen DeGeneres**

"You learn a lot in your teenage years. For instance, I learned that if you're ever being chased by a police dog, try not to go through a little tunnel, then onto a mini seesaw, and then jump through a ring of fire—they've trained for that, you see."
—**Danny McCrossan**

"Sometimes I'm afraid of bears. Sometimes I'm not. I must be bipolar."
—**Peter Sasso**

"I've always wanted to give birth …to kittens. It'd hurt less, and when you're done, you'd have kittens!"
—**Betsy Salkind**

"Watching a baby being born is a little like watching a wet St. Bernard coming in through the cat door."
—**Jeff Foxworthy**

"I don't see the point of testing cosmetics on rabbits, because they're already cute."
—**Rich Hall**

"I got a dog, a cocker spaniel. He swallowed a Viagra pill. Now he's a pointer."
—**Rodney Dangerfield**

"How great would it be if actors had tails, because tails are so expressive. I have cats and you can tell if they're annoyed. If they're scared, they bush their tail. If I had to play scared in a movie, all I'd have to do is bush my tail. I think that if actors had tails it would change everything."
—**Christopher Walken**

What do Scottish men wear under their kilts? Traditionally, nothing at all.

GOING MY WAY

Anyone can make a name for themselves with the things they do in life. It takes real creativity (and an accommodating undertaker) to make your biggest splash after you've departed this world.

Deceased: Lonnie Holloway of Saluda, South Carolina

Details: In 1973 Holloway bought a brand-new emerald-green Pontiac Catalina coupe. He'd purchased other cars over the years, but he really loved that Catalina and drove it for the rest of his life. And before he died in 2009 at the age of 90, he told his family he wanted to be buried in it.

Going His Way: The Rock Hill Baptist Church, which owned the cemetery where Holloway wanted to be buried, had no objection. So Holloway was propped up in the front seat of his Catalina with his favorite hat on his head, $100 in his pocket, and his hands gripping the wheel, and then a construction crane lowered the car into the ground. The trunk of the Catalina was filled with Holloway's extensive collection of guns (not because Holloway had asked to be buried with them but because "somebody might take them and shoot somebody," his cousin Johnny McCloud explained). The grave was covered with a slab of concrete to keep people from stealing the guns, the car, or the $100.

Note: Holloway and his Catalina were laid to rest right beside the grave of his wife, Alice, who died in 2007. Alice did not join her husband in the Catalina; she's still in her coffin alongside the car. (No word on whether that was her decision or Holloway's.)

Deceased: Irene Bowler of Ramsgate, Kent, in southeastern England

Details: Not long before she died in 1998 at the age of 76, Bowler read an article about people scattering the ashes of loved ones by putting them into fireworks and shooting them into the sky. She told her family that she, too, wanted to go out with a BANG!

Going Her Way: Bowler's daughter, Judith Summers, needed some time to adjust to the idea of having her mother made into a giant firework. But then she found a company called Theatrical Pyrotechnics that was willing to inter her mother in a rocket and shoot it 500 feet into the sky on the evening of her memorial service. "It was all very impressive," Summers told London's *Evening Standard* newspaper. "It went with a real bang followed by a spectacular starburst. I know it is unusual, but I suppose it is just another way of scattering ashes."

Deceased: James Henry Smith of Pittsburgh, Pennsylvania

Details: Before he died from prostate cancer in 2005 at the age of 55, Smith told his family that he didn't want an ordinary viewing with people filing past his open coffin. Instead, he wanted to go out the way he'd spent so many pleasant Sunday afternoons: dressed in his robe and Pittsburgh Steelers pajamas and watching his beloved Black and Gold on TV.

Going His Way: A room at the funeral home was redecorated to look like Smith's living room. Then he was dressed in his game-day robe and jammies and laid out, sitting in his recliner, legs crossed with a remote control in his hand and a beer and cigarettes within easy reach, in front of a television playing Steelers highlights. His favorite Steelers blanket was draped over the side of the chair. "I saw it and I couldn't even cry," Smith's friend Mary Jones told the *Pittsburgh Post-Gazette*. "People will see him the way he was."

Deceased: Jack Woodward, the former proprietor of the Boat Inn in Northamptonshire, England

Details: The Boat Inn has been in Woodward's family since 1877. He was born in the pub and tended bar there from the age of 14 until he retired. After that he was a regular at the pub until shortly before his death in 2008 at the age of 83.

Going My Way: In his will, Woodward asked that his ashes be buried beneath the pub's floorboards. His son Andrew, who took over the running of the inn, was happy to oblige. The spot in the floor is marked with a brass plaque that reads "Stand here and have a drink on me. Jack 1924–2008." Patrons of the bar have been having drinks on Jack ever since.

*   *   *

"The truth does not change according to our ability to stomach it."

—**Flannery O'Connor**

Q: What's brown and sounds like a cowbell? A: DUNNNG!

EYEBALL BLING

We decked out Uncle John with all of these interesting fashion accessories, and—well, he got a lot of funny looks. (Try it on your favorite friend or relative.)

EYE-CATCHING JEWELRY

You may have thought that there was jewelry for every possible body part: fingers, wrists, neck, toes, ankles, ears, lips, bellybutton, private parts—but now you can wear jewelry on your eyeballs, too. Dutch designer Eric Klarenbeek sells a line of contact lenses that come with thin metal wires attached to the center of the lenses. The wires hang down and can be adorned with the jewels of your choice. So you can walk around with a short string of diamonds hanging from each eyeball (or, if you're really chic, just one). "People who have worn my eye jewelry are amazed at its comfort," Klarenbeek says. "You can't feel the wire dangling, it doesn't affect your sight, and the lens moves along gently with your eyeball." Asked what would happen if someone were to tug on the wire connected to a contact lens, Klarenbeek said he was quite sure that it would not cause your eyeball to fall out. They cost about $300 per lens.

LEFT-HANDED UNDERPANTS

When it comes to men's underwear, left-handers have always been at a disadvantage. The vertical opening at the front of most briefs and boxers, which allows men to "go" without dropping their drawers, is made with right-handed people in mind. Watch a lefty try to take a simple tinkle while wearing right-handed underpants and you'll think he's been drinking, or missing several fingers. British underwear company Hom has come out with a new design—drawers with a horizontal rather than vertical opening, making it just as easy for a lefty to open as a righty. "In our view," said one retailer, "this is a vital step toward equality for left-handed men."

NICE CUP IN BRA

Ladies, if you've ever found yourself thinking, "I wish I had a bra that could be easily converted into a five-foot putting green," wish no more. British lingerie maker Triumph has introduced the Nice Cup in Bra (it was made for the Japanese market). When it's worn, it's a functional, green, corsetlike bra. But when you get the urge to putt a few golf balls, just take the bra off, unroll it—and it becomes a putting green. The bra's cups become holes at the end of the green. It even has pockets for extra balls and tees, and if you sink a putt, a recorded voice says, "Nice shot!" The Nice Cup in Bra also comes with a miniskirt printed with the words "Be quiet" that can be converted into a flag to hush the crowd while you're concentrating.

WINKING PANTS

Do you want to be able to wink at people behind you while you're walking down the street...without turning around? Well, thankfully, some enterprising clothes designers in Everett, Washington, have invented "Winkers," pants that have eyes painted on the butt, just under the crease, so that as you walk, the eyes seem to open and close. So you "wink" as you walk. Winkers cost between $140 and $160.

THE VENDING MACHINE SKIRT

Let's say you're walking on a sidewalk dressed in an ordinary skirt, when... *Here come the bad guys! They're chasing you! Run! Hide!* Too bad you weren't wearing the Vending Machine Skirt. Designed by Tokyo designer Aya Tsukioka, it looks like a normal skirt, but when you need to become invisible, it quickly unfolds into a large, rectangular piece of cloth that looks like a soda vending machine. Just hold it in front of you and hide behind it, the idea goes, and you'll blend into the scenery. "Vending machines are on every corner of Japanese streets, and we take it for granted," says Tsukioka. "That's how I came up with the idea for this dress."

*   *   *

THREE REAL CLASSIFIED ADS

• "Easy-going athletic SJM, 41, seeking SF, looks not important, must be tall, slim and attractive."

• "PIG! I saw you at Tiki Bobs. You grabbed my butt and I told you if you did that again I'd kill you. You did. I need your address now."

• "This large personal ad cost $340 to run. Needless to say, on our first date, we'll be going dutch."

William Shatner, Hollywood's biggest ham, doesn't eat meat.

THE MEANING OF LI-FI

If you've ever tried to set up a wireless router in your home or just tried to access the Internet in a Starbucks using your iPad, you're familiar with the list of Wi-Fi networks that pop up when you do. Most have pretty boring names, but some people go for laughs when naming theirs.

The LAN before time

Area 51

Your Bathroom Shower
Needs New Tiles

Help Me Pay For It

The Meaning of LiFi

Secret CIA Intelligence
Underground Military Base

Why Phi?

Holy *$#% We're Online

The Dingo Ate My Wi-Fi

FBI Surveillance Van #42

RCMP Surveillance Horse

It Hurts When IP

IfYouGuessMyPassword
IHaveToRenameMyDog

Mom Click Here For Internet

Alien Abduction Network

Global Thermonuclear War

SHUT YOUR DOG UP
OR I WILL CALL THE COPS

IP Freely

Caitlin stop using our Internet!

HeyUGetOffMyLAN

NCC-1701

Abraham Linksys

.— .. ..-. ..
(morse code for WiFi)

I'm Under Your Bed

Nuclear Launch Detected

Secret Federal Witness
Protection Safehouse

I'm cheating on my WiFi

John Wilkes Bluetooth

c:\virus.exe

Router—IHardlyKnowHer

Bill Wi the Science Fi

LAN of Milk and Honey

"I failed kindergarten because I couldn't spell my last name." —Zach Galifianakis

GOVERN-MENTAL

Five-time presidential candidate Eugene McCarthy said, "The only thing that saves us from the bureaucracy is inefficiency. An efficient bureaucracy is the greatest threat to liberty." (Looks like our liberty is safe.)

SENIORS IN SENSIBLE SHOES

Australia's leading relationship counseling body has a suggestion to older women who have outlived their husbands and are worried about burying another man: Try a woman instead. "As women get over 60, opportunities to find a man diminish substantially. Men marry younger women and they die about eight years younger, so there is a real male shortage," said Relationships Australia spokesman Jack Carney. "And as women get even older it gets much worse, so we ask them to entertain the idea of lesbian relationships."

A KILLER MISTAKE

When U.S. Representative Michele Bachmann kicked off her presidential campaign in 2011, she did so from Waterloo, Iowa. "John Wayne was from Waterloo," she boasted in her speech, "That's the kind of spirit that I have, too!" One problem: It was John Wayne *Gacy* who was from Waterloo—a serial killer who murdered 33 people. John Wayne the movie star was from another town on the other side of Iowa.

A SNAFU AT HQ

After the U.S. armed forces invaded Iraq and squashed the existing army, it fell upon the Americans to create a new Iraqi army, one that was better run, better organized, and more inspiring to the average man on the street. Thus was born the New Iraqi Corps. It was inspiring, but not in the way the U.S. authorities had hoped. Why? Make an acronym of "New Iraqi Corps" in English and you get the innocent-sounding "NIC." But translate "New Iraqi Corps" into Arabic and make an acronym out of that, and you get something a little more...spicy. How spicy? Well, let's just say that if there were a U.S. military unit called the Fabulous Underwater Corps, it'd have basically the same problem in English as the New Iraqi Corps has in Arabic. Result: The New Iraqi Corps was renamed the New Iraqi Army.

Gelotology is the study of laughter. (We thought it was *laughology*. Oops.)

MISSING THE POINT

A Russian tightrope walker was told to wear a hard hat while performing his act in Britain—this despite the fact that the man does his act without a net. Goussein Khamdoulaev, a performer with the Moscow State Circus, traded in his usual Cossack hat when the circus was told by insurers that it had to comply with new workplace rules put in place by the European Union. What value the hard hat would have if Khamdoulaev fell from the traditional tightrope height of 50 feet is unclear.

BUSHWHACKED!

• In 1989 President George H. W. Bush was giving a speech in Poland when it started to rain. He ordered a Secret Service guard—who was holding Bush's raincoat—to give it to an old woman on the other side of the fence. The press praised the president for his selfless generosity. Sixteen years later, Bush admitted that the raincoat wasn't his; it belonged to the guard…who was just about to put it on.

• In 1991 the White House held a two-day conference to promote President Bush's new economic agenda. During the panel discussion, however, the invited financial experts were a bit befuddled by the television monitor in front of Bush. In big letters, the message displayed on the screen read: "Financial Challanges for Today and Tomorrow!" (What's a "challange"?)

• In 2006 an anonymous aide to President George W. Bush reported that the commander in chief "can't get enough of fart jokes." And not only that, Bush often greeted young aides with a "21-trumpet salute," just to alleviate some of the stress they may be feeling about meeting the president.

DUEL THE RIGHT THING

In Kentucky, whenever a politician takes office, he or she must recite an oath that was written in 1847, which reads, in part: "I, being a citizen of this state, have not fought a duel with deadly weapons within this State nor out of it, nor have a sent or accepted a challenge to fight a duel with deadly weapons, nor have I acted as second in carrying a challenge, nor aided or assisted any person, thus offending, so help me God." In 2012 state representative Darryl Owens proposed a law that would delete the outdated dueling provision from the oath. His reason: "Every time we get to that part of the ceremony, laughter erupts." The bill failed.

Hogwarts motto: *Draco dormiens nunquam titillandus* ("Never tickle a sleeping dragon").

WHO SMELT THE IRON?

We all make dumb comments now and then, which we hope nobody notices, or that if they do, they're not writing them down. The people who made these bloopers weren't so lucky. Believe it or not, these are real.

KIDS' FAKE EXCUSES FOR SCHOOL ABSENCE

"Please excuse Mary for being absent. She was sick and I had her shot."

"Please excuse Ray Friday from school. He has very loose vowels."

"Please excuse Jimmy for being. It's his father's fault."

"Please excuse Harriet for missing school yesterday. We forgot to get the Sunday paper off the porch, and when we found it on Monday, we thought it was Sunday."

DOCTORS' MEDICAL REPORTS

"Patient was tearful and crying constantly. She also appears depressed."

"Patient has left his white blood cells at another hospital."

"When she fainted, her eyes rolled around the room."

"Discharge status: Alive but without permission."

COMMENTS FROM VISITORS TO U.S. NATIONAL PARKS

"We had no trouble finding the park entrances, but where are the exits?"

"The coyotes made too much noise last night and kept me awake. Please eradicate those annoying animals."

"Too many rocks in the mountains."

"Where does Bigfoot live?"

STUDENT SCHOOLWORK

"The inhabitants of Moscow are called Mosquitoes."

"A census taker is a man who goes from house to house increasing the population."

"Most of the houses in France are made of plaster of Paris."

"Iron was discovered because someone smelt it."

"The four seasons are salt, pepper, mustard, and vinegar."

QUESTIONS FOR CANADIAN FOREST RANGERS

"Where does Alberta and Canada begin?"

"Can you help? My husband's driving me crazy and he won't shut up."

"Do you have a glacier at this visitor centre?"

"Is this a map I'm looking at?"

"Don't all Canadians wear raccoon hats? Where can I buy one?"

"I've got the fifth sense: I smell dead people." —Robin Williams

WINNING QUOTE QUIZ

You can leave off your thinking caps for this one.

Speaker: Ronaldo, Brazilian soccer star
Quote: "We lost because we didn't…"
          a. "win"   **b.** "show up"   **c.** "cheat"

Speaker: Tony LaRussa, baseball manager
Quote: "When you're not winning, it's tough to…"
    a. "win a game"   **b.** "remember your name"   **c.** "place the blame"

Speaker: Chuck Knox, football coach
Quote: "Football players win…"
      a. "football games"   **b.** "baseball games"   **c.** "the lottery"

Speaker: David Garcia, baseball manager
Quote: "The only reason we're 7-0 is because we've…"
    a. "won all seven of our games"   **b.** "lost all seven of our games"
              c. "won all twelve of our games"

Speaker: Jimmy Hill, soccer announcer
Quote: "If England is to win this game, they are going to have to…"
    a. "score a goal"   **b.** "not score a goal"   **c.** "not score two goals"

Speaker: Alexander Haig, pundit
Quote: "The only way the Republican Party can hold the White House is to nominate a candidate who can…"
         a. "win"   **b.** "lose"   **c.** "seduce an intern"

Speaker: Isiah Thomas, basketball analyst
Quote: "A lot is said about defense, but at the end of the game, the team with the most points…"
         a. "wins"   **b.** "loses"   **c.** "seduces an intern"

All the answers are "a," of course.

Real (odd) book title: ***Tattooed Mountain Women and Spoon Boxes of Daghestan***

THE GREAT CARNAC

In a recurring Tonight Show *bit, Johnny Carson donned a cape and feathered turban and became "Carnac the Magnificent." Ed McMahon handed him a sealed envelope, which Carnac would hold up to his forehead. Then he'd say an "answer," open the envelope, and read the "question"—a groaningly bad punchline. A few examples.*

A: "Gatorade."
Q: "What does an alligator get on welfare?"

A: "Milk and honey."
Q: "What do you get from a bee that has an udder?"

A: "An unmarried woman."
Q: "What was Elizabeth Taylor between 3 and 5 p.m. on June 1, 1952?"

A: "Camelot."
Q: "Where do Arabs park their camels?"

A: "Rub-a-dub-dub."
Q: "What does a masseuse do to your dub-dub?"

A: "Supervisor."
Q: "What does Clark Kent use to keep the sun out of his eyes?"

A: "Head and shoulders."
Q: "What do you see if you open the trunk of the Godfather's car?"

A: "E-I-E-I-Owwwww!"
Q: "What did Old MacDonald say when he got a vasectomy?"

A: "Shareholder."
Q: "What did Sonny Bono used to be?"

A: "Disjoint."
Q: "What was dat hippie smoking?"

A: "Rose Bowl."
Q: "What do you say when it's Rose's turn at the bowling alley?"

A: "Follow the yellow brick road."
Q: "What are the directions to a urologist's office?"

A: "Three Dog Night."
Q: "What's a bad night for a tree?"

A: "Igloo."
Q: "What do you use to keep your ig from falling off?"

"HOLY OLEO, BATMAN!"

The campy 1960s Batman TV series generated 120 episodes...and 359 separate utterances of Robin's "Holy [blank], Batman!" catchphrase. (That's three per episode.) Here are a few choice examples.

"Holy taxidermy, Batman!"

"Holy bank balance, Batman!"

"Holy semantics, Batman!"

"Holy wedding cake, Batman!"

"Holy stewpot, Batman!"

"Holy rats in a trap, Batman!"

"Holy squirrel cage, Batman!"

"Holy chicken coop, Batman!"

"Holy travel agent, Batman!"

"Holy contributing to the delinquency of minors, Batman!"

"Holy Long John Silver, Batman!"

"Holy Bluebeard, Batman!"

"Holy Venezuela, Batman!"

"Holy hole in a doughnut, Batman!"

"Holy oleo, Batman!"

"Holy haberdashery, Batman!"

"Holy sardine, Batman!"

"Holy red snapper, Batman!"

"Holy costume party, Batman!"

"Holy floor covering, Batman!"

"Holy waste of energy, Batman!"

"Holy slipped disc, Batman!"

"Holy understatements, Batman!"

"Holy jelly molds, Batman!"

"Holy known unknown flying objects, Batman!"

"Holy bunions, Batman!"

"Holy astringent plumlike fruit, Batman!"

"Holy mashed potatoes, Batman!"

"Holy coffin nails, Batman!"

"Holy hors d'oeuvre, Batman!"

"Holy Benedict Arnold, Batman!"

"Holy potluck, Batman!"

"Holy remote-control robot, Batman!"

Mom: "Billy! Why are you sitting on the toilet and hitting yourself...

SLEEPWALKING IN THE U.K.

Time for some strange stories about sleepwalking. For reasons we can't explain, they all occurred in the British Isles.

A YAWN ON THE LAWN

One night in March 2005, Rebekah Armstrong of London awoke around 2:00 a.m. to the sound of a motor outside her home. She immediately noticed that her husband, 34-year-old Ian Armstrong, wasn't beside her in bed, so she went looking for him. A few minutes later she found him in their yard, mowing the lawn...in his sleep. He was also naked. "I dread to think how long he'd been there," she told the *Sun* newspaper the next day, "but he'd nearly finished." She was afraid to wake him in the middle of the task, so she unplugged the electric mower and left her naked husband walking back and forth across their lawn in the middle of the night pushing the now-quiet mower—and went back to bed. Ian climbed back into bed some time later. The next morning, Rebekah told reporters, she had to point out her husband's dirty, grass-stained feet to convince him that he'd actually mowed the lawn in his sleep.

WINDOW DRESSING

Rachel Ward, 18, of Horsham, West Sussex, went to bed around 9:30 one evening in May 2009. A few hours later, her parents heard her screaming for help and found her in a daze outside their home. The teen, who had no memory of how she'd gotten there, had apparently gotten up from bed, walked in her sleep across the bedroom, crawled out the second-story window, and fallen 25 feet to the ground below. Divots in the ground (she landed on a narrow strip of grass just a few feet from the asphalt driveway) indicated she'd landed on her feet. Amazingly, X-rays showed no broken bones. (When her parents found her, Rachel was wearing a "jumper"—the British term for a sweater—which she hadn't been wearing when she went to bed. She apparently put it on in her sleep before taking that leap.)

HIGH THERE!

In June 2005, a 15-year-old girl in London got up in the middle of the night, walked in her sleep from her home to a nearby building site, climbed 130 feet into the air on the arm of a crane, then walked across a narrow steel beam to a large concrete block that served as a counterweight for the crane arm. A passerby saw the girl and immediately called emergency services. Police feared the girl was suicidal, but when a rescue worker made it up the crane and reached her, she was curled up on the concrete block…fast asleep. The worker gently woke her up, ready to grab her in case she was startled, then got her to use her cell phone to call her parents. They kept the girl calm while a rescue ladder was sent to the scene, and after a delicate two-hour rescue operation, she was lowered to safety. After being checked out in a local hospital (she was fine), the girl was sent home. Her parents told police she was a regular sleepwalker.

IT'ZZZZZZZZZ ART

By day, Lee Hadwin is a nurse in Wales. By night, he's a sleep artist. When he awakes each morning he finds that during the night he's made as many as 10 elaborately detailed pencil drawings. His subjects range from humans to landscapes to fantastical creatures to intricate abstract designs. Yet, despite this, Hadwin claims to lack both an aptitude and interest in art. "It is the most extraordinary feeling to wake up and find myself surrounded by artworks and have no recollection of having drawn them," he told the *Daily Mail*. Hadwin's problem began when he was four (he drew on walls). As a teenager on a sleepover, he drew all over a friend's kitchen. Since his 20s, he's left art supplies scattered around the house for himself. He's agreed to have himself filmed for a documentary (while he sleeps) and to be observed by the Edinburgh Sleep Centre (while he sleeps).

ZZZ…OW…ZZZ…OW…ZZZ…OW…

Morag Fisher, 40, was staying at the home of a friend in Long Eaton, near Nottingham in central England, when she got up in the middle of the night and went on one of her regular sleepwalks. In her own home, such nighttime excursions ended with Fisher simply returning to her bed. But because she was staying at a friend's house…things didn't end well. The sleepwalking woman fell down a set of steep stairs and broke her jaw, nose, both cheekbones, one eye socket, a couple of ribs, and both wrists, and damaged vertebrae in her neck and back. Fisher's friend, 39-year-old Carl Muggleton, found her in a pool of blood at the bottom of the staircase and, fearing she was dead, called emergency services. Fisher had to undergo multiple surgeries, but she made what doctors called a remarkable recovery and was able to return home in less than two weeks. Bonus: Fisher slept through the entire ordeal and didn't wake up until she was in the ambulance. (There are now baby gates at the top of the stairs in both Fisher's and Muggleton's homes.)

Duct tape was invented during WWII as waterproof sealing tape for ammunition boxes.

BEN KINGSLEY'S HAIR

Critics agree: The 2005 sci-fi movie A Sound of Thunder *was one of the year's worst. Why? In addition to the laughable dialogue and cheesy special effects, there was that poofy white wig worn by British actor Ben Kingsley.*

"The usually-bald actor has been given a thick thatch so white it almost glows in the dark. Now that's scary."
—**Movie Mom's Review**

"Ben Kingsley sports a white wig that looks like a lump of cotton candy perched on his head."
—**CNN**

"It's 2055. Ben Kingsley has grown a head of 'Man from Glad' hair and presides over Time Safari, Inc."
—*Toronto Star*

"They keep going back to the same spot and shooting the same poor dinosaur, allowing director Peter Hyams to use the same sequence over and over, thereby saving money to pay for Kingsley's snowy-white Chia Pet head."
—*The Arizona Republic*

"Kingsley is forced to wear an out-rageous wig that makes it appear he has a massive White Persian cat perched atop his head."
—*Variety*

"Someone has also apparently gone back to the 20th century to retrieve a truckload of double-breasted chalk-stripe suits and—to judge from Mr. Kingsley's white pompadour—Jack Valenti's hair."
—*The New York Times*

"Ben Kingsley pits his hairdo against Edward Burns' space suit."
—**Roger Ebert**

"The saddest thing is watching an actor of Kingsley's caliber try and say his lines without being embarrassed…made even harder with the ridiculous wig he's forced to wear. Did these guys lose a bet or something?"
—**ThreeMovieBuffs.com**

"I'm talkin' pure white Cesar Romero Joker-style hair."
—**MovieJuice.com**

"Kingsley has scary hair. It's tall and white and exceedingly strange, like Donald Trump's collided with Siegfried Fischbacher."
—*USA Today*

Somebody had to: In '03 biologist K.W. Moeliker did a study on homosexual necrophiliac ducks.

HONK IF YOU LOVE BUMPER STICKERS

We keep thinking that we've seen every clever bumper sticker that exists, but every year readers send us new ones. Have you seen the one that says…

I'll rise, but I won't shine

I would never sell out unless I got a lot of money for it

YOU CAN PICK YOUR NOSE AND PICK YOUR FRIENDS, BUT YOU CAN'T WIPE YOUR FRIENDS ON THE COUCH

CLEAR THE ROAD, I'M 16!

A barrel full of monkeys would *not* be fun—it would be horrifying

All I want is less to do, more time to do it, and higher pay for not getting it done

When in doubt, mumble

EVERYTHING I NEED TO KNOW I LEARNED IN PRISON

Caution: Impending Doom

ONE MORE REPO, AND I'LL BE DEBT-FREE!

I do what the bumper stickers tell me to

LEGALLY, IT'S QUESTIONABLE, MORALLY, DISGUSTING. PERSONALLY, I LIKE IT.

Don't call me infantile, you stinkybutt poophead!

I *do* work for food

Follow your dreams, except that one where you're at school in your underwear

SHH! I'M LISTENING TO A BOOK

C'mon, give me the finger like you mean it

The closer you get, the slower I go

WATCH OUT! I'M LATE FOR DRIVERS' ED CLASS!

When life gives you lemons, shut up and eat your lemons

Sylvester Stallone's first acting role: the lower half of Smokey Bear in a Cub Scouts play.

WERE YOU RAISED IN A BARN?

Tell the truth—how are your manners? Maybe you need some help from these old etiquette books. You may not believe it, but we really didn't make these up.

"Although asparagus may be taken in the fingers, don't take a long drooping stalk, hold it up in the air, and catch the end of it in your mouth like a fish."

—*Etiquette* (1922)

"Do not move back and forth on your chair. Whoever does that gives the impression of constantly farting or trying to fart."

—*On Civility in Children* (1530)

"If a dish is distasteful to you, decline it, but make no remarks about it. It is sickening and disgusting to explain at a table how one article makes you sick, or why some other dish has become distasteful to you. I have seen a well-dressed tempting dish go from a table untouched, because one of the company told a most disgusting anecdote about finding vermin served in a similar dish."

—*Martine's Handbook of Etiquette* (1866)

"It is not the correct thing to put the spoon or fork so far into the mouth that the bystanders are doubtful of its return to the light."

—*The Correct Thing in Good Society* (1902)

"No decent person laughs at a funeral."

—*The Bazar Book of Decorum* (1870)

"When you have blown your nose, you should not open your handkerchief and inspect it, as though pearls or rubies had dropped out of your skull. Such behavior is nauseating and is more likely to lose us the affection of those who love us than to win us the favor of others."

—*The Book of Manners* (1958)

"Never put your cold, clammy hands on a person, saying, 'Did you ever know anyone to have such cold hands as mine?'"

—*Manners for Millions* (1932)

No thanks: *Formicophilia* is the fetish for having insects crawl around on your private parts.

"It is unmannerly to fall asleep, as many people do, whilst the company is engaged in conversation. Their conduct shows that they have little respect for their friends and care nothing either for them or their talk. Besides, they are generally obliged to doze in an uncomfortable position, and this nearly always causes them to make unpleasant noises and gestures in their sleep. Often enough they begin to sweat and dribble at the mouth."

—*The Book of Manners* (1958)

"Peevish temper, cross and frowning faces, and uncomely looks have sometimes been cured in France by sending the child into an octagonal boudoir lined with looking glasses, where, whichever way it turned, it would see the reflection of its own unpleasant features, and be constrained, out of self-respect, to assume a more amiable disposition."

—*Good Behavior* (1876)

"If you ask the waiter for anything, you will be careful to speak to him gently in the tone of request, and not of command. To speak to a waiter in a driving manner will create, among well-bred people, the suspicion that you were sometime a servant yourself, and are putting on airs at the thought of your promotion."

—*The Perfect Gentleman* (1860)

"It is bad manners, when you see something to nauseate you by the roadside, as sometimes happens, to turn to your companions and point it out to them. Still less should you offer any evil smelling object for others to sniff, as some people do, insisting upon holding it up to their noses and asking them to smell how horrible it is."

—*The Book of Manners* (1958)

"When not practicable for individuals to occupy separate beds, the persons should be of about the same age, and in good health. Numerous cases have occurred where healthy, robust children have 'dwindled away' and died within a few months, from sleeping with old people."

—*The People's Common Sense Medical Adviser* (1876)

"Applause is out of order at any religious service."

—*Your Best Foot Forward* (1955)

"It'd be a good idea." —Mahatma Gandhi, when asked what he thought of Western civilization

THE 25 YEARS OF PANTS

Take two brothers-in-law and add in one pair of unwanted pants.
Then toss in some competitive spirit and creative packaging.
And what do you get? A bizarre holiday tradition.

FOR ME? YOU SHOULDN'T HAVE

While he was away at college in 1964, Larry Kunkel received a Christmas present from his mom—a pair of yellow moleskin pants. One problem: They hardened up in the cold Minnesota winters. So the next Christmas, Kunkel decided to regift them to his brother-in-law, Roy Collette, who didn't want them either, so he gave them back to Kunkel the following year. And with that, a tradition was born.

For the next 25 Christmases, Kunkel and Collette devised new ways to stick the other with the pants. The rules: Only junk parts can be used for wrapping materials, expenses must be kept to a minimum, and if the pants are damaged the game will end. As each brother-in-law tired to outdo the other, the "gift boxes" got more and more elaborate. Some examples:

• a green, 3-foot cube that was a compacted 1974 AMC Gremlin (The tag said the pants were in the glove compartment.)

• a welded shut, 600-pound, green-and-red-striped safe

• an 8 x 2-foot truck tire filled with 6,000 pounds of concrete ("Have a Goodyear!" said the tag)

• a 17-foot, 6-ton model rocket filled with concrete

• a 225-pound steel ashtray made from 8-inch steel casings

• a 4-ton replica of a Rubik's Cube

• a station wagon filled with 170 steel generators all welded together

SLACKING OFF

Just when it was starting to seem as if the pants might outlive their owners, tragedy struck. In 1989 Collette sent the pants away to be encased in 10,000 pounds of glass. But as the molten glass was poured over the moleskin pants, they were incinerated. That Christmas, Collette sent Kunkel a brass urn filled with the ashes of the pants, accompanied by this epitaph: "Sorry, Old Man, here lies the pants."

Small talk: There are a quadrillion femtoseconds in one second.

NUDES & PRUDES

Nudity can be shocking…and so can prudery. But these characters demonstrate that whether you're dressed or naked, you can still be dumb (and funny).

NUDE…On Christmas Day 2003, Minneapolis firefighters with sledgehammers knocked down the chimney of Uncle Hugo's Bookstore and rescued a naked 34-year-old man who was trapped inside. The man claimed he had stripped naked in order to fit down the 12-inch square chimney, and that he was looking for some keys he had accidentally dropped down the shaft. Police didn't buy it—and charged him with attempted burglary. "He doesn't appear to be a hard-core criminal," said Lieutenant Mike Sauro, "just stupid."

PRUDE…Acting on a neighbor's complaint, in May 2004, police in Barnsley, England, ordered a local man named Tony Watson to do something about the naked lawn gnomes in his front yard or face arrest for "causing public offense." Watson, an ex-army sergeant, complied by painting bathing suits on the gnomes. "We have to take complaints from members of the public seriously," a police spokesperson told reporters.

NUDE…In 2004 a woman parking her car in Göttingen, Germany, was confronted by a man who complained about her driving. According to police, the man—who was completely naked—ran after her "to communicate his displeasure about the noise and time she had taken to park." The woman swore at the man, then ran into her house and called authorities.

PRUDE…In 1998 the U.S. Navy charged a career officer with indecent exposure and conduct unbecoming an officer following an incident at the Pensacola Naval Air Station in Florida. The incident: Lieutenant Patrick Callaghan, 28, had mooned a friend while jogging on the base. "There are people who are real offended when you take your pants down in a public street," Callaghan's commanding officer, Captain Terrence Riley, explained. At first, Callaghan faced dismissal from the navy for the prank, but officials let him off with only a letter of reprimand in the end.

Q: What's the difference between a bad golfer and a bad skydiver?…

NUDE... In January 2004, a businessman named Bill Martin bought a run-down nudist colony outside of Tampa, Florida, for $1.6 million and made plans to open a new business on the site. What kind of business? A *Christian* nudist colony. "The Bible very clearly states that when Adam and Eve were with God, they were naked," says executive director David Blood. "When people are right with God, they do not have to fear nudity."

PRUDE...A 51-year-old woman returning home from a date in 1991 kissed her friend good night and went inside her condo. The next day she received a notice from the homeowners association threatening her with a fine. The complaint read: "Resident seen kissing and doing bad things for over one hour." Kim Garrett insisted she only kissed her date once, then got out of his car and was back in the condo in less than a minute. "If they can judge my morals, which are not wrong, they can just keep passing rules," she said. "It will be just like living in Russia."

NUDE... In January 2004, Stephen Gough, 44, known as the "Naked Rambler," accomplished his goal of walking the length of the United Kingdom wearing only socks, walking boots, and a hat. His purpose: To encourage greater acceptance of the naked body. The 900-mile trip took a long time—seven months. Gough was arrested 16 times along the way and served two stints in jail for indecent exposure.

PRUDE... Mel Culver, a teacher in Waukesha, Wisconsin, asked the school district to remove the 2001 *Guinness Book of World Records* from all 17 elementary schools in the district. Why? The book contains photos of models wearing "the world's most valuable bikini" and "the world's most expensive bra and panties." "Boys are asking to go to the library for the sole purpose of looking at these pictures," Culver wrote in her complaint. "The news of the pictures is spreading like wildfire." (The review committee voted 9–0 to reject her request.)

*   *   *

"Humor is a reminder that no matter how high the throne one sits on, one sits on one's bottom."

—**Taki**

...A: A bad golfer goes: WHACK! "Damn." A bad skydiver goes: "Damn." WHACK!

THE LAST LAUGH

This article comes courtesy of history's all-time funniest comedian: The Grim Reaper himself—Mr. Death.

Hair Today, Gone Tomorrow. In 2001 British actor Hugh Grant's mother was dying from cancer. Like a good son, he stayed by her side during her final days…but then: "I got bored and started tormenting her. My personal favorite being secretly activating her hospital bed so that the head and legs both lifted to put her in an amusing jack-knife position. I blow-dried her hair on the day before she died, which was frankly not the success I had hoped for, and which may—I now concede—have finished her off."

Close to Her Heart. "A grieving Australian widow had her husband's ashes injected into her breast implants. Sydney woman Sandi Canesco, 26, took the bizarre step after her husband Dustin was killed in a car accident. 'It dawned on me that if I carried Dustin's cremated remains in my breast implants, I'd never really have to part with him at all.'" (News.com)

Can-do Guy. Dr. Fredric J. Baur was a food storage technician for Proctor & Gamble. His proudest achievement: the cylindrical Pringles potato chip can, which he patented in 1970. When he died in 2008 at age 89, his children honored his last request…and stuffed as many of his ashes as they could into a Pringles can, and the remainder in an urn. The two containers were buried side by side.

Ghost Rider: Do you happen to live in a haunted house? Ultraviolet, a company in England, offers "Spooksafe" insurance policies that will pay up to $100,000 for "death, injury or damage to personal effects caused by a ghost or poltergeist." (Or aliens.) According to Simon Burgess, chief underwriter, the company has already paid out on one ghost-related murder. "We had a firm of investigators look into it," he said, "and they were convinced that a ghost was responsible."

Don't Die with Your Mouth Full. In 1948 former major league baseball player Jake Powell was showing off his "skill" of being able to eat an entire steak in one bite. Result: He choked to death. Last words: "Watch this!"

DAMN YOU, STINK MAN!

Until recently, all movies made in Hong Kong—including "chop sockey"
low-budget martial arts films—legally had to have English subtitles,
because it was a British colony. But chop sockey producers
spend as little on translations as possible...and it shows.

"You're a bad guy, where's your library card?"

"How can you use my intestines as a gift?"

"Quiet or I'll blow your throat up."

"Check if there's a hole in my underpants."

"No! I saw a vomiting crab."

"Damn you, stink man!"

"You're stain!"

"Bump him dead."

"Suck the coffin mushroom now."

"A big fool, with a gun, go to war. Surrendered and turned to a cake."

"You bastard, try this melon."

"Noodles? Forget it. Try my fist."

"Brother, my pants are coming out."

"Get out, you smurk!"

"Don't you feel the stink smell?"

"Take my advice or I'll spank you without pants."

"You cheat ghosts to eat tofu?"

"I'm not Jesus Christ, I'm Bunny."

"You're bad. You make my busts up and down."

"He's Big Head Man, he is lousing around."

"She's terrific. I can't stand her."

"You daring lousy guy."

"Well! Masturbate in hell!"

"The fart of God. What does it mean? With a remarkable sound."

"Okay, I'll Bastare, show your guts."

"Suddenly my worm are all healed off."

"And you thought. I'm gabby bag."

What's *rhinorrhea*? The medical term for snot. (What's *rhinorhinorrhea*? Rhino snot.)

WHAT'S SO FUNNY?

Some comedy greats (and Bobby Slayton) on what causes an upside-down frown.

"Tragedy is when I cut my finger. Comedy is when you fall into an open sewer and die."
—**Mel Brooks**

"Comedy is tragedy plus time."
—**Carol Burnett**

"Humor is just truth, only faster!"
—**Gilda Radner**

"It's the duty of the comedian to find out where the line is drawn and cross it deliberately."
—**George Carlin**

"There's a thin line between 'to laugh with' and 'to laugh at.'"
—**Richard Pryor**

"If you can't laugh at yourself, make fun of other people."
—**Bobby Slayton**

"It's always funny until someone gets hurt. Then it's just hilarious."
—**Bill Hicks**

"Comedy is the art of making people laugh without making them puke."
—**Steve Martin**

"A lot of what makes sufficient numbers of us laugh, me included, is sometimes very broad, very low, grotesque, horrible stuff."
—**Madeline Kahn**

"If you want to make an audience laugh, dress a man up like an old lady and push him down the stairs. If you want to make a comedy writer laugh, push an actual old lady down the stairs."
—**Tina Fey**

"Sometimes things are really funny if you're earnest. If you're really serious, it's hilarious."
—**Christopher Walken**

"God writes a lot of comedy. The trouble is, He's stuck with so many bad actors who don't know how to play funny."
—**Garrison Keillor**

Richard Curtis: "What is the secret to great com—?"
Rowan Atkinson: "Timing."

"The safest place in an earthquake is a stationary store." —George Carlin

CORNER OF THIS & THAT

Believe it or not, all of these street names are real.

Old Guy Road
(Damon, Texas)

Pe'e Pe'e Place
(Hilo, Hawaii)

Wong Way
(Riverside, California;
in 1999 it was changed
to Wong Street)

Weiner Cutoff Road
(Harrisburg, Arkansas)

Rue du Hâ Hâ
(Chéroy, France)

Spanker Lane
(Derbyshire, England)

Awesome Street
(Cary, North Carolina)

Kickapoo Drive
(Fort Worth, Texas)

Farfrompoopen Road
(only road to Constipation Ridge
in Story, Arkansas)

Inyo Street
(Bakersfield, California; intersects
with Butte Street)

Butt Hollow Road
(Salem, Virginia)

Booger Branch Road
(Six Mile, South Carolina; also in
Crandall, Georgia)

Tater Peeler Road
(Lebanon, Tennessee)

His Way
(Lake Jackson, Texas;
behind a church)

Dumb Woman's Lane
(East Sussex, England)

Morningwood Way
(Bend, Oregon)

Unexpected Road
(Buena, New Jersey)

Kitchen-Dick Road
(Sequim, Washington)

Butts Wynd Street
(St. Andrews, Scotland)

Crotch Crescent
(Oxfordshire, England)

This Street, That Street,
and **The Other Street**
(three actual streets in
Porters Lake, Nova Scotia)

Fangboner Road
(Fremont, Ohio)

Divorce Court
(Heather Highlands,
Pennsylvania)

Psycho Path
(Traverse City, Michigan)

Q: How many surrealists does it take to screw in a lightbulb? A: To get to the other side.

HE WHO LAUGHS LAST

Well, you know the saying…

THE WORLD'S BEST ETHNIC JOKE

An Englishman, a Scotsman, an Irishman, a Latvian, a Turk, a German, an Indian, an American, an Argentinean, a Dane, an Australian, a Slovakian, an Egyptian, a Japanese, a Moroccan, a Frenchman, a New Zealander, a Spaniard, a Russian, a Guatemalan, a Colombian, a Pakistani, a Malaysian, a Croatian, a Pole, a Lithuanian, a Chinese, a Sri Lankan, a Lebanese, a Cayman Islander, a Ugandan, a Vietnamese, a Korean, a Uruguayan, a Czech, an Icelander, a Mexican, a Finn, a Honduran, a Panamanian, an Andorran, an Israeli, a Venezuelan, a Fijian, a Peruvian, an Estonian, a Brazilian, a Portuguese, a Liechtensteiner, a Mongolian, a Hungarian, a Canadian, a Moldovan, a Haitian, a Norfolk Islander, a Macedonian, a Bolivian, a Cook Islander, a Tajikistani, a Samoan, an Armenian, an Aruban, an Albanian, a Greenlander, a Micronesian, a Virgin Islander, a Georgian, a Bahaman, a Belarusian, a Cuban, a Tongan, a Cambodian, a Qatari, an Azerbaijani, a Romanian, a Chilean, a Kyrgyzstani, a Jamaican, a Filipino, a Ukrainian, a Dutchman, a Taiwanese, an Ecuadorian, a Costa Rican, a Swede, a Bulgarian, a Serb, a Swiss, a Greek, a Belgian, a Singaporean, an Italian, and a Norwegian walk into a fine restaurant. "I'm sorry," said the maître d', "but you can't come in here without a Thai."

AND FINALLY…THE WORLD'S FUNNIEST JOKE

In 2002 the University of Hertfordshire in England set up a website where people could read through and rate over 40,000 jokes. Their goal: to determine the world's funniest joke across wide culture, age, gender, and nationality differences. The winner—which proves that most people prefer their comedy on the dark side—comes from a 1951 routine performed by Michael Bentine and Peter Sellers:

Bentine: "Help! I just came in and found this man lying on the carpet in there."

Sellers: "Oh, is he dead?"

Bentine: "I think so."

Sellers: "Hadn't you better make sure?"

Bentine: "Alright. Just a minute."

[*Bentine leaves. Sound of two gunshots. Then he walks back in.*]

Bentine: "He's dead."

The closest living relative of *Tyrannosaurus rex* is the chicken.

We are pleased to offer over 120 e-book versions of Portable Press titles—some currently available only in digital format! Visit www.portablepress.com to collect them all!

- ❏ Bathroom Science
- ❏ The Best of the Best of Uncle John's Bathroom Reader
- ❏ The Best of Uncle John's Bathroom Reader
- ❏ Dad Jokes
- ❏ Do Geese Get Goose Bumps?
- ❏ The Funniest & Grossest Joke Book Ever!
- ❏ The Funniest Joke Book Ever!
- ❏ The Funniest Knock-Knock Jokes Ever!
- ❏ The Grossest Joke Book Ever!
- ❏ Instant Genius
- ❏ Instant Genius: Smart Mouths
- ❏ See Ya Later Calculator
- ❏ Strange Crime
- ❏ Strange History
- ❏ Strange Science
- ❏ Uncle John's 24-Karat Gold Bathroom Reader
- ❏ Uncle John's Absolutely Absorbing Bathroom Reader
- ❏ Uncle John's Ahh-Inspiring Bathroom Reader

- ❏ Uncle John's All-Purpose Extra Strength Bathroom Reader
- ❏ Uncle John's Bathroom Reader Attack of the Factoids
- ❏ Uncle John's Bathroom Reader Book of Love
- ❏ Uncle John's Bathroom Reader Cat Lover's Companion
- ❏ Uncle John's Bathroom Reader Christmas Collection
- ❏ Uncle John's Bathroom Reader Dog Lover's Companion
- ❏ Uncle John's Bathroom Reader Extraordinary Book of Facts
- ❏ Uncle John's Bathroom Reader Fake Facts
- ❏ Uncle John's Bathroom Reader Flush Fiction
- ❏ Uncle John's Bathroom Reader For Girls Only!
- ❏ Uncle John's Bathroom Reader For Kids Only!
- ❏ Uncle John's Bathroom Reader For Kids Only! Collectible Edition

- ❏ Uncle John's Bathroom Reader Germophobia
- ❏ Uncle John's Bathroom Reader Golden Plunger Awards
- ❏ Uncle John's Bathroom Reader History's Lists
- ❏ Uncle John's Bathroom Reader Horse Lover's Companion
- ❏ Uncle John's Bathroom Reader Impossible Questions
- ❏ Uncle John's Bathroom Reader Jingle Bell Christmas
- ❏ Uncle John's Bathroom Reader Nature Calls
- ❏ Uncle John's Bathroom Reader Plunges into California
- ❏ Uncle John's Bathroom Reader Plunges into Canada, eh
- ❏ Uncle John's Bathroom Reader Plunges into Great Lives
- ❏ Uncle John's Bathroom Reader Plunges into History
- ❏ Uncle John's Bathroom Reader Plunges into History Again

To demonstrate flaws in the patent system, in 2001 an Australian lawyer patented the wheel.

❏ Uncle John's Bathroom Reader Plunges into Hollywood

❏ Uncle John's Bathroom Reader Plunges into Michigan

❏ Uncle John's Bathroom Reader Plunges into Minnesota

❏ Uncle John's Bathroom Reader Plunges into Music

❏ Uncle John's Bathroom Reader Plunges into National Parks

❏ Uncle John's Bathroom Reader Plunges into New Jersey

❏ Uncle John's Bathroom Reader Plunges into New York

❏ Uncle John's Bathroom Reader Plunges into Ohio

❏ Uncle John's Bathroom Reader Plunges into Pennsylvania

❏ Uncle John's Bathroom Reader Plunges into Texas

❏ Uncle John's Bathroom Reader Plunges into Texas Expanded Edition

❏ Uncle John's Bathroom Reader Plunges into the Presidency

❏ Uncle John's Bathroom Reader Plunges into the Universe

❏ Uncle John's Bathroom Reader Quintessential Collection of Notable Quotables

❏ Uncle John's Bathroom Reader Salutes the Armed Forces

❏ Uncle John's Bathroom Reader Shoots and Scores

❏ Uncle John's Bathroom Reader Sports Spectacular

❏ Uncle John's Bathroom Reader Takes a Swing at Baseball

❏ Uncle John's Bathroom Reader Tales to Inspire

❏ Uncle John's Bathroom Reader Tees Off On Golf

❏ Uncle John's Bathroom Reader The World's Gone Crazy

❏ Uncle John's Bathroom Reader Tunes into TV

❏ Uncle John's Bathroom Reader Vroom!

❏ Uncle John's Bathroom Reader Weird Canada

❏ Uncle John's Bathroom Reader Weird Inventions

❏ Uncle John's Bathroom Reader WISE UP!

❏ Uncle John's Bathroom Reader Wonderful World of Odd

❏ Uncle John's Bathroom Reader Zipper Accidents

❏ Uncle John's Book of Fun

❏ Uncle John's Canoramic Bathroom Reader

❏ Uncle John's Certified Organic Bathroom Reader

❏ Uncle John's Colossal Collection of Quotable Quotes

❏ Uncle John's Creature Feature Bathroom Reader For Kids Only!

❏ Uncle John's Curiously Compelling Bathroom Reader

❏ Uncle John's Did You Know...? Bathroom Reader For Kids Only!

❏ Uncle John's Do-It-Yourself Diary for Infomaniacs Only

❏ Uncle John's Do-It-Yourself Journal for Infomaniacs Only

❏ Uncle John's Electrifying Bathroom Reader For Kids Only!

Actual product: the Happiness Hat. It stabs you in the head if you stop smiling.

❏ Uncle John's Electrifying Bathroom Reader For Kids Only! Collectible Edition

❏ Uncle John's Endlessly Engrossing Bathroom Reader

❏ Uncle John's Factastic Bathroom Reader

❏ Uncle John's Facts to Annoy Your Teacher Bathroom Reader For Kids Only!

❏ Uncle John's Fast-Acting Long-Lasting Bathroom Reader

❏ Uncle John's Fully Loaded 25th Anniversary Bathroom Reader

❏ Uncle John's Giant 10th Anniversary Bathroom Reader

❏ Uncle John's Gigantic Bathroom Reader

❏ Uncle John's Great Big Bathroom Reader

❏ Uncle John's Haunted Outhouse Bathroom Reader For Kids Only!

❏ Uncle John's Heavy Duty Bathroom Reader

❏ Uncle John's How to Fight a Bear...and Win

❏ Uncle John's How to Toilet Train Your Cat

❏ Uncle John's InfoMania Bathroom Reader For Kids Only!

❏ Uncle John's Legendary Lost Bathroom Reader

❏ Uncle John's Lists That Make You Go Hmmm...

❏ Uncle John's New & Improved Briefs

❏ Uncle John's New & Improved Funniest Ever

❏ Uncle John's Old Faithful 30th Anniversary Bathroom Reader

❏ Uncle John's Perpetually Pleasing Bathroom Reader

❏ Uncle John's Political Briefs

❏ Uncle John's Presents: Book of the Dumb

❏ Uncle John's Presents: Book of the Dumb 2

❏ Uncle John's Presents: Mom's Bathtub Reader

❏ Uncle John's Presents the Ultimate Challenge Trivia Quiz

❏ Uncle John's Robotica Bathroom Reader

❏ Uncle John's Slightly Irregular Bathroom Reader

❏ Uncle John's Smell-O-Scopic Bathroom Reader For Kids Only!

❏ Uncle John's Supremely Satisfying Bathroom Reader

❏ Uncle John's The Enchanted Toilet Bathroom Reader For Kids Only!

❏ Uncle John's Top Secret Bathroom Reader For Kids Only!

❏ Uncle John's Top Secret Bathroom Reader For Kids Only! Collectible Edition

❏ Uncle John's Totally Quacked Bathroom Reader For Kids Only!

❏ Uncle John's Triumphant 20th Anniversary Bathroom Reader

❏ Uncle John's True Crime

❏ Uncle John's Ultimate Bathroom Reader

❏ Uncle John's Uncanny Bathroom Reader

❏ Uncle John's Unsinkable Bathroom Reader

❏ Uncle John's Unstoppable Bathroom Reader

❏ Uncle John's Weird Weird World

❏ Uncle John's Weird Weird World: Epic

❏ The Wackiest Joke Book Ever!

❏ The Wackiest Joke Book That'll Knock-Knock You Over!

❏ Who Knew?

THE LAST PAGE

FELLOW BATHROOM READERS:
The fight for good bathroom reading should never be taken loosely—we must do our duty and sit firmly for what we believe in, even while the rest of the world is taking potshots at us.

We'll be brief. Now that we've proven we're not simply a flush-in-the-pan, we invite you to take the plunge: Sit Down and Be Counted! To find out what the BRI is up to, visit us at www.portablepress.com and take a peek!

Get Connected

Find us online to sign up for our email list, enter exciting giveaways, hear about new releases, and more!

🌐   Websites: www.portablepress.com

           www.bathroomreader.com

f   Facebook: www.facebook.com/portablepress

ⓟ   Pinterest: www.pinterest.com/portablepress

🐦   Twitter: @Portablepress

Well, we're out of space, and when you've gotta go, you've gotta go. Tanks for all your support. Hope to hear from you soon.

Meanwhile, remember…

Keep on flushin'!